The Real Lancashire

By the same author:

FAMOUS LAKELAND HOMES

FYLDE FOLK

LANCASHIRE GHOSTS

LANCASHIRE LANDMARKS

LANCASHIRE LEGENDS

WITCHCRAFT IN LANCASHIRE

The Real Lancashire

by

Kathleen Eyre

CLXX

Dalesman Books
1983

The Dalesman Publishing Company Ltd.,
Clapham, via Lancaster, LA2 8EB
First published 1983
© Kathleen Eyre, 1983

ISBN: 0 85206 740 2

To Lancashire, with Love

Printed in Great Britain by Fretwell & Brian Ltd.,
Healey Works, Goulbourne Street, Keighley, West Yorkshire

Chapter House, Cockersand Abbey.

CONTENTS

1. A Glorious Heritage 7
2. This Clever County 11
3. The Lancashire Twang 16
4. The Making of a County 20
5. Proud Preston 22
6. The Fylde 33
7. Lancaster 41
8. Tides, Mists and Tragedies 48
9. Morecambe Bay 50
10. Wildlife in Lancashire 56
11. Lancashire Rivers 57
12. A Gallery of Minstrels 79
13. Towers, Moors and Old Mill Towns 84
14. The Rossendale Valley 98
15. South-East Lancashire 105
16. Between Ribble and Mersey 117
17. Two Great Cities 137
    Acknowledgements 142
    Index 143

Cover photograph of Walton-le-Dale by Michael Edwards

THE HARRIS FREE LIBRARY, ART GALLERY & MUSEUM, PRESTON, is regarded as one of the finest Neo-Greco buildings in Britain. It is shown to advantage in this photograph of *c.* 1895 during the demolition of all the 17th and 18th century buildings immediately to its north (left) giving a view that has not been seen before or since. In the background (right) are old buildings demolished in 1896 ready for the laying of the foundation stone of the Miller Arcade in July of that year. Ald. James Hibbert, designer of the "Harris" (built 1882–1891), was an eclectic architect. He designed Fishergate Baptish Church in Romanesque style with Moorish additions; St. Matthew's Church in New Hall Lane, in the Decorated Gothic style; and Preston Royal Infirmary in a manner resembling French 18th century architecture.

1. A GLORIOUS HERITAGE

WHAT gradely folk they are whose roots strike deep into the good soil of Lancashire – and if you are puzzled about "gradely" it means all that is decent, upright, honest and properly becoming – and that's what they are, and cheerful with it, and hard-working, and clever as a cart-load of monkeys. No other county has so directly affected the destiny of Humankind for Lancashire was the dynamic heartland of the first Industrial Revolution which changed the course of civilisation, hustled the world into a new machine age, led to the splitting of the atom and the landing of man on the moon.

The diversity of this beloved county is a constant surprise. There is so much here to see, and do, and marvel at. So much history to probe, literature to savour; scenic contrasts to entrance the eye and refresh the spirit; splendid achievements to reflect upon with awe and admiration. The liveliest curiosity, in a long lifetime, would never exhaust this county's treasures. The nimblest mind need never relapse into boredom. Landmarks abound, riveting the eye, capturing the imagination; and every laneside, hill-top, hamlet, adds to an abundant harvest. The wildlife is superb. Country Parks and picnic sites are generously provided by the County and District Councils and Lancashire has some of the finest art galleries and museums in the kingdom.

This single volume cannot offer more than a synopsis . . . a tantalising glimpse of great lives, a delightful dip into important events, a review of all those Lancashire interests which have enslaved my attention for all but my first handful of years. I grew up, went to school, became aware of the world here; made all my friends, in Lancashire; found my life's work in the pursuit of its history; and in the absence of any ancestral obligation to love the place, developed a deeper passion for Lancashire than many a native born.

This is an immensely lovable county, unique in its very personal links with the Sovereign, steadfast in its devotion to old legends and traditions. Here, noble consciences were stirred and great reform movements came bravely to birth. Writers and artists have drawn inspiration from this northern region where sublime western sunsets and dreamy emerald pastures, and brooding black mosslands and boundless moors contrast sharply with dismal industrial grime and the clatter of Mammon.

The townsman moves purposefully about his business. The countryman feasts his eye on the delights of Nature. The stranger is bowled over by the transcendant beauty of Lancashire and astonished by the wealth of its history. From signpost pointers the long past leaps out in place names, half a hundred of them British, many more Anglian and Norse, not a few left over from the long Roman occupation. Normans left their castles; the imprint of early Christian activity remained in perhaps five hundred wayside or "weeping" crosses erected after the Conquest, many falling in later centuries to the vandals. Yet, unheeded by preoccupied passers-by, many an ancient base socket remains in situ.

Last century, T. Harrison Myres, a Preston architect, studied Lancashire's wayside crosses, rescued many and restored several, notably in the Fylde. A Norman font at Mitton was unearthed by him in 1897. From a private garden he rescued and returned a 17th century font to Penwortham in 1906. He was responsible for restoring the "Seath Bushell" brasses to Preston Parish Church 47 years after dishonest workmen had flogged them to a marine store dealer for 8½d. apiece during the rebuild of 1854. Here was a man after my own heart, whose enthusiastic writings and lectures enriched the lives of thousands, and I am perfectly certain that he hugely enjoyed and savoured every moment of his span. Recently, a stranger telephoned to enquire where he might start to accumulate a photographic record of all the surviving Lancashire village stocks. Colne, Woodplumpton, Broughton-in-Amounderness, Poulton-le-Fylde, Standish, Hest-with-Slyne . . . offhand, enough sprang to mind to set him happily off on his searchings which should keep him engrossed for the next year or two. Indeed, the investigations and discoveries continue unabated, every town and village producing its faithful chronicler whose patient probings enrich the Lancashire saga.

This red rose county has everything for deep soul satisfaction. There are fine old country churches, literary shrines, memorials to native genius. You can drink real ale in grand old country pubs; rub shoulders with half the working population of the north on the sands, or along the Golden Mile, at Blackpool. Because it was, and to a considerable extent, still is a Catholic county, it is the most haunted region, claiming more spooks to the square mile than any other area of the kingdom. White, Black or Grey Ladies (and even one Green Lady, at Mossock Hall, near Ormskirk) still float about, long after serving as cover-ups for illicit priestly comings, sojournings and departures, during the persecutions. Celestial radar systems are over-worked averting collisions between all the boggarts, phantoms, elves, fairies, wraiths and spectres of every shape and description which have amused or plagued Old Lancashire from end to end, from time out of mind!

Lancashire deserves more credit than it is accorded for the wealth of its historic halls and houses. There are lovely examples of "black and white" at Samlesbury, Rufford, Hall-i'th-Wood and Turton; at Worsley where a lovelorn Duke planned his canals; at 15th century Ordsall Hall, Salford, with its Gunpowder Plot associations and a background of dockland gear where once were dreamy pastures and sweet woodlands; at Speke Hall near the wide Mersey, where priests from the Continent were secreted in a virtual warren of runs, hides, galleries and peep-holes before striking out on perilous missions; at 15th century Wythenshawe, the once moated mansion of the Tattons and Simons, far to the south of Old Lancashire, and that rescued gem from the 1300's, Baguley Hall nearby, one of the most antiquated half-timbered properties in the north-west.

The latter-day Planner – often synonymous with the uglifier of the landscape, the perpetrator of those hideous and often disastrous tower blocks, and the perverse and pointless shifting of boundaries – must accept that a stroke of his capricious pen will never destroy old allegiances fiercely upheld. Reluctantly, one loosens hold of Lakeland Lancashire, the bit that flew away and dropped down over Furness, and concedes that it always seemed illogical to depart from Lancashire, only to re-enter it within Lakeland. Nevertheless, during that great upheaval of 1974 – the point and purpose of which have entirely eluded me ever since! – we lost what Cumbria won . . . great stretches of breath-taking natural beauty; Hawkshead and those links with the schoolboy Wordsworth; the glorous ruins of a great sandstone abbey; the Priory Church at Cartmel, and Holker Hall (pronounced "Hooker"), where hot air balloonists congregate and the grounds riot with colour – daffodils first, rhododendrons and azaleas in May, roses in June-time! We cannot forget that they were ours, once! Lancashire's treasures!

Still, there are plenty more where open doors welcome the eager traveller, some publicly, others privately owned. Study the long lists available. I will mention only the, perhaps, less well known, like Chingle Hall, near Goosnargh, an early moated Mass centre with several hides and extravagant claims as to its antiquity and its hauntings. And yet, I have encountered there a curious atmosphere that stirs the senses and I have never failed to enjoy a visit. Thanks to local enthusiasm, the Pendle Heritage Centre, based at Park Hill, Barrowford, has preserved the 1661 stone hall of the Bannister family whose line goes back to the Conquest, whose descendant, Dr. Sir Roger Bannister, broke the four-minute mile.

Thurnham Hall, ancient seat of the Daltons, has opened recently after massive restoration; even has a Cavalier robot designed by Lancaster University, an all-talking, eye-blinking, unnervingly human 17th century guide that gives an excellent commentary and suits its movements to the vocal performance. I clearly picture John Dalton arriving here, weary and penniless, on foot after tramping from London following his release from prison, punishment for engaging in the 1715 Rebellion. The servants had fled; the place was unnaturally quiet; his wife was gathering faggots in the woods like any common cotter, and both had so grievously suffered that neither recognised the other. Fines crippled the Daltons for generations; their line is all but, and possibly totally, extinct, but their historic home has been secured, we hope, for ever.

A county of contrasts indeed! . . . of endless fascination! They joke about Widnes where "it used to rain dilute hydrochloric acid", and I begin wondering if this can be true, and long to go and see! Prescot, they say, was the clock and watch making centre of the kingdon from c. 1600 until Swiss and mass-produced American goods flooded the market from the 1860's onwards, and I itch to visit that museum. A friend gabbles so excitedly about the exhibits at the Pilkington Glass Museum that I prepare to visit St. Helens where the cast glass process was introduced in 1773, though Romans had been making glass in south-west Lancashire centuries before that.

There are scenes that must be viewed again, and the loveliest of villages from the Yealands in the north to

THURNHAM HALL, south of the Lune estuary, before the present owners embarked on major renovations. It was the home of the Dalton family, Catholics and Jacobites, whose descendants resided here until modern times. The property was refaced in the 1820's, the private chapel (ground floor right) being added 30 years later.

Hale in the south, the "beautifullest village in all England", Jane Carlyle described it in a letter home in 1844. Such beauteous thatched properties there to linger by, some three centuries old, others built in the 1930's, and a giant's grave to visit in the churchyard, and his home, still there, of John Middleton (1578-1623) who stood 9ft. 3ins. in his socks and created a stir in the land when local gentlemen kitted him out in the height of fashion and traipsed him to London to challenge James I's champion.

Lancashire has produced the greatest men and the grandest women in the world and these gradely folk have made this region special. I have much still to learn, many notes and undigested fragments to be followed up and enquired into. But there is the assurance that so long as brain and limbs function and friends are spared who share my deep love of Gaunt's domain, this Lancashire, whose honorary daughter I am proud to be, will satisfy every desire of heart and mind and soul; and in gratitude, and as long as I have breath, I will write and sing in praise of Lancashire, the beloved county.

— **Kathleen Eyre.**

OLD THATCHED COTTAGES AT HALE near the banks of the wide Mersey. Cruck cottages of whitewashed "clam, staff and daub" were traditional in west and south Lancashire where stone was scarce and timber was fairly plentiful. The framework cottage (above) dates back to 1665.

2.   THIS CLEVER COUNTY

A QUICK GLANCE through this county's record of "firsts" in every field of human achievement confirms that Lancashire left precious little for the rest of the world to accomplish! . . . though probably it takes a lady born in the West Riding to assert that; the Red Rose chap simply cannot be bothered to boast!

Turn to the evidence of history . . . to those Lancashire men who tipped the scales at Agincourt, at Bosworth Field, at Flodden; to those staunch Catholic families who, in times of severest persecution, put forward more candidates for the priesthood than the rest of England put together. Lancashire know-how invented all those textile machines, pioneered the factory system, canals, the first passenger railway in the world, the Co-operative movement, free libraries, life insurance. Lancashire had the first gas street lighting in the land, at Chapel Street, Salford in 1805, two years before London's Pall Mall; and the first electric trams in the country (Blackpool, 1885, and still going strong!) Liverpool has the oldest Children's Hospital, and the first School of Tropical Medicine in the World (1898); and tea-heiress, Miss Annie Horniman, founded England's first Repertory Theatre at Manchester in 1907. Lancashire had the first motorway in the kingdom, by-passing Preston (1958), the largest bus station in Europe, the world's widest bridge, and the world's first computer assembled at Manchester in 1947. A random selection! Not bad for starters!

Take libraries, for instance. Humphrey Chetham's at Manchester, first in the kingdom, possibly in Europe, housed in a building 550 years old, rich in priceless treasures, and available to "all well affected persons" since 1653! The John Rylands Library, a widow's memorial to her St. Helens-born husband who founded a weaving business at the age of 18, died in 1888 leaving a fortune and is remembered now in that magnificent building housing some of the oldest documents in the world. Since the merger with Manchester University in 1972, "Rylands" has achieved world status, famed for its superlative examples of calligraphy, its ancient papyri, its rich ivory bindings encrusted with jewels, the oldest copy of the Nicene Creed, the earliest fragment of the New Testament. A Lancashire chap, Wm. Ewart of Liverpool, pressed the Public Libraries Act through Parliament in 1850 and immediately Salford opened the country's first Municipal Free Library!

Old Lancashire has the highest peal of bells in the world, in the largest cathedral in the kingdom (Liverpool Anglican) and the oldest dated bell (1296) in the country. Charles II financed Greenwich Observatory in 1675 but Sir Jonas Moore, a Lancastrian Scientist and Mathematician, inspired and master-minded the whole project. The iron trade was revolutionised by Henry Cort of Lancaster, and a Middleton clergyman-scholar, who worked out a scheme of annuities for clergy-widows "and others", originated the idea of Life Insurance. He was Wm. Assheton, a graduate of Brasennose College, Oxford, co-founded in Tudor times by a Lancastrian, Dr. Wm. Smyth, Bishop of Lincoln, born at Widnes c. 1460 and probably educated in the Stanley household at Knowsley.

In pioneer aviation, Lancashire led the way again. In the year that Louis Bleriot flew the English Channel (1909), Blackpool organised the first British Flying Meeting of all time, at Squire's Gate, and among those intrepids was A. V. Roe, the doctor's son, born at Patricroft in 1877, who designed the Avro Biplane in 1912. At the second event in 1910, C. Grahame-White, in the teeth of a strong wind, carried a sackful of letters and dropped it over the side, the first air-mail! . . . and in June 1919 the whole world thrilled to the exploits of John Wm. Alcock and Arthur Whitten Brown, both of Manchester, who flew the Atlantic in a flimsy contraption powered by a 360 h.p. Rolls Royce Eagle engine. Alcock, whose family lived in St. Annes for a while, attended Heyhouses School and later worked for a grocer, delivering orders on an old push bike. His early death during a flight to Paris was "a very sad affair to St. Annes folk", an old school chum told me.

Women's position in society owes much to Lancashire and the Fighting Pankhursts. Emmeline Goulden, a Mancunian cotton merchant's beautiful daughter, had the glorious good sense to marry Dr. Pankhurst, a kindly and liberated Barrister who not only championed her cause but promoted the Married Woman's Property Act which put paid to many a fortune-hunting Victorian! The struggle for Women's Suffrage against disgraceful male prejudice was "crowned with victory" in 1918, a triumph dearly bought by such as Christabel Pankhurst and Anne Kenny, the courageous Saddleworth mill-girl, who were flung into Strangeways Gaol, Manchester, for presuming to ask pertinent questions at an election meeting in 1905. There are plans now to preserve Mrs. Pankhurst's house in Nelson Street, Manchester.

John Rawsthorne of Manchester prepared the gum for the world's first adhesive postage stamps in 1840. "Mercerising" was invented at Great Harwood and the use of asbestos was developed at Rochdale. Liverpudlian Henry Booth invented the spring buffer and other railway devices still in use; young Edward Entwistle from Wigan drove the first locomotive on the Manchester/Liverpool Railway in 1830, at the age of 15; George Bradshaw, a Pendleton printer and engraver, compiled those first fascinating time tables in 1839. Lancashire has the nation's oldest Building Society properties in Club Row, Longridge (1793), near Preston; the oldest bound volume in the country, at Stonyhurst College; (St. John's Gospel, copied for Boisil, Prior of Melrose, and later retrieved from St. Cuthbert's coffin); the world's greatest horse-race, the Grand National, founded in 1839, run at Aintree! And on 3rd April 1982, a 26-year old became the first woman jockey to complete the course, only 8 finishing out of a field of 39 (a lass from Lancashire, too, Geraldine Rees of Tarleton, wouldn't you just know!)

Last century Lancashire gave the nation two great Prime Ministers, Sir Robert Peel of Bury and Liverpool's Wm. Ewart Gladstone; and among many Red Rose men who accomplished much for humanity's sake and deserve to be remembered are Sir James Kay-Shuttleworth who founded the modern educational system and pressed for sanitary reforms in the terrible slum areas; a Rochdalian called Roberts who fought to keep youngsters out of the mills; George Long of Poulton-le-Fylde, a Fellow of Trinity College, Cambridge and Professor of Greek at London University, a respected scholar who diffused knowledge among the under-educated by editing the Penny Cyclopaedia, delivered to the door in penny instalments. The Government rewarded him with a pension for his lifelong services to literature and he died in 1879. And above all, Joseph Livesey who championed the poor, founded the Teetotal Movement, wrote and spoke against injustice and oppression, founded the country's first illustrated halfpenny weekly, "The Struggle" (1842-5) before launching the "Preston Guardian" (1844).

Charles Towneley of Towneley furnished some of the most valuable exhibits in the British Museum; Henry Tate, of Chorley, the grocer's boy turned sugar refiner, gave cube sugar to the world and the Tate Gallery to the nation (1897), and the researches of another Chorley chap, Nobel Prize Winner, Sir Walter Norman Haworth (1883-1950) gave us cheap Vitamin C . . . while over at Wrightington Hospital the courageous pioneers in the replacement of joints have earned the gratitude of thousands and the admiration of the world.

In 1978, the world's first test-tube baby, Louise Brown, was ushered into consciousness by Mr. Patrick Steptoe and his brilliant team, not in London or New York, with all the accompanying razzmatazz, but without fuss or palaver, in the General Hospital at Oldham, Lancs! And just think what courageous Pat Seed, M.B.E., has done for cancer-sufferers the world over! The gutsy, unquenchably cheerful Lancashire lass from Manchester and the Fylde responded to a virtual death sentence by working flat out and raising an astronomical sum for a body scanner and a unit to house it at Christie's Hospital, Manchester.

The world's most celebrated broadcaster, Alistair Cooke, was born in Manchester, educated at Blackpool Grammar School. David Lloyd George first saw the light of day at Chorlton-on-Medlock, and Burnley-born "Butch" Cassidy spent his childhood at Accrington before moving across the Atlantic. As for world-renowned writers, one would know neither where to begin nor to finish. Lionel Angus-Butterworth's "Lancashire Literary Worthies" (1980) has skimmed off the first hundred but there are as many more again waiting to be listed. Mancunians Thomas de Quincey and James Agate are there; and Beatrix Potter, creator of "Peter Rabbit", boasting Lancashire descent from "generations of yeomen and weavers, obstinate hard-headed matter of fact folk!" Preston's Stanley Houghton, who worked closely with Allan Monkhouse of "The Manchester Guardian" and Harold Brighouse of "Hobson's Choice" fame, died at 33, leaving us the immortal "Hindle Wakes".

Who could ever forget Walter Greenwood who gave us "Love on the Dole", or Richmal Crompton of Bury who created the Brown family's lovable young scamp, "Just William"? Yesterday's schoolgirls idolised Angela Brazil whose best-sellers may never have been written but for those holiday adventures around Morecambe Bay, while film and T.V. producers still fall for "Little Lord Fauntleroy" that took the world by storm in 1886; yet, its author, Mrs. Frances Hodgson Burnett, a Cheetham Hill shopkeeper's daughter who grew up in Salford, emigrated to America during the Great Cotton Famine, but never lost her love of England and had a rich capacity for wrapping her tongue round the Lancashire dialect.

I must stifle the urge to write volumes about those whose works have immeasurably enriched my life and whose lives were spent in this historically exciting county. The great Dr. Thomas Dunham Whitaker earned fame in his own time; so did Edward Baines (1774-1848), born at Walton-le-Dale, educated at Preston Grammar School, who went into printing, bought up the "Leeds Mercury", at the age of 27, and turned it into a success story. For his great history of Lancashire, Baines drew on material supplied by Edwin Butterworth who undertook most of the leg-work, and his sons, Edward and Thomas Baines; and though the results have been described as "disjointed and ill-proportioned", those four sumptuously bound volumes with splendid engravings will always occupy an honoured place on my bookshelves.

In addition to Lancashire's own clever children, there were many famous "off-comed-uns" whose potential only developed in the Red Rose county. One of Newcomen's earliest steam pumps was working at Fairbottom, near Ashton-under-Lyne, c. 1710, and going strong until 1840. Folk called it "Fairbottom Bobs" and in 1929 Henry Ford bought it and shipped it across the Atlantic. In 1784 James Watt patented, but never actually created, the steam hammer, but a young Scotsman James Nasmyth, did . . . after assuming managership of a Patricroft foundry and designing parts for the steamship "Great Britain" in 1837.

I think of an 11-year old tearfully leaving home at Rothwell, Northants, last century, and heading by rail for Manchester, having already earned his living for 3 years, to take up employment secured for him by his brother. Grim years followed, carrying tools, delivering boots in a barrow, spending leisure bowed over lessons at night school. The youth went home after fraternal disputes, trained as a shoemaker and at 16 returned to Manchester where, in 1865, he opened a Boot and Shoe Shop at 298, Oldham Road, with a brother in law's help. That, briefly, is how William Timpson (1849-1929) founded his famous chain of shoe shops.

When preparing "Famous Lakeland Homes", I remember lingering beside a cottage in the remote Cumbrian community of Eaglesfield, where a colour-blind Quaker scientist was born in 1766, John Dalton who propounded the Theory of Atomic Energy. He was teaching at 12, assistant master at Kendal at 14, and at 27 he took up a Professorship at Manchester's New College. For fifty years he dominated the "Lit. & Phil. Society" which enhanced the city's scientific reputation, a gentle bachelor whose genius, stimulated by great minds drawn to that Lancastrian power-house of original thinking, flowered so gloriously and set him among the immortals. A unit of electrical energy was named after one of Dalton's most distinguished pupils, James Prescott Joule, son of a Salford brewer. And in 1919, after coming from New Zealand to become Professor of Physics at Manchester University, Ernest Rutherford achieved the ultimate ambition of splitting the atom.

I sometimes wonder (with that authors' Bible ever at my elbow) if Peter Mark Roget, the Swiss physician who worked at Manchester Infirmary in 1804, would ever have embarked on his famous "Thesaurus of English Words and Phrases (1852)" but for his close association with the city's famous Portico Library, and I have no doubt whatsoever that it was quietude at Hornby that enabled Dr. John Lingard (1771-1851) to concentrate for 40 years on his R.C. History of England.

"Worth a Guinea a Box? . . . remember the slogan coined by old Thomas Beecham, the Oxfordshire farm-lad who rolled powdered herbs into pills and hawked them around Oxfordshire markets . . . a fantastic character who achieved fame and fortune only after settling in Lancashire, near Wigan's Market Place first, St. Helens later where the business really took off under the shrewd management of son Joseph. "Dr. Beecham", retired at 72 at Southport, caused quite a stir when pointed out as the man whose clever little pills had relieved constipation on both sides of the Atlantic, and it was the Beecham fortunes which financed his famous grandson's musical career.

Around 1880, one of the great heart specialists of all time, Scots-born James Mackenzie, came to practise among the working folks of Burnley, and for 30 years in that industrially polluted area, studied case histories which inspired him to create a "Pulse Writing Machine" recording heart-action. It earned him international recognition, and fame lured him to London's Harley Street, but he never forgot those Lancashire mill-workers who made his achievements possible.

On April Fools' Day, 1904, the first model of the World's Finest Motor Car was shoved out of a workshop in Cook Street, Hulme, into the Spring sunlight by Henry Royce, a mechanic from Lincolnshire, who arrived in Manchester jobless and with £20 in his pocket.

Nor should we forget that Charles Dickens, who found his Cheeryble Brothers in Lancashire, used the Preston Strike of 1853/4 for "Hard Times", the novel that drove him "three parts mad". Disraeli, Mrs. Gaskell, Charlotte Brontë and many others drew heavily upon Lancashire for their novels, while Nathaniel Hawthorne, for four years U.S. Consul at Liverpool, wrote "Our Old Home" (1863) based upon his impressions of England. "The Condition of the Working Class in England" by Fredrich Engels is a savage denunciation of that "whited sepulchre", early Victorian Manchester, with its blackspots like Hulme and Ancoats and "Little Ireland", near the Medlock, "most horrible . . . of all" Engels, surely the original Angry Young Man, came from Germany in 1842 to work for his father's Patricroft cotton firm, spent much time noting humanity skulking in "ruinous cottages" . . . in "dark wet cellars" . . . in "measureless filth and stench". He went home after two years but returned for two more decades in 1850, being often visited by Karl Marx, and both resorting to the Reading Rooms at Chetham's.

A young Nottinghamshire Chancery Barrister who came to Manchester and took up a Professorship at Owen's College (forerunner of the University which he helped to expand) will ever be remembered for that world-famous hospital which stands to-day as a symbol of high hope and which took its name from Richard Copley Christie (1830-99).

Those who don't know Lancashire will find it hard to believe that this county, from end to end, is alive with Music! The folks who wear the red rose do not have to travel far to hear the most glorious choirs, the most pulse stirring bands, the most respected orchestras in the world, the most dedicated amateur groups whose standards would not disgrace the Albert Hall! Musically speaking, Sir Charles Hallé (b. 1819) put Manchester on the map when the French Revolution of 1848 drove him across the Channel into England. Nine years later, he founded the Hallé Orchestra, known the world over; he also helped to establish Manchester's Royal College of Music, and Lancashire became his home for ever.

Chetham's School of Music at Manchester, brought itself brilliantly to the notice of the whole nation during the 1982 prestigious "Young Musician of the Year" competition, televised by B.B.C. Three of the four finalists were Chetham's pupils and the winner was the Head Girl, 17-years old Anna Markland, pianist, from the Wirral. Those finals from Manchester's Free Trade Hall will not be forgotten in a hurry by many millions watching in from all over the country.

The late Sir Thomas Beecham was a genuine Lancashire product, born at St. Helens in 1879, educated at Rossall School (another of whose famous Old Boys was Leslie Charteris, author of "The Saint" series), a racy and rugged individualist and raconteur and "the greatest maker of music this country ever produced". By plundering those Beecham fortunes, he created the London Philharmonic Orchestra in 1932 and will long be remembered for a lifetime of "ravishing sounds". Oldham gave to the world Sir Wm. Walton, one of our greatest conductor/composers, and also Dame Eva Turner of the huge and magnificent voice; while at Higher Walton in 1912 was born that beautiful, fun-loving Lancashire lass, Kathleen Ferrier, who grew up in Blackburn, and whose superlative singing is still recalled with tender pride. The whole world of music mourned her early death in 1953.

Eighteenth century Lancashire produced artists of the calibre of Liverpool's George Stubbs, celebrated painter of horses, and George Romney who produced 23 portraits of Emma, Lady Hamilton, and who was a serious rival to Reynolds and Gainsborough. Romney would have considered himself a Lancastrian; only boundary changes have swept him, posthumously, into Cumbria! More recently, and more controversially, Augustus John, L. S. Lowry and Helen Bradley earned fame and fortune and during the last few years Richard Ansdell, R.A., the Victorian artist who specialised in animals and the windswept outdoors in style sometimes reminiscent of Landseer's, has evoked a revival of interest. He was born in Liverpool, built a summer residence (now Starr Hills Methodist Home for the Aged) among the dunes at the edge of old Lytham Common c. 1860 for the joy of watching the glorious sunsets; and in due course the large district of Ansdell in Lytham-St. Annes adopted his name. Apart from these internationally acclaimed ones, the county has an impressive roll of superbly gifted regional painters whom no rewards would tempt away from the fount of so much inspiration, and whose works have brought me so much joy. Let me mention just one, whose exquisite fantasies have delighted me since childhood along the Fylde coast, Patience Arnold who is still happily beavering away in her Lakeland studio with all the old delicacy and purity of style.

Lancashire gave the world superb 18th century furniture by Gillow, Unilever, moulded hot-water-bottles, the C.H.A. & Holiday Fellowship, Crosswords, Leyland Vehicles, Beatlemania, and the old G.F.S. that befriended many a young servant girl away from home for the first time. It was founded in Toxteth, Liverpool, birthplace of one of the world's greatest astronomers, Jeremiah Horrocks, and lamentably in 1981 the setting for terrifying street violence. And remember, the world's first sugar-coated pills were produced in Lancashire by a family firm whose linctus "Tackles that Tickle!", Parkinsons of Burnley, still operating in the 5th generation!

Above all, Lancashire has given us laughter! The twang is a great vehicle for humour, graphic description, the apt word. It is warm, and broad, and unambiguous. It is candid, but not unkindly, and it comes from the guts, rather than from the head. The Lancashire comedian is funny before he opens his mouth, unlike so many who stand at a microphone and ream off a string of memorised jokes. Liverpool, whose citizens think, talk and sound like no-one else on earth! . . . specialises in acrid, dead-pan humour. (They will tell you that you have to be a comedian to live there!) . . . but its list of funny men includes stars like Rob Wilton, Arthur Askey, Ted Ray, Tommy Handley and Ken Dodd. The county's list sweeps in Gracie Fields and the droll Hylda Baker; and Thora Hird and Dora Bryan, the two George Formbys, that irrepressible "Rochdale Cowboy", Mike Harding with the deceptive innocence twinkling behind those absurd goggles, Norman Evans ("Over the Garden Wall"), Eric Sykes, Eric Morecambe, Jimmy James, Roy Castle, Al Read, Les Dawson and the monstrously funny Frank Randle. My great favourite used to be Dave Morris, the straw-boatered de-bunker of officialdom who pilloried the Civil Service for seasons on end on South Pier, Blackpool. Nowadays, I fall about when Cannon and Ball appear on television and who couldn't have sprung from anywhere but Lancashire!

Comedy and this county have become synonymous but it is also appropriate to recall that Lancashire has an inexhaustible fund of Compassion! So many great and worthy causes for the betterment of mankind were championed here. And tormented, as I shall ever be by the items I have had to leave out, I will close this section with another "first" that touches my heart most nearly. In the aftermath of the Penlee Lifeboat disaster which brought in donations from all over the world, we rest assured that the R.N.L.I. is in good heart, and financially healthy. It was not always so. And in October 1891, Saturday crowds in Manchester and Salford were startled to see two lifeboats and their crews, mounted on carts, being dragged through the streets before proceeding to Belle Vue where they were launched on the lake before an audience of 30,000, many of whom had never set eyes on the sea! This first "Lifeboat Saturday", now held annually, raised £5,500, that day, increased the annual revenue of the R.N.L.I. by £40,000 and pulled the Service out of the financial doldrums.

The organiser was (Sir) Charles Macara, son of the Free Kirk Manse, who migrated from Fifeshire to Manchester at the age of 16 in 1862 to work for the House of Bannerman, a cotton concern founded by a Perthshire farmer. Macara made good, married into the family, moved to a promenade residence at St. Annes-on-the-Sea in 1884 and formed a close friendship with the lifeboat crew of the "Laura Janet", all 13 of whom, along with 14 from Southport's "Eliza Fearnley" perished in the Ribble estuary on 10th December 1886 while attempting to reach the German barque "Mexico" (whose entire company was miraculously saved by the Lytham contingent).

This, the greatest tragedy in the whole history of the Lifeboat Service, shook the world, stunned two communities on the Lancashire coast, broke the heart of Charles Macara who had loved those heroes like brothers. For years afterwards, he lectured and wrote about the R.N.L.I., promoting interest, raising the much needed funds. On the very morning after this awful disaster, you can be very sure that a new crew volunteered and signed on. And among them was a beloved old chum of mine, the late Henry (Harry) Melling of St. Annes whose old Dad, in anxiety for his lad, threatened to turn him out for his temerity. He wasn't even old enough; had to lie about his age to be accepted; spent the rest of his life in the Service and was the last Coxswain of the last St. Annes Lifeboat which operated until the Station closed down in 1925. For many years, his son "Billy" Melling, whose funeral packed the parish church in Spring 1981, joined his father in the lifeboat, the two of them risking death while saving life on so many heroic errands of mercy. The Lancashire lifeboats from north to south have a proud record of service and a prodigious list of lives saved at sea. It has been my privilege to know, and love, and record the memories of many of these self-effacing Supermen whose modesty, whose courage, whose sense of comedy were a true blend of all that is best in this wonderful county.

3.   THE LANCASHIRE TWANG

*" I am always sorry when any language is lost because
languages are the pedigree of nations ".*
Samuel Johnson.

IDEALLY, we would all be bi-lingual – fluent in standard English, equally at home with the regional patois. The Yorkshireman is a splendid example, addressing customers with formal correctness, and "thee-ing" and "tha-ing" with the best of them when talking to his workmen.

The Lancashire man is of another ilk and couldn't disclaim his origins even if he had a mind to. As soon as he opens his mouth, the "r's" give him away every time – and, incidentally, turn his tortured French into purest comedy!

There is an uncompromising honesty about "th'owd Lonkysheer" which is a grand, or "gradely" language to relapse into in moments of excitement. Insults that would be bitterly resented in standard English are somehow acceptable, and even very funny, in th'owd Lanky twang. Standardised B.B.C. English sounds clipped and cool and bloodless compared with the rich, gutsy dialect of the county. Besides, dialect is a language in its own right, rooted in history, having its own wild notes and cadences, employing words handed down from Celtic, Anglo-Saxon, Norse, Danish and Norman French forbears. It doesn't have to apologise for itself, for it is the honest folkspeech of the natives, recognisable instantly though varying even from one village to another. It is a full-bodied, broad-chested speech contemptuous of the long "a" (let them talk of "grahss" in the drawling south), and none too keen on the letter "l" which, except at the beginning of words, is shed wherever possible ("schoo'", "foo'", "baw'", "wilta be towd?"). "H" is another problem; best drop it altogether (Hexcept when you are eer to Hopen a bazaar!) "R" is pronounced, indeed it is emphasised, wherever it is written, not as the Scot rolls it, nor as the Geordie strangles it, but as it was meant to be sounded – "th'moRnin StaR wuR bReet an' fuRR".

The Lancastrian does odd things with the "ou" sound which becomes more distorted the further east you travel, "out" becoming "eawt" or even "eht", according to district. The short "o" is often interchanged with the short "a" – "mon" for "man"; "con" for "can" – "conti lend us thi 'ommer?" "he's wesht his honds". There is great delight in shortening words of two syllables – "ta'en" for "taken"; "ne'er" for "never"; "o'er" for "over", and similar satisfaction in extending the metrical content of monosyllabic words like "poor" which in Lanky becomes "poo-er". "Who" "Whooa"; "alone" – "aloo-an"; "clothes" – "cloo-az", and so forth. "Hoo", for "she" (from "Heo") is pure Anglo-Saxon and the housewife sweeps "t'pad" (path) as did her Norse progenitors.

That supremely lazy and totally unattractive glottal stop which T.V. plays have done so much to popularise in the last twenty years is an urban product. In forty years of research, I have never heard an old Fylde native resort to that ugly little hiccup which became almost as obligatory as the wearing of denim in the Swinging 'Sixties. I reckon both English and the dialect would be a whole lo(t) pre(tt)ier withou(t) i(t)! (Producers please note).

In this part of the world you will hear "brunt" and "brids" (burnt and birds), both good Anglo-Saxon words, and Wycliff used them in his 14th century translation of the Bible. Those scars on Pendle's side were caused by water-"brasts" (bursts) long ago. Our every-day word "nice", meaning agreeable or dainty, becomes "nesh" in Lancashire, from A.S. "hnesc" – meaning tender, soft, delicate or sensitive. We shiver in a "nesh" wind, or refer to that spoiled, spineless lad as "browt up too nesh for owt!"

"Nobbut", meaning "only", which also appears in that early Bible, is a great favourite, as is "welly" (Middle English "well-nigh" or "nearly"), and in dialect you allus say "allus" (not always). They speak of "e'en" (eyes) and "shoon" (shoes or boots) and in summer they take the degging-can and "deg" or dampen the garden – as Scandinavian immigrants were doing here, centuries ago. They don't squint, they "sken"; they don't gulp their food, they "gollop" it; and "if owt guz wrang" – be it machinery, household articles or thatch on the roof – they "fettle" it. (When in good health, they "are i' fine fettle"). They say "happen" (pronounced 'app'n) instead of "perhaps" or "possibly", tack on the word "like" for emphasis and use the double negative whenever possible ("ah, wouldn't give 'em nowt!" . . . "They cornt do nowt wi' him, like!")

Shrewd sayings have travelled down the generations, crackling with native wit and humour. "Bread etten is soon fergetten" (ingratitude). "As peart as a dog wi' a tin tail". "If he wor a slice o' tooast, he'd land butter side up" (a lucky person). "When they wor cwortin, he loved her that mich, he could hev etten her. Afther they wur wed, he wisht ta God he hed!" "Troubles come thick an' three fold". "Doo-ant cut tort-tha, then tha weyant hort-tha' (don't peel towards yourself, then you won't hurt yourself). "Hunger is t'best sauce". "Too mich of owt is good for nowt". To be very rich is to be "bow-legged wi' brass", and brain-weary is "pow-fagged". "A bellowin' ceaw soon fergets id cawf". "A creakin' doo-er hangs long on th'hinges!" "Stroke wi' one hand, strike wi't'other".

All of which proves that the down-to-earth Lanky man "wasn't behind the doo-er when they wur givin' t'brains eawt!" Nor did he lack ingenuity when concocting nick-names to apply to his neighbours, a few uncomplimentary, all amusing, many handed down the generations, as in the case of "Bill-o' Jack's" or "Dick'o'Ned's-o'Bob's". I talked to an old chap who, when he was a little lad at Sunday School, was invited out for tea by one of the scholars. When they arrived at her back door, her old grannie called out: "Whoo-a's-ta getten theer?", to which the little girl replied: "Elizabeth Cookson's-Janey Barrow's-Johnny Clarke!" "Oh!", said Grandma, placing the stranger at once. "Well, then. Coom thee enduss an' set thee deawn on th'squab, an' put thi fute on th'kather!" The lad sidled sheepishly in, seated himself on the sofa (squab) but didn't know where the devil to put his "fute" (foot) until the old lady indicated that, in return for having his tea out, he was expected to put his foot on the cradle rocker and lull the newest infant to sleep.

From Marton Moss, outside Blackpool, to the moorland regions bordering the Pennines, nicknames abounded and were so generally used that folk were often puzzled to recollect the correct nomenclature of their neighbours. The "Mossogs" had a grand collection of by-names, all handed down – the Websters being "Ducks", the Boardmans – "Shanks", the Eaves's being "Chickins" and the Harrisons – "Tossies". (See my "Seven Golden Miles" for a full list). Thus, Elizabeth Webster would be known as "Lily Duck"; a third or fourth generaton "James Harrison" became "Jimmy Tossy", and Richard Boardman – "Dicky Shank".

Inspiration was drawn from physical peculiarities in cases like "Red Nob", "Ducky-legs", "Littlethick", "Smiler", "Owd Boco". Tom of the Fold would become "Tum Fowt"; "Flattener" was a good boxer; but explanations for names like "Owd Gobbler", "Owd Pills", "Owd Corks", "Shiggles", "Flimmins" died with their owners.

Whole townships had their nicknames, such as Bowton Trotters, Snuffy 'Arroders (Great Harwood), Eccles Cakers, Burry Puddin's, Darren (Darwin) Salmon, Blegburn (Blackburn) Duddoos, Owfen (Westhoughton) Keaw-yeds; Ozzies or Gobbin-landers (Oswaldtwistlers), Owdham (Oldham) Roof-Yeds; Middleton Moonrakers, etc. (for a comprehensive list read "Lancashire Nicknames and Sayings" by Bob Dobson – Dalesman publication).

One wonders why parents of a hundred years ago bothered to dream up two perfectly acceptable Christian names when the likelihood was that they would be slurred together, as in Marthalice, MurryAnn, S'rran, Marthannah, Murryalice. Similarly, surnames were contracted, particularly in the country areas of Fylde and Over-Wyre. Having started off as – Tomlinson, Atkinson, Jenkinson, Hodgkinson, Metcalf, Lawrenson, Myerscough, Threlfall, Catterall, Fairclough, Hull, Banks, Hayhurst, Curwen or Gaulter . . . they finished up sounding like: "Tumliss'n, Akissa', Jenkyss'n, Husskiss'n, Medcawf, Larns'n, Maska, Trelfa', Cattra', Feercla', Hoole, Bonk, 'Urst, Curran or Gawter. Thus, Henry Banks became "Harry a Bonk"; Richard Hull – "Richert a Hoole"; Edward Whiteside (the first company-housekeeper in Blackpool) – "Ethart a-Whiteshut!"

Locally, Poulton-le-Fylde becomes "Poot'n, Skelmersdale – "Skemmers'l" or "Skem"; Westhoughton is "Owfen"; Stalmine is "Stawmin"; Walkden "Wogden". Worsley – Wazzly. Burscough – "Bosca" and Burnley – "Brunley". There are dozens more you can find out by talking to the natives.

The stranger notices the softening of "d" and "t" when they occur in the middle of a word. Wandering becomes "wantherin'"; ladder – "ladther"; burden – "burthen". He soon realises that "mun" means "must" – "Ah mun ged agate" (I must get moving), whereas "munt" or "moo-ant" means the opposite – "Eigh! Tha munt do that , lad!"

Those who condemn the dialect as slovenly, ill-begotten English mouthed by the ignorant for the edification of the contemptible, should remember that many dialect words and phrases can be traced directly back to dear old Geoffrey Chaucer. Is anyone presumptuous enough to dismiss "The Father of English Poetry" for using words like: "Hastow" (hast thou), "Artow" (art thou); "lig" (lie down); "skryked" (shrieked); "Ax" (ask); "Lappe" (fold); "Mixen" (midden) – even the very respectable Tennyson used that! "Cote" (cottage or shed) – as in Cottam, meaning "Huts", a village near Preston; "Warch" (ache) – "Hesti getten t'belly-warch?" These words crop up in "Canterbury Tales" and in country districts are still in use to-day, particularly by the older generation. Let us hope the youngsters are taking heed and cleaving to their birthright.

Even now, I reckon Chaucer, with his quick ear and lively wit, would be in his element in this county, though he hailed from the south, was educated at Oxford/Cambridge (they both claim the honour), knew John o' Gaunt and enjoyed the great Duke's protection. How he would love our verbal gusto and sharp asides. You wouldn't find him puckering his handsome brow in real or pretended puzzlement at some of the comical expressions tumbling forth. He would be far too busy capping one phrase with another and enjoying the exercise hugely, for this was his very own lingo. In comedy, the Lancastrian has powers akin to Chaucer's and in quick wittedness, I doubt if he has any equals!

Blackpool's Sep Smith was a prime example. Born in 1879 with a caul over his face and a hint of Romany blood in his veins, Septimus grew up blessed with a nimble wit and lively tongue that got him into more scrapes than a few during his brief schooling. When the teacher accused him unjustly of some small mischief, he didn't pass over that lightly. Instead, he sat on her and threatened her with a brick, and was expelled . . . a situation which he probably dismissed with contempt and a hundred well-chosen sentences . . . in rhyme! He went into the building trade, loved boats, bargains and babies better, remained a bachelor, however, – his only romance came to grief – and went into buying and selling. Made a fortune but always wore second-hand suits and a sixpenny hat with a feather ("What's th'use o' paying all them guineas for new 'uns?), opened a warehouse crammed with just about everything, and agitated to get Cowley Road re-named "Manners-and-Sense" Road. Moved to "Sep Avenue" which the Council promptly labelled "Dover Road", though Sep was always busy tacking up the old name during the night.

He was a genuine one-off, always good for a laugh, writing and talking in rhyming couplets which he shot off the cuff so rapidly that no-one could record them, even in shorthand. Whether on the top deck of a bus, in the Magistrates' Court or on the electioneering platform, he aired his independent views with vigour and hilarity. He made several attempts to get on the Council, never succeeded, but kept the populace in a state of helpless merriment in the process. His election addresses, all in rhyme, of course, were sold in thousands. Free toilets for ladies, making up-hills run down-hill and vice-versa, straightening all the bends in the roads and challenging the world, including Yorkshire! . . . no wonder his campaign meetings were always crammed to the doors.

During one of these gala occasions a heckler with a fruity voice called out: "Hey, Sep! How monny too-az hez a pig?". Quick as a flash came the answer: "Ah dooan't knaw, lad, but tek thi booits off an' Ah'll count 'em". Another time, he knocked up a hand-cart out of oddments. A friend called and admired it. "By gum, Sep", he says, "that's a good 'un! how've ya med it?" "Out of me heyd, lad", chuckles Sep. "An' thur's enough wood left ta mek another just like it!" Until the end of 1958 he was a familiar figure in the town, never wore overcoat or socks, even in winter, always had pockets-ful of sweets for the folks he met on the buses, rolled up at hospital with gifts for new babies or sick people, wrapped up in newsprint, a man both parsimonious and generous to a degree, and for all his garrulity, always clean spoken. They talk about him still!

Under-statement, exaggeration and colourful similes add vigour and interest to the language. "Ah'm nobbut middlin'", means "feeling pretty awful". A weakling "couldna knock skin off a rice puddin'". "He started off nobbut middlin, and tapered off!", describes the hopeless apprentice, while "Gormless as Soft Mick", "as mich use as a chocolate poker" . . . or as "glass tacks an' a rubber 'ommer" . . . or "a knitted tay-pot" signifies the ultimate in inanity.

The terseness of the twang also makes sentiments abundantly clear. At a Candlemas Hiring Fair, lads and lassies hung about, waiting to be "tekken on". A farmer with a poor reputation, having weighed up the prospects, spotted a likely-looking youth and began to haggle. When all seemed settled the farmer warned: "I'se want thi character, tha knaws! See me when tha's getten it an' we con fix up, like!" They met later. The farmer asked: "Hesta getten thi character?". "Naw!", replied the youth, "but Ah've getten thine, an' Ah'm nooan coomin'!"

Note how the Welshman fights to retain his language. I can't always approve the way he goes about it but, at the same time, cannot help admiring his devotion to an excellent cause. Bi-linguality is the answer, I feel, and a study of philology in day-schools might help to cleanse the English language of Americanised slang punctured with grunts, glottal stops and hackneyed catch-phrases gleaned from cinema or television; and at the same time lead to a better understanding of the historic Lancashire dialect which can prick a conscience, administer a good telling-off, convey a world of tenderness or reduce an audience to tears or gales of laughter, in a sentence!

I recall the late Ronald Digby, retired schoolmaster and editor of "A Rossendale Anthology" talking about the visiting celebrity who came to address the whole school on the subject of "The English Language". For an hour and a half they listened politely to a mellifluous voice expounding on the correct use and pronunciation of English. Sitting at the back, the master, a dialect scholar and devotee, felt his heart slowly sinking. But when it was over, in the headlong rush to get out of the assembly hall, one young Accringtonian was heard calling urgently to another: "Hey, Jonty! Hesti getten thi Shakespee-urr?". "And that", he confided, "fair warmed my heart".

The Fylde dialect, I am sorry to say, is disappearing rapidly now. Blackpool and her sister resorts attracted too many incomers for it to survive unadulterated and the internal combustion completely transformed the rural way of life. It is, to my mind, the prettiest of all the Lancashire folk-tongues, Anglo-Saxon, basically, with fragments of Irishised Norse for spice and flavour; and you can still track it down in Marton Moss or the quieter Over-Wyre region. Some of it is recalled in my "Fylde Folk – Moss or Sand" in tales like that of "Owd Betty" who used to catch the "Markut Special" train from Moss Side to Preston every Saturday morning. Her husband's weekly ration of "twist 'bacca" was always on her list, but one week she purchased an extra ounce, crammed it into the jar and said nothing. The following Saturday, finding the jar empty, she asked: "Wheer's aw' thi 'bacca getten to?" "Ah've smooked id", said Jem. "Why!", she accused, "Ah bowt thee an extry lot last Set'da!" "Didta?", exclaimed Jem. "Ah thowt id needed some geddin' through this week!"

That happened long before my time. More recently, my heart leapt at the sight of two elderly farmers meeting outside the village shop in the charming little Norse village of Wrea Green. They surveyed one another quizzically, eyes twinkling, good health shining out from two honest old faces. "Na-then, Johnny! Howrta gait?" (how are you getting on) enquired one. After a pause (for weighing up, like), the other commented: "Noo-an as weel as thee, bi t'look on thee!" . . . a compliment implied, warmth, affection and good humour all expressed in one short phrase! And that, I can tell you, fairly warmed my old cockles!

4. THE MAKING OF A COUNTY

THE SURVEYORS who compiled the Domesday Book (1080-6) had many hazards and discomforts to contend with – gloomy forests, trackless wastes, impenetrable marshes and rivers without bridges. With waning enthusiasm, they covered what is now Lancashire, but sketchily and, having reached Preston in the Hundred of Amounderness, they probably summoned the townreeve, enquired what lay between there and the coast, noted it down, and left it at that. Obviously, they never set foot in Lytham or they would have seen the church in existence. At least five others were omitted from the Survey which listed 18 Lancashire churches, whereas 24, or more, would have been nearer the mark.

And that, of course, is a deliberately misleading statement because in Domesday there was no Lancashire as we know it. The northern portion was lumped in with Yorkshire and the area south of Ribble was included in Cheshire. The first steps were taken to establish Lancashire after the Conquest when William rewarded his supporter, Roger of Poitou, with the area around Morecambe Bay and the land betwixt Ribble and Mersey. Roger chose Lancaster as his base since it guarded the road into Scotland. When he fell from grace in 1102 his estates reverted to the Crown.

A lifetime later there were odd references to the "county of Lancaster" and from 1182 the name "Lancastra" was applied to that remote region between Mersey and Duddon. Seven years later, the none too savoury Richard I bestowed the Honour of Lancaster on his rapacious brother, John Lackland, Count of Mortain, the King John of inglorious memory. His son, Henry III, bestowed the Earldom of Lancaster, with special privileges, on his youngest son Edmund who died in 1296. In the next century, local civil strife broke out when Edmund's son, Thomas, Earl of Lancaster, fell out with the Sovereign, causing a polarisation of loyalties among the county's powerful families, and an incident referred to as the Banastre Revolt (1315). Sir Adam Banastre of Shevington and his friends clashed with supporters of the rebel Earl Thomas. It was an unhappy time for Lancashire, rendered worse by pestilence and poor crops, and the uneasy peace that followed was rudely shattered in 1322 when Robert the Bruce and his raiders swept down as far south as Chorley.

But with the inevitable swing of history, Earl Thomas's son Henry of Lancaster was rewarded for his allegiance to Edward III with the Dukedom of Lancaster with full palatinate powers. In his kingdom-within-a-kingdom, except for national taxation, he wielded almost unlimited jurisdiction. It lapsed when he died in 1361 but was revived sixteen years later in favour of Edward III's fourth son, John of Gaunt, so named because he had been born at Ghent. This mystical and romantic figure, "Time-Honoured Lancaster", fathered Duke Henry who dethroned Richard II and occupied the throne of England as Henry IV. Thus, in 1399, when "Old Gaunt" passed on, the palatinate was linked with the Sovereign; and the wily Henry was assured of a useful power-base to fall back on in case anyone with gall enough tried to prise him off his throne! That, of course, did not happen, and to-day the Lancastrian enjoys his unique link with the monarch and feels a special pride when the loyal toast is proposed to "The Queen, the Duke of Lancaster".

"They win or die who wear the Rose of Lancaster"

In those distant crazy days when knights charged about like bundles of animated ironmongery, hacking each other to pieces, it was only possible to distinguish friend from foe by the wearing of a linen surcoat embroidered with a recognisable emblem. The Plantaganets adopted a sprig of broom blossom from the plant Genista though, according to an old school book, they also favoured a golden rose. "Just when the red and white forms of it" were used by rival branches of the family had long been forgotten but the habit was established before the Wars of the Roses which culminated in a victory for the house of Lancaster at Bosworth in 1485. Those hostilities had erupted in spasms for thirty years, a job for mercenaries, no principles being involved. Two powerful cliques wished to control the government of the country. It was as simple as that.

There is a persistent legend that rivals from Lancaster and York were strolling in some palace gardens when one plucked a red rose and the other a white rose for his badge. The "English Illustrated Magazine" of June 1889 may shed light on the subject in the story of the Savoy, between the Strand and the Thames, of which only the beautiful Savoy Chapel survives with its small churchyard and unbreakable links with Lancashire. Count Peter of Savoy settled here, built a house in 1246, laid out pleasure grounds and passed his days happily. He had arrived ten years earlier in the train of his niece, Eleanor of Provence, bride of Henry III who took kindly to his accomplished and courtierly uncle-in-law, sent him on missions abroad and, for his greater dignity, gave him several acres "outside the walls of our city of London in a street called The Strand". The friars of Mountjoy inherited when Count Peter died but Queen Eleanor bought back the estate, kept it in repair and left it to her youngest and "most dear son", Edmund Plantaganet, Earl of Lancaster, while his father, the King, permitted this favourite son to fortify his property with a wall of lime and stone. Honours and possessions were heaped upon this Earl Edmund, nicknamed "Crouchback", who brought from Provence those red roses which his descendants adopted as their emblem.

Roses bloomed at the Savoy long after Edmund's death, when John o' Gaunt, son in law of the Duke of Lancaster, was savouring the good life, turning the Savoy into a palace befitting the first man in the land. Chaucer was a constant visitor. In fact, he lived on a ducal allowance of £10 a year. And when friend Wyclif was summoned to appear before the Bishop of London for his alleged "sins", Gaunt accompanied him and threatened to thrash the prelate. The enraged Londoners, who detested Gaunt, retaliated by ransacking the Savoy Palace, burning, looting, slashing at his best jewelled coat with axes and raiding his cellars, "and so was all whatsoever destroyed" during the Wat Tyler riots. The property then reverted to the crown and to the Duchy of Lancaster, being carved into eligible building sites, including a plot for Henry VII's hospital "for nedie pouer people" in that place called "the Savoie besid Charing Crosse".

Only the Savoy Chapel survived, hemmed in now, engulfed by "the roaring loom of Time". Yet here, seven centuries ago, the proud symbol of Lancasire first bloomed, the Red Rose brought over from "the sunny pleasances of Provence".

5. PROUD PRESTON

Old Unicorn Inn, Walton-le-Dale.

"PRIESTS TOWN" . . . I love the place! Attended Commercial College there in the 'Thirties, worked at County Hall during the war years. Probably didn't appreciate what a history-packed place it was, then. Just loved its atmosphere, its warmth, its busy-ness and the magic of the markets. Browsing round the stalls offered free lunch-time entertainment. "Stockings, tenpence a pair!" (4p), bellowed an old-timer. "And if there's a one-legged woman, I'll split a pair!" . . . "Lace, tuppence a hank that goes round twice (but don't ask me round WHAT!"), followed by a broad wink. On non-market days there were the shops, art galleries, the library, and nervous hoverings at the entrances to mysterious and forbidding yards. Names like Fishergate, Friargate, Stoneygate, Main Sprit Weind and Old Cock Yard hinted at past romancings. Miller Park, and Avenham Park where eggs are rolled on Easter Mondays, were pleasant for strolling; the Ribble gurgled by and over by the docks, great cranes unloaded raw materials from all parts of the globe. The railway station in war-time was a sea of uniforms from the allied forces and gallant W.V.S. ladies dispensing tea and buns, round the clock, to millions passing through.

Peace brought an attack of "Shopping Precinct" fever. Old properties were cleared, ring roads appeared and what is thought to be the largest bus station in Europe, together with multi-storey car parks and the Guildhall which ought to have been ready for the Guild Merchant of 1972, but wasn't, because of industrial disputes. The Guild Court, therefore, was held in the old Public Hall, once the hub of the cotton trade, and I was there on the front row of the gallery within arm's reach of the flower of the Lancashire nobility and gentry. Lord Derby sat beneath my right hand. The then Cardinal Heenan and a bevy of Catholic prelates in red or purple beyond my left. Memorable was the sight of Preston Freemen, four generations from the same family, from ancient Grand-dad and middle-aged Dad to the young father of a swaddled babe, all rising or being held aloft to make their solemn obeisances to the Court. My host, an enrolled Freeman, could trace his line for 400 years through the parchments lodged in the Town Hall. The benefits once enjoyed by his forebears were nullified by the Municipal Reform Act of 1835 which imposed a uniform system and abolished old trading privileges. Nevertheless, he would have risen from a sick-bed to have his name entered, along with those of his son and grandson. Without any obligation, there is every hope that the next Preston Guild Merchant will be celebrated in September, 1992, commencing on the Monday following the Feast of the Decollation of St. John the Baptist.

The Guild, from Anglo-Saxon "Gild", meaning money, was an association of townsmen. It protected craftsmen from competition from incomers or "foreigners" who only operated by permission of the Guild Merchant and by payment of fees. Members, however, were bound to high standards of workmanship and materials and the conscientious training of craft apprentices. Burgesses also enjoyed privileges and immunities, having command over their markets and being free "quietly and honourably" to traipse with their merchandise, free from "toll, passage, pontage" through the monarch's dominions.

The Guild Merchant probably originated in 1179 by Royal Charter of Henry II. The next recorded Guild was in 1328 and subsequent celebrations were irregular until 1542 when twenty year intervals were decided upon and Guilds were regularly held until the second world war caused a postponement from 1942 to 1952. By that time, the old Guildhall had been burned down in 1947, a serious set-back, coupled with general apathy. Nevertheless, preparations went ahead and the 1952 Guild was a proud and happy milestone in Preston's history. I can only remember the 1972 celebrations which were exciting, colourful, spectacular and eternally memorable as a feast for eye and ear.

*　　　*　　　*　　　*

Late in the first century the Romans had a small military station on the alluvial flats between the A.6 and the River Darwen which empties into the Ribble at Walton-de-Dale. Experts once dismissed it as of no account until 1855 when workmen turned up "Scotch pennies" which were Roman. Excavations brought up pottery and other fragments (Vol. VIII of the Historic Society of Lancs. & Cheshire's Transactions) and a more recent probe (Vol. 109) in 1947-8 points to two periods, the first timber buildings having to be replaced, c.120 A.D., after a fire. The site, with a civilian settlement adjoining, was a natural choice. A navigable river, fordable at Penwortham, Walton-le-Dale and Cuerdale, linked it with Ribchester. Centuries dragged by before the bridge "having V great arches" was constructed at Walton.

Principal township of the Hundred of Amounderness, Preston, high on the Ribble's north bank, began to develop after the Roman withdrawal. It was halfway along the trade route between London and Scotland. It was familiar to warring factions passing through or fighting within its environs. From the 1320's it was also the administrative centre for the Duchy of Lancaster. Yet it was, and still is, a stronghold of the Old Faith. Lands here were given to the Ripon monks under Archbishop Wilfrid in 705 and a church was dedicated to his memory. That early St. Wilfrid's was rebuilt in 1581 and re-dedicated to St. John the Divine and in 1855 it was almost entirely replaced to a design by Shellard.

From earliest times, trading went on in the shadow of the church, a reminder that the Almighty was watchful of secular affairs also. A stone's-throw away, the Market place developed where proclamations were made, villains were pilloried, where itinerants prayed at the cross and bull and bear baitings drew lusty crowds. Preston had survived Anglian invasions which absorbed the Romano-British, Norse intruders who settled and became farmers, and the upheavals after the Norman Conquest when Earl Tostig's possessions were given to Roger of Poitou. Normans brought monasticism into the county and in the 12th century the Benedictines of Evesham established a daughter house at Penwortham, a handful of monks managing the estate. In 1123 Stephen gave land at Tulketh to the Order of Savigny which removed to Furness, amalgamated with the Cistercians and established a magnificent sandstone abbey, ranked second only to Fountains.

A 13th century hospice dedicated to St. Mary Magdalene was founded in the Maudlands and grey-clad Franciscans settled in the heart of Preston, labouring in poverty and preaching to the townsfolk. Their collegiate building with chapel and cloisters, acquired after the Dissolution by "that devourer of monastic lands", Sir Thomas Holcroft, was occupied by the Breres of Bowland. It became a House of Correction until the gaol was built at the foot of Church Street in 1790.

Old Preston had its share of royal visits. Athelstan passed through en route to another battle with the Northumbrian danes, liked what he saw, bought and gave it to the Church of York. His triumph at Brunanburgh in 937 routed a coalition of Scots, Irish, Welsh and Danes in a battle that raged from sun-up to sun-down, leaving kinglets, princes, earls and commoners slaughtered on some bloody field which has not yet been decisively located. Many have claimed the Brunanburgh site, from Bromborough to Burnley, Banbury to Burn, from Burnham, Brownedge, Bourne and Brunton, to a site near the M.1 between Rotherham and Sheffield Until firm evidence is produced to the contrary, my imagination clings stubbornly to the possibility, if no more, of Athelstan's forces slashing "with swords mill sharp" within sight of the Ribble before the survivors took flight

" In their nailéd barks . . .

On roaring ocean

The mystery was revived on 15th May 1840 when labourers, repairing the river bank at Cuerdale where a memorial now stands, uncovered a lead-lined chest containing 10,000 silver coins minted between AD.815-928 and 1,000 ounces of ingots and ornamental items. It was declared to be Treasure Trove, claimed by the Crown, not before numerous samples had vanished! The rest was shared out between the British Museum and other bodies and Preston lost the opportunity of displaying, in its entirety, one of the most amazing discoveries of Anglo-Saxon silver. Was this the treasure chest of an army in flight? The loot of a marauding band, ditched in blind panic? Or some vast personal fortune wrecked here by chance? Who will ever know? As for Brunanburgh, the mystery remains, tantalising as ever.

In 1306 Edward I issued two proclamations here during a march to Scotland and in 1322 Robert the Bruce came and burned the town, having first destroyed Samlesbury Hall which stood among the trees beside an old ferry crossing. When the Southworths rebuilt c. 1325 they picked a less obvious site deep in the woodlands. To-day, traffic hurtles along the Preston-Blackburn road within feet of this beautiful "magpie" building which recusancy fines obliged the Southworths to sell to Thomas Bradyll in 1678. The hall, famous for its legend of star-crossed love and an inconsolable White Lady, houses the Lancashire Branch of C.P.R.E., and is a favourite venue for exhibitions and functions. It was near-derelict in 1925 and was rescued in the nick of time by its "Friends" who tackled the restoration. It has splendid quatrefoil timbering, a great hall with a fine oriel window and connections with Saint John Southworth, the Lancashire Martyr.

Incidentally, Samlesbury's riverside parish church of St. Leonard the Less was roughly handled by the Bruce and his lusty fellows. Natives dreaded the tartan brigade and, at the alarm, headed with their valuables to the nearest refuge. Pele towers became a feature of the region and many of our historic houses developed from them later. Attacks were sharp and short, kilted ruffians piling their loot on to carts and driving stolen livestock before them. Samlesbury's little 12th century sandstone church offered the only protection but the attackers burst in, snatched valuables and vestments and pressed on to Ribchester, frightening villagers out of their wits and purloining anything that could be carried or driven.

Samlesbury's church feels ancient, still has original sand-stone portions in its gable-ends. It was "in ruine and indangering people" in 1558 and Lord Derby and his "louing friends . . . with there charity" paid for the rebuilding. Call in, if you have a taste for old country churches. Its floor is uneven – generations lie buried beneath – the 17th and 18th century box pews are a credit to forgotten local craftsmen, particularly the de Hoghton pew of 1688 and those of the Petres of Dunkenhalgh, 1719 and 1725. The choir occupy the west end where once sat the sad orphans who toiled at the Roach Bridge factory. Plenty of bygones here from Norman font and medieval bell, to a chained bible and relics of the Southworths. The old box pews have earned their right to lean and sag after centuries of service and one is surprised that tower and porch were only added in 1899.

Locals will point out the "Witch's grave" with a smashed stone and iron spikes beneath, a desperate widower's attempts to stop his first wife's hauntings (and he with his eye on another!) So runs one story! Others say the iron spikes were driven in to keep a witch quiet. Certainly, there was an outburst of hysterical prattle over "supposed" witches at Samlesbury in 1612. Several were conveyed to Lancaster and tried there but the chief prosecution witness, the mischievous adolescent, Grace Sowerbutts, was dismissed as "an impudent wench delivering a strangely devised accusation".

*   *   *   *

Preston returned a Member of Parliament in 1295 and elected a Mayor in 1327. Edward III, who had a soft spot for the place, deemed the richest of the county's royal boroughs, granted another Charter in 1328. He had passed through in 1333 with his army on his way to Scotland. The Dissolution of the monasteries caused rumblings of unease and again, Prestonians slept fitfully when the Armada threatened in 1588. Notables rushed in to discuss defences with Lord Strange. Fortunately, apart from a minor alarm when a westerly gale grounded a Spanish vessel off Rossall Point, near modern Fleetwood, all passed off serenely. 1617 was memorable for James I's visit. He was received with acclamation in the Market Place, accepted a purse of gold and the obeisances of the municipal worthies, dined right heartily with the Mayor and corporate body at the Moot Hall and left the following day for Hoghton Tower, a formidable pile six miles away, poised above the Darwen.

Sir Richard de Hoghton, "Honest Dick", was host for the three-day royal visit. Jovial, hospitable and addicted to Rhenish, he spent recklessly on improvements to the ancestral home and stocks for the cellars. New stables and royal apartments for the king and his long-time favourite, "Babie Steenie", Duke of Buckingham, had been built and a red velvet carpet had been woven to cover the steep drive up to the Tower. Two months earlier, Royal Jamie, en route to London from Scotland, proposed to travel by way of Kendal, Hornby Castle, Ashton Hall, near Lancaster, Myerscough Lodge, home of the Tyldesleys, leaving there on 14th August 1617 for Preston. Incidentally, on 11th August, Mr. Shuttleworth of Barton Lodge, dreading the dubious honour of a royal stop-over, burned his house to the ground as the cheapest way out of a dilemma.

During that fabulous Hoghton weekend, the king hunted stags, visited Sir Richard's "Allum Works" near Blackburn, championed his subjects' lawful Sabbath recreations and touched a few for the King's

HOGHTON TOWER, a romantic and castellated fortress set upon a hill overlooking the River Darwen, was largely built by Thomas de Hoghton in the 1560's. The gatehouse gives access to a courtyard and "royal" stables specially built for the visit of James I in 1617. The gabled stone house had fallen into ruin 200 years ago but was restored during Victoria's reign.

Evil. Between drinking, dancing, dining and divine worship, he received petitions, knighted a very splendid loin of beef before departing for Lathom, attended by the gentry of Lancashire, many of whom received knighthoods. Sir Richard waved them off, collected a few bosom pals and descended to the cellars to drown deep sorrows after the costliest junketings in the history of his line. Hoghton Tower, now wooded about, is still there, full of history and well worth a visit, under the care of the 14th Baronet, Sir Bernard de Hoghton.

When James' son, Charles I, fell out with Parliament, Royalists flocked to Preston Moor in the summer of 1642, talked a lot, but took no action. Later in the year, they offered men and money for a Royalist garrison at Preston, and not a whit too soon, for in February 1643 Roundheads stormed the town, killing and capturing before moving on to occupy Hoghton Tower where, soon after, a powder store exploded, causing great loss of life. Lord Derby rushed over with relief troops but the Manchester men were approaching which drove him "quite away, out of the countie".

Fortune's tides swung hither and yond, Lancashire towns holding out or being recaptured for the King or for Cromwell. Uneasy peace came in 1645 and prevailed until 1648 when Scots moved south to the king's assistance. Again, Preston provided a backcloth to the action. The Duke of Hamilton's Royalists awaited reinforcements led by Sir Maramduke Langdale. Cromwell, meantime, racing along the Ribble valley, then hotly pursuing Langdale's troops through Chipping Vale and Longridge, engaged the King's men on Ribbleton Moor, taking prisoners and horses and driving the remainder into the town. The Royalists, hoping to counter-attack, rushed towards Walton-le-Dale but, by nightfall of 17th August 1648, had been chased over Darwen bridge and put to flight, only to be overtaken, trounced at Wigan and defeated at Warrington. During the action, Cromwell slept at the Unicorn Inn, Walton-le-Dale as Scottish blood stained the waters of Darwen. The Parliamentarians were cock-a-hoop and early in 1649 took the drastic step of beheading their sovereign.

In that year, hundreds perished by pestilence and famine and travellers kept well clear of stricken Preston. No thought now of Civil War with all its bitterness and sorrow. The problem was how to escape or survive the plague. Troubles had not finished yet. In 1651, Royalists commanded by the Earl of Derby, rallied round the dead monarch's son, (Charles II), and made a final bid for the Stuarts, passing over

Walton bridge and heading for Wigan where, at a spot marked by a monument, Sir Thomas Tyldesley fell mortally wounded. The drama was all but played out. Charles II fled overseas after the Battle of Worcester. The Earl of Derby was executed at Bolton and Royalists licked their wounds and kept a low profile until the monarchy was restored in 1660. Charles II left no legitimate children and his brother, James II, notorious for Catholic sympathies, was deposed in 1688, to the dismay of Lancashire Papists, High Anglicans and Tories. They were Jacobites, derived from the Latin form of James, "Jacobus", and in 1701 they formed a frivolous fraternity with a serious purpose, the "Mock Corporation of Walton" which met regularly at the Unicorn, kept records, elected a Mayor, municipal officers and other ridiculous title holders. The insignia and wands of office were kept at the hostelry which, by rumour, was a smugglers' roost and contraband depot. Illustrious personages came here, supped, caroused and plotted to restore a Catholic Stuart during the reign of Protestant Queen Anne. The Earl of Derwentwater, the Duke of Norfolk, important Lancashire knights and diarist Thomas Tyldesley, grandson of the famous leader, were all prominently connected. When Queen Anne died and George of Hanover arrived to a bungled reception in 1714, the Earl of Mar raced north to rouse the chieftains who summoned the clansmen, formed an army and moved south. Down they swept by Penrith, Appleby, Kendal and Lancaster, arriving in Preston on 9th November 1715 when James Edward Stuart was proclaimed James III beside the old Market Cross.

Preston was an elegant town, in those days, patronised by fashionable society in the winter season. A few, all Catholics and not as many as expected, joined the high-spirited rebels who had become cocky enough to mind little "but courting and feasting". Ladies flirted with the officers while the Commanding Officer, General Forster, dallied pleasantly, unaware, perhaps, that Hanoverian forces under Generals Wills and Carpenter, were drawing nearer with every hoof beat. They reached Preston on 12th November 1715, found the town barricaded, and "lay upon their arms" overnight after setting fire to a few barns and houses.

And where was General Forster during these critical hours? In bed, apparently, taking it easy, instead of conferring with his officers and preparing his troops for a do or die effort on the morrow. By noon next day, the situation was hopeless. The Jacobites were totally surrounded by Hanoverians and by 3 o'clock, were discussing surrender terms in the Mitre Inn in the Market place (site of Harris Library). Furious rebel officers were tempted to shoot the incompetent Forster who was taken prisoner the following day, a "Black Monday", indeed! More than 1500 common soldiers, mostly Highlanders, were locked up in the freezing cold of the Parish Church on bread and water, waiting to be escorted to Lancaster Castle. Their officers, shocked beyond belief, surrendered to the Hanoverians, the shame of their ignominious collapse with scarcely a blow struck conveyed to the townsfolk who looked on aghast (though you would scarcely gather this much from some of the historical accounts which lay more emphasis on London, where trials subsequently took place, than on Preston, where it all happened!)

Some of the Lancashire Catholics got away with it, including John Dalton of Thurnham Hall, Edward Tyldesley of Myerscough and Richard Towneley of Burnley. Others were shot, hanged or transported and in towns throughout the county rebels were executed during 1716 when confiscations and fines crippled some families for generations. Preston claimed £6,400 for damage suffered during the action which was still fresh in the memory when Bonnie Prince Charles made his bid thirty years later. Preston Catholics cheered him right lustily and rang the church bells. Few, however, fell in with the rebel cause though they sang him off with "The King shall Have His Own Again" when he left after a night's stay. That was 28th November 1745. Three weeks later he was back, hotly pursued by Hanoverians, heading for bloody massacre on Culloden moor in April 1746. There was no further serious attempt for the Stuarts, though Jacobitism survived among the Lancashire Papists, in sentiment only, and "The Mock Corporation" still met as late as 1820, though with no solemn purpose.

Preston had specialised in linens "for many ages" before Cotton came, causing resentment and suspicion among the township's "little maisters". There was a factory along Moor Lane, near Gallows Hill, in 1777. Then, in 1791, John Horrocks, aged 23, of Edgworth, a quarry master's son, started up in muslins, operating from Turk's Head Yard as a putter out of yarns to handloom weavers. The following year he built his famous "Yard Factory", east of the township, and within a decade he had 7 factories in Preston, houses for his work-force, and had fought a Parliamentary election. He was returned for Preston in 1802 at the second attempt and died two years later at 36, worn out by pressures of industrial and public life. His

ARKWRIGHT HOUSE, the oldest surviving town house in Preston, was built in 1728 for occupation by the Headmaster of the nearby Grammar School built in 1666 (site now occupied by premises immediately to the right), and succeeded by new school premises in Cross Street in the early 1840's. Whereupon, Arkwright House became a public house, the Arkwright Arms, in memory of Arkwright and Kay who, in 1768, rented a room here and perfected his spinning machine, the Water Frame, in 1768. In the 1890's, Temperance Reformers purchased the premises for a model lodging house but after 1950 it stood empty and derelict until the "Friends" embarked on a massive restoration project, assisted by Manpower Services Commission, the Architectural Heritage Fund and Lloyds Bank. Princess Alexandra formally opened the premises on 4th July, 1980.

activities doubled the population of Preston in a dozen years and thousands turned up for his funeral at Penwortham. The business to-day specialises in textile conversion.

One of Preston's most famous sons was Sir Richard Arkwright (1732-92), thirteenth child of a humble tailor living in the Lancaster Road area. Richard went to Bolton to learn a barber's trade, taught himself how to make wigs, travelled around buying human hair and heard spinners bemoaning the want of a machine to speed up spinning in order to keep pace with Kay's Fly-Shuttle.

Arkwright was "a sharp 'un", a bungler with the pen, perhaps, but a good reader, with a business sense and an aptitude for putting ideas into practice. He had no training in mechanics and may well have indulged in a spot of industrial espionage, 18th century version. There lived at Leigh in the 1760's an inventor called Thomas Highs whose near neighbour, John Kay (not to be confused with the Fly-Shuttle inventor) was a watchmaker by trade. Highs had tried several methods of spinning with some success and was tempted to discuss his experiments with neighbour Kay, never suspecting that his confidences would be revealed to Arkwright, nor even less that the two of them would soon be working hand in glove. Arkwright, accompanied by Kay, moved to Preston about 1768 and persuaded John Smalley, a liquor-dealer and house-painter, to join him "with hand and purse". They experimented in a room in Stoneygate rented from the headmaster of the Grammar School. The three-storey property, built in 1728, restored 1978-9 and administered by Lancashire County Council, is "the oldest surviving town house" in Preston. It was a pub called the "Arkwright Arms" in the 1840's and Temperance Reformers bought it for a lodging house fifty years later. In the late 1940's it was derelict and might have disintegrated but for the faithful Friends who, to their everlasting credit, preserved it for Posterity. The room where the experiments took place, to the dismay of neighbours who suspected Diabolism, was restored during the reclamation of this important national monument.

Arkwright took out patents in 1769 and 1775. Meantime, like Hargreaves, he had suffered the machine wreckers at his Chorley factory. Immediately, he moved to Nottingham, approached Jedediah Strutt the celebrated stocking-maker, and established a mill powered by horses. But the Derwent's waters soon attracted him to Cromford, when the machine was re-named The Water Frame and later, when steam-operated, the Throstle. The rest is history. Arkwright, High Sheriff of Derbyshire, a wealthy man who had provided homes and employment for thousands, was knighted by George III in 1786. He died before he was 60 and in the process of building Willersley Castle, leaving two richly endowed children. One might have pictured a restless, lean-faced, hard-driven fellow rather than the "plain, gross, bag-cheeked, pot-bellied" character described by Carlyle. Clearly, he had enjoyed a good pasture. Doubtless, he cut corners and was a tartar to work for. But he founded the factory system and the drive which promoted the Industrial Revolution made him the first tycoon in modern history. Preston is justly proud of her competent son and Arkwright House, opened by H.R.H. Princess Alexandra on 4th July 1980, now functions as an Art Gallery and Lecture Centre.

*   *   *   *

The Teetotal Movement was born in the old Cockpit behind the Parish Church on 1st September, 1832, when a reclaimed alcoholic, Dicky Turner, a painful stammerer, leapt to his feet pleading for T-T-Tee-TEEE-total Abstinence as against Drinking in Moderation. They adopted the word "Teetotal" on the spot and seven signed the pledge, including Joseph Livesey, an ardent and lifelong campaigner for the movement.

Livesey was born at 146 Victoria Road, Walton-le-Dale in 1794 and at seven had lost both parents of the "wasting sickness". He was reared by a grandfather who clattered on the handloom in the cellar (look for a village shop with two commemorative plaques above the entrance). Life was a grind, poverty and premature death were rampant, schooling was scant. Infant hands were busy winding bobbins and borrowed books had to be pored over by firelight. It was worse still when grandmother died and those bitter early years left painful scars.

Joseph married Jane Williams, a splendid partner for 53 years, mother of many children (nine survived) and helpmeet in the cheese business which became more profitable than weaving. Joseph travelled around, buying in and selling at Preston, Chorley, Blackburn and Wigan markets. In both town and country, the sufferings of working folk due to the Corn Laws nearly broke his heart.

The Liveseys opened a cheese shop in Church Street, Preston, supported a Sunday School where adults could learn to read and write, did much to relieve the crushing despair all around. It was a losing battle. Living standards had slumped to a sub-human level. Degradation screamed from every dingy den, every damp cellar and rag-stuffed hovel. Bread prices still soared and thousands were dying of starvation. Morale cracked, desperation reigned and decent sober citizens began to purchase oblivion in beershops and pubs. Sad gaunt faces were everywhere and only the repeal of those Corn Laws would ease the plight of the people. Livesey combined tender heart and powerful conscience with great moral courage. He slammed politicians, monopolists and bloated landowners, alike. In righteous anger, he wrote without fear or favour and having ventured into letter-press printing, he founded "The Struggle" in 1842, the country's first illustrated halfpenny weekly which continued until Livesey launched the "Preston Guardian" in 1844.

"The Struggle" is a compelling saga of the times and cannot be read without an uncomfortable stirring of the emotions. Here are ragged crowds queueing up at the soup kitchen; youngsters risking death, scrabbling for coals on the tramway; widows wandering from house to house seeking "a meal's meat"; fathers clearing off to America leaving their families chargeable to the parish; morality gone by the board; self respect defeated by the apathy of starvation; bailiffs distraining on "poor folks' traps" for non-payment of rent; and mountains of goods, obelisk-high, being auctioned for coppers in the Market Place, thrice-weekly! In a stark hovel where an under-nourished asthmatic has just breathed his last, a child sadly informs us: "My daddy is upstairs in a box". "And this", says her mother, clutching an old black rag about her thin shoulders, "is the only shawl I have to follow him to the grave!"

Crime, poverty, drunken accidents or suicides, Livesey spares us none of the horrors he was compelled to witness. When only pawn tickets were plentiful, he saw three bedsteads knocked down for 11½d., and a pair of bed-steads for 10d., whilst hundreds slept on straw and rich men's coat buttons burst with over-

JOSEPH LIVESEY 1794–1884 (top left) of Walton-le-Dale and Preston, Founder of the Teetotal Movement, Champion of the Poor.

EDWIN HENRY BOOTH 1829–1899 (top right), the Bury-born founder of a Lancashire grocery empire, whose home and main interests were based at Preston.

SIR RICHARD ARKWRIGHT (right), Preston's famous son, whose energy, ingenuity and practical talent secured his own fortunes and raised British manufactures to unparalleled standards of excellence and superiority.

feeding. He lashed at Poor Law officers whose callous abuse of the supplicants was "disgraceful to humanity". He followed the aged and decrepit who begged sooner than enter the dreaded Workhouse; "We are hawf-clemmed to deeath!", murmurs a 77-year old woman with a "very ill-pinched" husband who spins a little yarn, and a mother weeps for her son, in gaol for debt because "the shop-keeper would not wait". His wife and four children were living upon 4s.0d. a week! "Sometimes", she sighs, "they haven't a bite to eat!"

In an agony of dry tears, Livesey points out that gaol birds are better off than honest workers and he rails against wages going "to purchase high-taxed food". "Starvation Fever" was rife. Accrington folk ate a calf which had sickened and died and in Pendle Forest a crowd came at night and dug up a dead cow, taking even those parts which "smelled strongly of the medicine". This was no rumour. Livesey tracked down the incident, had it verified, brought it to the attention of the House of Commons.

Countryfolk were no better off. There were kiddies, sad silent little ghosts, standing beside their father whom poverty had worn down almost to a skeleton. There were cottages crumbling, farms deserted, dirt and disease flourishing in unholy concert. He longed for a magic wand or a seat at Westminster. Instead, he preached cleanliness to those who had no towel and could not afford soap; urged total abstinence on those whose road to oblivion lay through the alehouse; urged morality on those who slept, like animals, on chaff, or straw, or shavings, on the floors of damp stinking cellars; and stormed at the privileged who knew nothing of "scanty meals" and "meagre fare" and never learned how to "love one another, as we ought".

Even the young Queen was not spared, she daily showered with gifts from all parts of the kingdom. "Why should she not know the real condition of the humblest of her subjects", demands Livesey, pointing an accusing finger at tattered sheets and patched shirts flapping in the back yard of a poor weaver. Tracts and pamphlets poured from Livesey's pen and were circulated via the penny post. He became a power to be reckoned with and in 1842 he joined a delegation to Sir Robert Peel who, four years later, was obliged to repeal the Corn Laws, at the cost of his premiership.

The "Preston Guardian" (later "Farmers' Guardian") was later taken over by the Toulmins who acquired the "Blackburn Times" and founded the "Lancashire Evening Post" in 1886. George Toulmin was a former pupil and a disciple of The Grand Old Man of Teetotalism and the name is still connected with newspaper production.

The Liveseys who lived for twenty years in an ivy-covered farmhouse at Holme Slack, built "Lake View Villas", Bowness (where Jane died at the age of 73), and moved to 13, Bank Parade, Preston, where the widower died in September 1884. He had stumped the Temperance platforms of the nation, had stirred the hearts of millions, had taught many to read and write, and had helped to promote the Mechanics' Institute in 1828, fore-runner of the Harris Institute which became Harris College in 1956 and Preston Polytechnic in 1973. A portion has, appropriately, been named "Livesey House".

Livesey left over £9,000, a remarkable achievement, considering the times. He died aged 90, greatly loved and revered and thousands turned up for his funeral, including a schoolgirl whom I met, in her 93rd year in 1964 when she recalled the occasion. The sewing lesson was in progress. The headmaster came in and instructed the scholars to don cloaks and bonnets and join their fellows, in silence, on the footpath outside. "For soon", he told them, "the funeral of a very great man will come by and I want you to see it, and remember it, for ever!" And she did! The hearse preceded a cavalcade of carriages carrying Mayor, Justices, parsons, politicians, while 400 followed on foot to the cemetery where Joseph and his Jane were reunited after a lifetime of service.

*   *   *   *

Who was the man called Harris . . . a name impossible to avoid in Preston? He was born in 1804, son of the Rev. Robert Harris, Vicar of St. George's and Principal of the Old Grammar School on Stoneygate. He had a facial disfigurement, a nervous tic, trained as a lawyer in his uncle's Chapel Street practice, and never married; lived instead with his unmarried brother and sister at 13, Ribblesdale Place; worked till the age of 70, then retired to Whinfield Lane, Ashton. The kindly fellow endowed infection wards at Preston Royal Infirmary and died in 1877 leaving the then fantastic fortune of £300,000 to be spent on public buildings in memory of his family.

The Corporation undertook to clear a mess of old buildings around the Market Place, which provided a site for the Harris Library, Art Gallery and Museum, one of the finest Classic edifices in the north of England and a noble ornament to the town centre. Alderman James Hibbert designed it in a style reminiscent of St. George's Hall, Liverpool, with a central lantern and a pediment, gloriously sculpted by E. R. Mullins, on voluted columns. This fine building houses some of the best art treasures in the kingdom, besides fascinating relics from Preston's long past. Human skulls, Bronze Age canoes, red deer antlers, bones of Urus, the wild ox, extinct before the Romans arrived, were all plucked from the silt when Preston Docks were formed. There are fragments and cinerary urns from the famous Bleasdale Circles discovered in 1898 by Thomas Kelsall, a farmer from Higher Fairsnape, and later declared to be unique in that the Bronze Age timbers, perhaps 3,000 years old, had survived . . . the first timber circle to be discovered in Britain! It was classified as an Ancient Monument in 1925 and concrete posts have replaced original timbers.

The glory of the "Harris" and a goldmine for the researcher must be the library of Dr. Shepherd, an honorary Prestonian, who came from Kendal, lived in Friargate, practised with Christian charity in the town and was twice Mayor of Preston. This compassionate, fun-loving Jacobite ("Mayor of the Mock Corporation" in 1733) was also an omnivorous reader. He died childless in 1761, leaving thousands of volumes to the Corporation, with money to upkeep them for the benefit of the citizens. They are now safely lodged in the Reference Section of the "Harris".

*   *   *   *

Another remarkable man who made his mark in Preston was Edwin Henry Booth, born posthumously at Bury in 1829, his father, a doctor, having perished in a street accident. Early years were blighted by a drunken stepfather from whose house he finally fled to Bolton at the age of eleven. He started work as a tailor's errand boy, became a draper's assistant working for bare keep and switched to the grocery business, then an "art and mystery" requiring a thousand skills. A spiteful apprentice and an unjust employer drove him to Preston, where he had a half-sister, and where he secured a new post with an ambitious grocer who hoped to expand. Edwin expected to become the first branch manager; but Fate stepped in and at eighteen, after training with a firm of Liverpool tea-blenders, he was jobless, without prospects, and with his dreams in ruins.

It was 1847, the year after the railway was brought through to Blackpool. Edwin bought a cheap day excursion ticket and spent the day there, spotted an outhouse on the lane leading to the new Market House, arranged to rent it and start up in business. Without capital and with stock loaned by his previous employer, he opened in time for the season and by combining quality goods with a courteous manner, quickly collared the principal trade of the resort. He married Susannah Phillips, a corn miller's daughter from Colne, opened his first branch at Chorley, moved to Preston in 1859 and branched out all over the county. Yet Preston was the Booths' home and good causes roused their compassionate interest. The plight of poor unhappy children particularly touched Booth's tender heart. Many were destined for the Workhouse until a committee was formed to provide clothing and comforts for deprived youngsters and kindly folk encouraged the unfortunates to attend Day and Sunday Schools and to grow up in the Christian tradition.

Booth's grand dream was to build an orphanage that would offer a happy home and good prospects and he approached Mr. Harris unsuccessfully on several occasions. He applied again, to the Trustees, when the terms of the Will were announced, and they granted £100,000 from the Harris fortunes, resulting in the Harris Orphanage at Fulwood where generations of otherwise lonely children have grown up in family homes and with the assurance of bright futures.

Against all the odds, Edwin Henry Booth succeeded by honest trading and sheer hard work. His home life was supremely happy. His residence was Avenham Tower, an attractive Italian-style villa, built c. 1847, at the corner of Bank Parade overlooking the green slopes of the park. Yet, always, he thought of those less well off, worked actively for the Blind, for the Deaf and Dumb and for the community in general. He rescued the local Electric Supply Company from financial disaster, chartered the first clipper to bring tea into the new Preston Dock, and died, admired and loved, at the age of seventy in 1899.

*   *   *   *

I do not apologise for devoting much space to Preston. It is a place that cannot be dismissed briefly and its history proves that. There it always was, at the heart of the action, an administration centre, a royal stop-off, a battlefield, a parade ground for the medieval guilds, a market town still, a centre for the Arts, a living memorial to heart-stirring events that made this nation great!

Stray off Fishergate into Turk's Head Yard and picture young John Horrocks, oil can in hand, tending his machines before striking off into fame and fortune. Wander through fine squares filled with Solicitors' and Insurance Brokers' offices, where the nobility and gentry had their town houses and picture fine ladies in sedan chairs being carried to assemblies at the old Bull Hotel. Up Stoneygate, strain your ears for the hum and clatter of Arkwright's experimental machine, or in St. John's Place catch faint echoes from the old Cockpit built, they say, by Lord Derby, closed last century and now vanished.

You will not see the docks as I remember them as a schoolgirl. They closed in November 1981, yet in memory I can still picture great ships unloading cargoes of Scandinavian timber and china clay from the West Country. How permanent it all seemed! Later came the banana trade and names like Fyffe and Geest plastered everywhere; and container ships, and the Larne Ferry laden with holiday makers and their vehicles, before the Irish troubles, going to Belfast. Preston merchants formed the first Ribble Navigation Company in 1838, a second in 1853, attempting to discipline the capricious Ribble. Preston Corporation took over in 1881, the Prince of Wales (Edward VII) laid the foundation stone of the Albert Edward Dock four years later and in 1892 the Duke of Edinburgh, in the steam yacht "Aline" broke the ceremonial blue ribbon. Times changed. Industrial disputes, continual silting and costly dredging combined to close the Port of Preston which had been losing the ratepayers £1M a year.

How quiet old Ribble's estuary seems without its convoys arriving and departing and the pilot cutter chugging busily between vessels, off Lytham; and huge ships, apparently on wheels, gliding through green fields away across Freckleton marshes. What will happen to this dockland, stripped of its giddy cranes and gantries, its railway and warehouses, its yards once piled heavens high with timber; its oil storage tanks, its juggernauts thundering off in all directions? A housing estate, perhaps? A marina for pleasure craft? How tame compared with the tea clipper age and the great days of sail!

Preston, predominantly Catholic, has an abundance of churches of all denominations. The limestone spire of St. Walburge's R.C. Church (1852) designed by the inventor of the Hansom cab, soars giddily towards the heavens behind the railway-side pigeon lofts. St. Mark's acquired a fine tower in 1870. Free churches are plentifully scattered and the Mormons who were proselytising here in the 1830's and '40's, during the lifetime of Joseph Smith, and who secured many converts, particularly from Longton, during those depressed times, have a church in Ribbleton Avenue. In Bow Lane, behind the County Hall, where the Lancashire County Records are stored in a modern building, the old obsolete Christ Church (1836) has been cleverly incorporated into a new Conference Centre and office block. It was one of several churches erected by Preston's Vicar for 23 years, the Rev. Roger Carus Wilson, brother of the dreaded Mr. Brocklehurst of "Jane Eyre", based on the Vicar of Tunstall.

Preston has many literary associations. At 7 Winckley Street, Francis Thompson was born, the brilliant self-destructing opium-addicted poet and mystic who penned "The Hound of Heaven" and other notable works. Though he afterwards chose to forget it, Robert Service, famous for Yukon ballads like "The Shooting of Dan McGrew" first saw the light of day in Christian Road, while author of 49 books and idol of yesterday's schoolgirls, Angela Brazil, was born at 1 Westcliffe Terrace (now part of the railway) in 1869. Aloysius Smith, the origin of "Trader Horn", a roamer, a raconteur, an eccentric slip of a fellow with a straggly white beard and a broad-brimmed Stetson, was baptised at St. Ignatius' Church in 1861. Ethelreda Lewis turned his recollections into a runaway best seller in the 1930's. Mrs. Gaskell and Charles Dickens both drew inspiration for their novels from the patient sufferings of the Preston cotton operatives during a seven months' strike leading to a "lock-out" (the phrase was coined here) in 1853-4. Dickens was appalled and heart-sick at what he witnessed. Manufacturing centres seemed to him sheer "hell holes"; the fortitude of the workers impressed him deeply; and similarly, Edwin Waugh wrung the hardest hearts with harrowing tales of the Preston operatives during the great Cotton Famine of the 1860's. Proud Preston, they call it! Its record has much to be proud of!

Folds Farm, Marton Moss.

6. THE FYLDE

THERE are two distinct Lancashires, separated by the Ribble. The southern half, "workshop of the world", looks drab and toil-worn except where moorlands still support their bird choirs and workers breathe again in blossomed nook and posied dell, as poets would have us remember. North of the river lies that green and gently undulating field or "Fylde" . . . from the Anglo-Saxon meaning simply – the level green plain. Before counties were fixed, when administrative areas were Hundreds, the Fylde was the flat coastal portion of the Hundred of Amounderness.

Nowadays, millions hurtle up the M6 and the M55 into Blackpool heading for the seaside and a conglomeration of delights and excitements contrived by Man. Most rush home by the same route, never discovering the charm, the captivating sweetness of this little land of winding lanes and larksong; of hawthorn hedges laced with honeysuckle and the haunting scent of May blossom in early summer; of sheep grazing and lambs frisking, of cattle with bulging udders clip-clopping homewards to be milked and corduroyed farm lads chewing straws; of gulls soaring and screaming after the tractor in some furrowed field; of farmsteads half as old as time; of quaint cottages where healthy generations have lived and loved; of whitewashed walls and the occasional thatch!; of hamlets half a-snooze, of villages bonny as a picture; of motorists queueing for the best ice cream in the Universe; and little market towns with street stalls, in the old tradition; of British, Anglian and Norse names on signpost pointers; of delightful pubs and churches with 1,000 years of history; of toll bridges across the silvery Wyre to that separate world, level as a Dutch landscape, and Pilling's needle-sharp spire visible for miles before you approach it; of coast roads perilous to the unwary and mud-flats animated with the patterings of sea-birds; of humble homes, proudly tended and lofty halls, aloof behind their estate walls; of starr-grassed dunes, of sea and sand and shingle; of mosslands rippling with green growth and acres of tomatoes ripening under glass; of children's laughter behind the school railings, of ancients ruminating as the world trundles by; and, of all things in this beauteous place, the windmills!

Here, I have to confess partiality for the place that has been my home and my heart's delight for the best part of a lifetime. I share the enthusiasm of Allen Clarke (1863-1935) who migrated from the mills, the works, collieries, forges and smokey towns of the south-east to this magic "Windmill Land", as he called it. His father had been thrown out of work for presuming to join a Union, and the privation turned "their Charlie" into a Socialist. One Whitsuntide, his father brought him from Bolton on a cheap rail excursion to Blackpool. It was an eye-opener! A Lancashire where folk wore the bloom of health and lived long; where the air was bracing and unpolluted; where life went at a gentler pace and Industry had not annihilated Nature's music.

His first glimpse of a white windmill thrilled him to the soul; Treales Mill, an attractive home now, the first along the railway from Preston. To-day, coming in by road, you might first spot Clifton-with-Salwick's tall white tower mill, now a licensed restaurant; or entering by M.55 be greeted by Little Marton Mill on the outskirts of Blackpool, a Scouts' H.Q., now and a memorial to that wondering, wide-eyed laddie whose books and poems would romanticise the Fylde. From half-timer in a cotton mill, Allen Clarke won a scholarship to Hulton Grammar School, went into teaching, won recognition for his Lancashire poems and pieces, published "Tum Fowt" sketches in 1891, "The Bolton Trotter" weekly for the next three years. He contributed articles to the "Liverpool Weekly Post", "Blackpool Gazette" and other publications and in the plenitude of his energies and ambitions, he flitted Fylde-wards at the end of the century.

Paper-back and hard-back guides, annuals, periodicals and stories of Blackpool and his beloved "Windmill Land" made him one of the most widely read writers of his day. Trippers and cyclists were lured

BLACKPOOL — THEN (above) *c.* 1900, and NOW (left), on any fine summer's day.

Note how the modern Golden Mile has superseded the tall terrace boarding houses of the former South Beach. After the local authority cleared all the alfresco performers off the beach in the early years of this century, the "catch-pennies" drifted off but the "regulars" negotiated with the property owners, rented their front gardens and set up in business. The garden walls gradually disappeared and the Golden Mile, notorious for its human peepshows in the 1930's, developed. The old properties have since been wiped off and replaced in glass and concrete.

here by his romantic sentimental style and many joined the Speedwell Cycling Club and the Rambling Club which he founded. He was also a founder-member, at Rochdale in 1909, of the Lancashire Authors' Association; and even found time to stand as a Socialist for Rochdale (1900), only to be defeated by a Liberal. His homely, artless poem, "A Gradely Prayer" sold in thousands printed on post-cards and towards the close of his life he read his "Bill Spriggs' Sketches" on the wireless. Milling crowds of faithful fans attended his funeral at Marton in December 1935.

The Fylde also has two contrasting halves. From all that is sweet and verdant, the motorist finds hmself in no time wrestling with one-way systems, nosing through holiday crowds, heading for the nearest car park, anticipating a few hours at the seaside. He comes, literally, in his millions, with his car-load of excited youngsters and elderly relatives who were first brought to Blackpool as babes in arms, and wouldn't dream of going anywhere else. He mingles with third-generation New Zealanders, coming "home" for the first time and having Blackpool high on the list of places to be visited. They will devote a week to Blackpool; two days to anywhere else! "We daren't go home, otherwise!", they will tell you, these visitors from half-way across the globe! Southerners often know nothing at all about the Fylde; even pronounce it "Flyde", as in "lice", or "Fild", as in "thrilled". Yet, Blackpool is the north's premier holiday resort and its history, told in my "Seven Golden Miles", has all the pace and excitement of a thriller!

In 1600, there were perhaps half a dozen families of fisherfolk living in clay and cobble huts along the cliff-tops; they belonged to the parish of Bispham, to the Manor of Layton. There was no village, scarcely a hamlet, only a tiny fishing settlement near the dark-coloured water outlet from Marton Mere, the "blacke poole" noted in the baptisms register for the first time in 1602. During the next hundred years, less than 20 surnames crop up in a vast sparsely populated area and, except for an 18th century sea-bathing craze which caught on with Royalty and filtered down to the lowest orders, Blackpool might have remained at a standstill forever! But by the 1740's the first sea-water fanatics had trickled into the place, had made do with primitive conditions, had gone home loud in praises of Blackpool's health-giving properties. It was the start of health-seeking at Blackpool; the entertainments industry leapt ahead with the coming of the railway in 1846 and the immediate offer of cheap Sunday excursions when miners and mill-folk, who had no expectation of recovering health in a few short hours, looked forward to a rattling good time.

Before the cinema killed off Music Hall, Blackpool was the heart and centre of Entertainments in the Western World! The brightest and best, the most controversial and the most famous from the realms of Comedy, Concert Platform, Music, Circus, Drama, Ballet, Sport and the spoken word, counted it an honour to receive a Blackpool booking while a summer season engagement was the ultimate accolade. They HAD to be the world's best too or, like Sarah Bernhardt in 1882, they got the "bird" and demands to have their money refunded (the embarrassed directors coughed up the following Monday morning).

Magic names from the past read like a theatrical Debrett – Caruso, Kreisler, Tettrazini, Melba, Patti, Butt; Marie Lloyd, Florrie Forde, Gus Elen, G. H. Elliott and a thousand Music Hall "greats". Tom Mix was here, W. C. Fields, the Tower Circus juggler who went into comedy; Charlie Chaplin, Houdini, Dietrich, Garbo, Fairbanks Senior, Coward, Novello . . . the list is inexhaustible. Oscar Wilde lectured here, so did Horatio Bottomley; Charles Dickens staved off a breakdown with a few days at Blackpool and Blondin fell off the rope here in 1895, his penultimate performance.

Blackpool's version of the famous Eiffel Tower was erected in 1894 and still going strong; three Victorian piers, the Opera House – claimed to be the largest theatre outside the capital – and the restored Grand Theatre, a masterpiece by Matcham, with lashings of gilt and red plush redolent of the great days of live entertainment. Television killed off much that we would like to have kept, splendid palaces of entertainment, magnificent ballrooms, the old tatty Golden Mile, a seedy but utterly fascinating 200-yard stretch of the Promenade with its freaks and fantasies, its spielers, its spendthrifts with whom it was a point of honour to go home skint! . . . the haunting smell of onions, hamburgers, strong ale and fish and chips. Now everything is more clinical, with glass and concrete, and slot machines and electronics, and no soul! I think I preferred the hullaballoo-raising dreadful displays of "Starving Brides and Bridegrooms" and the Ex-Rector of Stiffkey, the Rev. Harold Davidson who was unfrocked for dubious behaviour on the 1930's and promptly agreed to be exhibited, peering out of the bung-hole of a barrel along the Golden Mile! Queues miles long stopped the traffic and made a fortune for the ex-cleric and Luke Gannon, the peepshow impresario of that era. Tasteless, brash, call it what you like, but it went down famously with the masses from hardworking Lancashire and Yorkshire.

Blackpool was the first place in the country to have trams (1885) and it looks like being the last! They thunder along the wide promenade giving great delight to enthusiasts and a new experience to the youngsters. The sands are washed clean twice daily, the beach is beautifully level and free of rocks, and Blackpool, like Fleetwood and Lytham (and, formerly, St. Annes) has a fine Lifeboat record. Blackpool's famous Illuminations which extend the season to late in October and have been labelled "The Finest Free Show on Earth" attract many more millions, besides those who, out of season, come to the resort for Conferences and Cultural activities.

Blackpool, incidentally, can conjure up 250,000 beds at a moment's notice. So, if you are jaded, fed up, have a few pounds to spare, come to Blackpool where those famous landladies will provide bed and board more cheaply, cheerfully and expertly than anywhere in the British Isles. They have been at this game a long time, are dab hands at coaxing roses back into pallid cheeks and they will wave you off fully expecting to see you again, next season.

To the south lies Lytham-St. Annes, amalgamated in 1922 and swept into the new Fylde Borough in 1974, two towns beautifully complementary yet entirely different. "Lidun" of Domesday had been settled c. 700 by the Angles and its history was recorded from the 12th century when the Benedictines of Durham received the Manor as a gift from Richard Fitz Roger and sent two or three monks to manage the estate. Lytham had close links with St. Cuthbert, whose body, carried by Lindisfarne monks, rested for a while here c. 882 before the crossing over the Ribble Estuary to North Meols (Churchtown, Southport) and Halsall. Decades after the Dissolution, the estate was purchased, lock, stock, church, cottages and all rights and privileges whatsoever, for £4,300 by (Sir) Cuthbert Clifton of Westby in 1606 who set about building the first Lytham Hall. Its frontage was devastated by fire c. 1750 and over a period of a dozen years was rebuilt to John Carr of York's design, resulting in the finest Georgian mansion in the whole of Lancashire.

The last of the family at Lytham, Harry Talbot de Vere Clifton who had been absent from home for more years than most could remember, died in November 1979 divorced and childless and having dissipated a patrimony worth millions and said to have brought in £7,000 a day. The Guardian Royal Exchange Group purchased the estate in 1963, turned the Hall into offices and filled the park with modern properties, providing useful employment in the process. The last Clifton to reside at the Hall until her death in 1961 was Mrs. Violet Clifton, nee Beauclerk, author, poet, traveller, friend of Royalty, patron of the Arts, who wrote "The Book of Talbot", the biography of her husband, John Talbot Clifton (1868-1928). He died in Teneriffe and is buried on his Kildalton estate on the Isle of Islay. They were two wild romantic spirits, restless, full of adventure, immensely tall and with intellects far above the ordinary, she being descended from Charles II and Nell Gwynne and having fears for "her father's sanity", he being cursed with a speech impediment and scarlet tempers. In 1950 Mrs. Clifton turned her back on the high life, entered the Convent of the Poor Clares founded in the grounds of Arundel Castle by Flora, Duchess of Norfolk, a relative of the Cliftons, and lived in that austere bare-foot community as Sister Mary Seraphim for several years. We met in the summer of 1955 at Lytham, her movements at that time uncertain until our conversations convinced her that tenants longed for her return and for a Clifton, at last, to be back at the hall. Shortly afterwards, she returned, took up residence in a suite of rooms, resumed her visits to the tenantry and received a never-ending procession of historians, scholars, artists and admirers. They were her "golden years", she informed me as we worked together, re-cataloguing family portraits, receiving parties at the Hall, reminiscing and, in my case, recording. She wrote a foreward for my "Sand Crown", the Lythan-St. Annes Story and lived to see "Seven Golden Miles" the Blackpool Story in print before her death in Novemver 1961.

The story of St. Annes began as a spontaneous inspiration in the brain of a Lancashire cotton man from the Rossendale Valley. Elijah Hargreaves walked through the empty acres at the west end of Lytham in 1874, while holidaymaking in Blackpool, conceived the idea of a new elegant resort and persuaded 7 colleagues in cotton to help him form a company which was named after St. Anne's Chapel of Ease, built 1872-3 for the fisherfolk and farmers, by Lady Eleanor Cecily Clifton. Building operations commenced in 1875 and national newspapers went to town on publicity for the romantic venture that provided the Lancashire coast with "a new elegant watering place". It set out shamelessly to cater for carriage folk and gentry and quickly earned the title of "Opal of the West". The story of the pioneers' early struffles is as dramatic as any saga of the western prairies and a tribute to the kind of sacrificial zeal which seemed to die out with Victoria.

To the north of Blackpool there were accommodations for bathers at "Cleaveles" in the 1780's but no thought for 60 years of the splendid school at Rossall founded in 1844 largely for the sons of Anglican clergy. "Rushale" was included in Domesday, the coastline then projecting much further out to sea. At the Dissolution, the Abbey of Dieulacres granted a long lease of the estate to the Catholic Allens whose son William (1532-1594) grew up in the old hall, became a Fellow of Oriel College, Oxford at 18, went into the priesthood and was marked out for preferment by Mary Tudor who appointed him Canon of York. His hopes collapsed on the accession of Protestant Elizabeth, however, and he fled to the Continent, founded the English College at Douai, set about training priests to re-convert England, entered into numerous conspiracies designed to replace Elizabeth with Mary Queen of Scots, and when the Armada threatened, even exhorted the nobility and gentry of England to rise up and support Philip of Spain, so zealous was he for the restoration of the Old Faith. Even ardent Catholics jibbed at that; Allen, who was made a Cardinal, became a sharp thorn in Elizabeth's flesh, hunted by the Queen's officers when occasionally he stole back to the Fylde, visiting friends and in-laws like the Heskeths of Mains Hall. He even entertained Edmund Campion, the Jesuit leader, at Rossall on several occasions.

In 1583, Edmund Fleetwood threw Widow Allen and her daughters out and they took refuge in Rheims under the Cardinal's protection. He died at last in Rome having drunk deep of the bitter cup of exile and regretting, perhaps, the sheer fanaticism which had cost him support and in some quarters had rendered his memory obnoxious. The Fleetwoods became Lords Paramount in the area; their heiress married a Hesketh from Rufford whose descendant, Peter Hesketh, adopted the old patronymic and on receiving a Baronetcy in 1838 became Sir Peter Hesketh-Fleetwood, M.P. By this time, he was in the grip of town-building fever, draining sandy wastes haunted by rabbits and sea-birds at the mouth of the Wyre and planning a resort and harbour to be known as "Fleetwood". It was one of the earliest English examples of town-planning, the Architect was Decimus Burton who is supposed to have marked the streets out with a plough, and when the Preston and Wyre Railway was opened in 1840 building projects leapt ahead, and fishermen from over the Ribble and pioneers from all parts hurried to get in on the ground floor.

This splendid scheme plunged the landowner into such dire financial straits that he had to abandon the ancestral home to school purposes. It opened in 1844 and there was even a sister scheme to found a similar establishment for girls Over-Wyre but somehow that project was neatly dropped in the river! Little that is original can be seen to-day at Rossall School, apart from a quaint battlemented 18th century gazebo, but it has a fine reputation and has turned out some illustrious old boys including the late Sir Thomas Beecham, the Lancashire grandson of an Oxfordshire pill-roller. S. P. B. Mais, a master at Rossall before the First World War, described Blackpool as "the most alive and most amusing seaside resort I know", adding "but its hinterland, unlike that of Brighton, is not attractive!" Well, I cannot argue about Brighton but I am up in arms when he suggests "the Fylde is not what I should call soothing!" Indeed, for the perfect description I resort to the French "douce" meaning kind, sweet, soft, gentle, fresh and quiet. Add the word "green" and you have it exactly. Where could the man have been looking???

Truly, if I were to be confined to a single county, I would choose Lancashire; and if to one portion of that county, it would have to be the Fylde. Familiarity never stales its variety for me. I love its dunes and shorelands, its waves lapping, its rivers running with the tides. I love its street markets, Kirkham and Garstang on Thursdays, Great Eccleston on Wednesdays, and prospects of a revival at Poulton-le-Fylde. I love its villages, Elswick, Weeton, Singleton, Freckleton and that Norse charmer, Wrea Green, where they play cricket on summer Saturdays and car loads come to feed the ducks on the Dub at the other end of the village green; where St. Nicholas's Church gleams in the sun, next to the Grapes Inn, once called the Dumpling, where you can spot the old cock-sod in spring in a circle of gold and purple crocuses planted by the local children. Come here in late June and recapture the spirit of Merrie England when the travelling fair settles on the green and everyone dresses up and joins the fancy dress parade round the village. There is even a spot of thatch, and more elsewhere at Westby, at Treales and Wharles, Weeton and Larbreck (Well Lane), and along the road to the Crematorium at Lytham-St. Annes. Norfolk reed nowadays, not the old traditional wheat-straw, but bonny for all that!

A TRANQUIL STRETCH OF THE PRESTON/
KENDAL CANAL (above) near Salwick.

POULTON-LE-FYLDE town centre (left) showing
the Market Place with cross, stocks, fish-stones
and whipping post overlooked by the late
Perpendicular tower of St. Chad's Church which
was largely rebuilt in the 1750's by Roger
Hesketh who had married Margaret Fleetwood,
the heiress of Rossall. Poulton, an old market
town, was described in the 1830's as a
"Metropolis" attracting trade from all over the
world through its port, Skippool on the Wyre.
Today, generous free car parks ensure its
popularity as a shopping centre.

MAINS HALL, SINGLETON (opposite top), one of
the county's famous houses (now a guest-
house) was the ancient seat of the Roman
Catholic Heskeths who were prominent in
Lancashire affairs. Priests were harboured,
including Cardinal Wm. Allen, a brother-in-law;
Jacobites took shelter here during the 1745
rising; and the future George IV came here in
pursuit of the widowed Mrs. Maria Fitzherbert
who had fled north to escape his attentions. The
old house, considerably rebuilt in the 18th
century, had several hides and a chapel
transferred to the barn dated 1686.

PILLING OLD CHURCH, built 1717, with a sun-
dial over the door commemorating the Rev.
George Holden (1766) who first calculated the
tide-tables which are still used today. Its
message reads: Thus ETERNITY approacheth.

Grand old churches, too, at St. Michael's on Wyre, one of only three listed in Domesday under Amounderness (others at Kirkham and Preston). Locally, they regard St. Helen's, Churchtown (Kirkland), an ancient and hallowed place, as the "Cathedral of the Fylde". All Hallows, Bispham, is late 19th century and the third on the site, but the carved sandstone Zodiac arch, re-tooled, is Norman, original and possibly unique. The churchyard is solid with corpses, known and unknown, washed up on the beach from wrecks at sea.

Shard tollbridge over the Wyre overlooks the 18th century Columbarium of historic Mains Hall (now a guest-house) where Cardinal Allen came visiting his in-laws, the Heskeths, and Jesuits and Jacobites once sheltered; and leads to that flat and melancholy Over-Wyre landscape similar to that south of the Ribble, yet possessing a plaintive charm. Pilling offers much, from the site of a medieval church at Newer's Wood to the "old" church of 1717 which was left standing, not far from the Victorian replacement with its compelling spire. There was a human settlement here during the Bronze Age and early inhabitants laid a trackway of tree-trunks across the squelching acres of Pilling Moss which, like God's grace, was said to be "endless!" Ancient squabbles between the Abbots of Cockerham and Cockersand, about boundaries, are commemorated in a Crawley Cross overlooking a ditch and Bone Hill Farm was the setting for a notorious 19th century Baby Farm where luckless servant girls "in trouble" were sent to get the business over and no-one enquired too closely what happened to the fruits of illicit passions.

You can drive for hours, crossing and re-crossing the track of "The Pilling Pig", the old Pilling-Garstang railway which ceased operating altogether in 1950, having suspended passenger services in 1930. Wardleys Creek, a busy little port 200 years ago, Preesall, Staynall, Stalmine, Knott End across the water from Fleetwood, Hambleton where new and ancient properties rub shoulders, all pleasant for Sunday afternoon explorations.

Poulton-le-Fylde had the foresight to provide plenty of free car parks, making it the most popular place in the Fylde for half a day's shopping. The town centre is dominated by the old Church of St. Chad, with its grounds dramatically carpeted with crocuses in Springtime. That other old market town, Kirkham, which was busy manufacturing sail-cloth for the Royal Navy in the 18th century, is built on seven hills, so they say, and I can believe it! Find the windmill, turned into an attractive home on Carr Hill, and you have located the site of a Roman station, its purpose impossible now to determine because of post-war school and bungalow developments.

For a blissful taste of unspoiled Old England, stroll along the Preston-Lancaster Canal towpaths or hire a cruiser and chug gently along at 4 m.p.h. Seek out the Eagle and Child pubs at Weeton, Wharles and Inskip, and remains of many windmills of which there must have been two dozen merrily at work. Lytham's (1805) on the famous Green is a gem! So is Thornton's Marsh Mill (1794), built by Bold Fleetwood Hesketh and opened on certain days, and Pilling Mill, another home now (1808), beside the Broadfleet. The Rev. George Holden, Curate of Pilling's "Old" Church for 9 years from 1758, sat on the bridge nearby for hours on end observing the tides and compiling "Holden's Tide Tables", still used to-day.

So much to enchant the eye and lift the heart! So much more, and a whole way of life, swept away by the internal combustion engine that brought buses into the villages and tempted countryfolk into the towns.

A Fylde cottage, Marton Moss.

7. LANCASTER

TWO MILLENIA of action packed history, a Norman castle all but a thousand years old, perched on a knoll with the Lune swirling usefully at its foot; a beautiful early 15th century Priory Church of St. Mary occupying an ancient Christian site; and memories of a Roman fort here and pre-Christian settlers long before that. All these figure in Lancaster's story; and the pride of achieving City status, at last, on Coronation Day, 1937, all those long years after the detested King John, when Earl of Mortain, granted a borough charter in 1193 followed by another in 1199, after his accession.

Everything has happened in this old county town once linked by Roman roads with Walton-le-Dale, Manchester and the south, and with "Portus Setantiorum" on the coast somewhere near the mouth of the Wyre. A veil descends from the Roman withdrawal until the Normans found the place in ruins, probably as a result of Northumbrian invasions. But the Conqueror recognised its strategic importance as a bulwark against the rampaging Scots and he gave town and castle to Roger of Poitou for a stronghold. Roger built the Lungess Tower, 80ft. square with walls 3 yards thick, as living quarters during times of sieige and a beacon site in times of stress, as in Armada year, 1588. The intimidating gateway is atttributed to John o' Gaunt whose son, King Henry IV, linked the Duchy with the Crown.

Gaze unmoved, if you can, upon those ancient formidable stones, every one reeking of human tragedy and despair. Lancaster was the county's only assize town from 1176 until 1835 and it is claimed that more wretches received the death sentence here than anywhere in the kingdom.

I think of Abbot John Paslew and his friends awaiting execution for their part in the Pilgrimage of Grace in 1536; of George Marsh, the Protestant Martyr, who was gaoled here before being taken to Chester to be burned at the stake in the reign of Mary Tudor; of the Yorkshireman, Henry Burton (1579-1648) whose Puritanism brought him before the Star Chamber Court where he was fined £5,000, ordered to be pilloried and to have both ears cut off after which he was flung into solitary confinement at Lancaster without the comforts even of pen and paper. Wide gaps between the floorboards of his cell admitted the stench and a "hellish noise, night and day" from witches immured in a noisome chamber below. Fortunately, after his arch-enemy Laud fell from favour in 1640 he received damages for the loss of his ears and was restored to his benefice. The Jesuit Edmund Arrowsmith was less fortunate. He joined the English mission in 1613, came to Brindle in 1624, embraced martyrdom at Lancaster four years later. When George Fox, founder of the Quaker movement, was incarcerated here for refusing to take a Bible oath, in 1664/5, the putrid atmosphere hung like a fog or "as dew upon the walls" and throughout the "long cold winter till the next Assize" his garments and bed covers were rain-soaked and his limbs "much numbed" and greatly swelled. Literally hundreds of God-fearing men and women suffered a similar fate for presuming, devoutly and honestly, to interpret the Christian message.

In addition were malefactors who were branded with a red hot iron; debtors who, until 1869, were lodged here in comfort and waited upon, so long as they could pay; petty criminals or downright villains, awaiting the death sentence, some of whose misdemeanours to-day would scarcely invite the wag of a magisterial finger. Public hangings on Gallows Hill were popular with the crowds who swarmed on to the moor, enlivening the proceedings with crude and raucous jests. Prisoners and their coffins travelled on a tumbril from the Castle to the scaffold, fortified by one last merciful drink at a hostelry en route. One victim, anxious to get the business over, declined the offer and by an ironic twist of Fate had choked his last when a messenger galloped up with a free pardon!

The most notorious gaolbirds were the Lancashire Witches from Pendle and Samlesbury whose alleged nefarious practices in 1612 whipped the north of England into a frenzy of superstitious fear. Nowadays, those arch-rivals, Demdike and Chattox, whose families were at loggerheads and whose accusations and wild counter-charges brought them all to grief, would be tenderly cared for in some home for confused geriatrics. Instead "Nineteene Notorious Witches" were cooped up, men and women together, in an underground cell below the Well Tower from Easter 1612 until the August Assizes, those proceedings,

Lancashire heritage

(Above left): Lancaster Castle, John o'Gaunt Gateway. (Above right): The Ashton Memorial. (Below, left): The Judges' Lodgings — now a Museum of Childhood and of Gillow furniture. (Below right): The restored Music Room in the City Centre. Photographs by Ian Ward, kindly supplied by Charles Wilson, Lancaster City Architect & Planning Officer.

conducted with indecent haste and without appeal, being carefully noted and afterwards recorded by Thomas Potts, Clerk to the Justices. Some of the old anguish, I fancy, lingers on and maybe in the quiet hours, is heard again the senile cackling of Old Demdike who died in her cell before the trial and thereby cheated the hangman.

After the collapse of the first Jacobite Rebellion in 1715, many hanged, many more were transported to the American Colonies, and of 400 supporters flung into this chill, cheerless prison, 50 died, adding to the catalogue of miseries for which John o' Gaunt's old palace provided the backcloth. In later years hangings were carried out in a corner overlooking St. Mary's Churchyard and great were the crowds who turned up for these grisly spectacles.

Mementoes of the barbaric past have survived in ill-ventilated, unlit dungeons where recalcitrant prisoners or lunatics were once locked behind a massive studded door, heavy with bolts and locks; in branding irons, in branks, or scolds' bridles, to compress the tongues of vituperative females; in chains and shackles, in rings and staples in the foul den where the so called Lancashire Witches spent the last months of their god-forsaken lives.

By contrast, the lofty Shire Hall contains a magniicent array of shields of the High Sheriffs of Lancashire and Constables of the Castle from Bertram de Bulmer in 1129 to the present day . . . over 600 of them, a colourful pageant of Lancashire heraldry. Some of the ancient pomp and ceremony is revived when the hanging of a new High Sheriff's shield follows a service in the Priory Church, and out come the trappings and robes, the dignified expressions and emblems of office. For the invited guests it is a never-to-be-forgotten experience. For chance onlookers it is an unexpected thrill and a reminder, if we needed it, that when it comes to ceremonials, no-one can touch the British and that nowhere in the realm is Her Majesty's dignity more jealously preserved than in her own Dukedom of Lancaster.

Who was this Gaunt whose spirit still dominates the place, whose statue was set over the gateway entrance only last century? We are told he only visited Lancaster twice and left no visible mark on the place. He was a king's son who fathered a king, though he never occupied the throne of England; yet his power and influence ranked him second only to the monarch. He was a determined and ambitious man, enormously wealthy, with prodigious energies which extended to his love life. He first married Blanche, the Duke of Lancaster's daughter and acquired through her a son Henry Bolinbroke (Henry IV) and also the Dukedom. His second alliance to Peter of Castile's daughter, Constance, produced a large family whose governess, Catherine Swynford engaged in an adulterous relationship with Gaunt. As a result, four love children were born at Beaufort, after which they were named, and afterwards legitimised by Gaunt's nephew, Richard II. From that strain descended Margaret Beaufort, mother of Henry VII.

The Scots came rampaging through Lancaster in Gaunt's time (1389), burning and spoiling as they had done in 1322. There were anxious times during the ebb and flow of the Civil Wars and tense excitements during the two Jacobite Rebellions. Lancaster has some splendid 18th century town houses once occupied by nobility and gentry in the social season and during the Assizes when everyone of note flocked to the county town to exchange gossip, carouse with companions, enjoy the court-room dramas and to "sup with ye judges". The Conservative Club with its torch-extinguisher used by link boys long before street lighting belonged to the Duchess of Hamilton under whose roof Bonny Prince Charlie was given hospitality during the '45. Before the first hints of restoration, I was conducted through an 18th century Music Pavilion at the far end of Sun Street and allowed to gaze sorrowfully upon Italian plasterwork of about 1730 which had fallen, it seemed, into irremediable decay but, thanks to the unconquerable human spirit, miracles have been accomplished. The former beauty has been recaptured and the place is useful again and a joy to the eye.

East of Castle Park, where 17th and 18th century mansions of socialites and wealthy merchants clustered as close as they dared to the Castle walls, China Street runs down towards St. George's Quay, once a-bustle with trade from tall-masted ships and sailors, and the city's oldest pub, the Carpenter's Arms, where the dreaded press-gangs pounced on the unwary and ships' carpenters brought their thirsty gullets. China Street passed the splendid town house of the Beaumonts. From 1825 until a few years ago it was reserved for Judges' lodgings during the Assizes. Now it is a Museum housing among other things the late Barry Elder's collection of dolls, formerly displayed at Carr House, Bretherton, and the open space in front was the site of the Roman basilica.

The Palladian style Custom House (1764), a serene and dignified building, hints at the importance of Lancaster's busy overseas trade when Richard Gillow's father was importing mahogany, plentiful in the West Indies and useful as ballast for ships. He founded the furniture-making firm whose products found their way into the finest houses in the country and the name of Waring and Gillow is still honoured.

Lancaster has some glorious buildings including the old Town Hall (1783), now a splendid Museum, handsome houses, Georgian and earlier, in Castle Park and Church Street, and a dignified property, now occupied by the City Architect's Department, which stood brooding and blighted for forty six years after a gruesome double murder hit the headlines in the 'Thirties. Here, at No. 2 Dalton Square, Dr. Buck Ruxton, a Parsee Indian who ranks with Dr. Crippen in the annals of crime, carved up his wife Isabella and their Scottish maid, Mary Rogerson, motored northwards with his gory bundles and tossed them into a Scottish ravine. Decades after Ruxton was hanged, sight-seers still recalled those macabre goings-on but no-one was prepared to move into that greystone townhouse which gazes over Dalton Square gardens and a statue of Queen Victoria to the impressive new Town Hall, a gift to Lancaster by the first Baron Ashton in 1909. In the same year, Lord Ashton indulged his fondness for opulence and style in that massive Portland stone monument, or folly, or architectural flight of fancy which dominates the Lancaster scene. Originally, it was a memorial to his first wife; after two subsequent remarriages "to deceased relatives". It cost £87,000, a fortune at the time, has a copper dome, balconies giving superb views, hopeless acoustics and no practical application. It is absolutely useless, utterly magnificent and Lancaster's appearance is considerably enhanced by the "building", the "structure" or the "jelly mould", as I have heard it called by locals. It casts an elegant shadow over Williamson Park, all 38 acres developed out of abandoned stone quarries on Lancaster Moor and donated to the town in 1878 by Alderman James Williamson, the linoleum king and father of the multi-millionaire, Lord Ashton who lived at "Ryelands", a mansion surrounded by 40-odd acres and now a social centre and public park, on the other side of Skerton Bridge. Like many excessively rich men, he was inclined to be eccentric and even touchy. An account of his offer to purchase the old St. George's Gardens and present them (re-named Ashton Gardens) to the new town of St. Annes-on-the-Sea, for which he had a great affection, almost degenerates into pure farce. The year was 1913, Lord Ashton had purchased a bungalow with extensive grounds in the sand-dunes in the growing resort of St. Annes and he had been elected President of the Old Links Golf Club.

St. George's Gardens, designed as a money-spinner, was a financial disaster and rapidly falling into dereliction. The proprietors had disbursed over £15,000 in ground rents and further sums demanded by the landowners sent the price up to £21,350. The town wanted the Gardens, ratepayers were chary of paying and telephones were somewhat indistinct at that time. One tea-time, after a full day on Council business, the Chairman, Local Chemist J. H. Taylor, received a call on his line at "No. 8, St. Annes". In throaty whispers and an atmosphere of cloak-and-dagger melodrama, Lord Ashton requested the Chairman to catch a train that evening and come to his home at Ryelands, Lancaster without revealing a single hint of his errand, even to his wife. Obediently, Mr. Taylor set off for MANCHESTER, arriving at Victoria Station and taking a taxi from there to Messrs. Rylands, Wholesale Warehousemen in the city, assuming that Lord Ashton was probably a director of the firm. Needless to say, the premises were closed, the night porter looked blank and the Chairman, blushing to the roots of his hair, made a beeline for the telephone office and the Lancaster directory and confirmed his worst suspicions. He tried to phone through to Lancaster, without avail, and the last train to the coast was about to leave. He left it to the call office boy to get a message through to Lord Ashton with his abject apologies, travelled home with his heart in his boots thinking his clumsiness might have jeopardised the bequest to the town, and still leaving his wife entirely in the dark about what was happening, slept fitfully, rose at crack of dawn and almost fell into the mouthpiece with relief when the telephone rang at eight o'clock the next morning and a message from his lordship invited him to catch the first train to Lancaster where a motor-car would be waiting to run him out to "Ryelands".

Meantime, a perplexed wife and a batch of council colleagues must have been wondering what on earth had got into their Chairman who, after a two-hour interview with Lord Ashton and a discussion of every angle concering this momentous bequest, made another telephone call to "No. 2, St. Annes" (Council Offices) where the Committee had assembled, suspecting that something of importance was going on. The news was received with "wild delirium" by the normally sober councillors, among whom was my Great

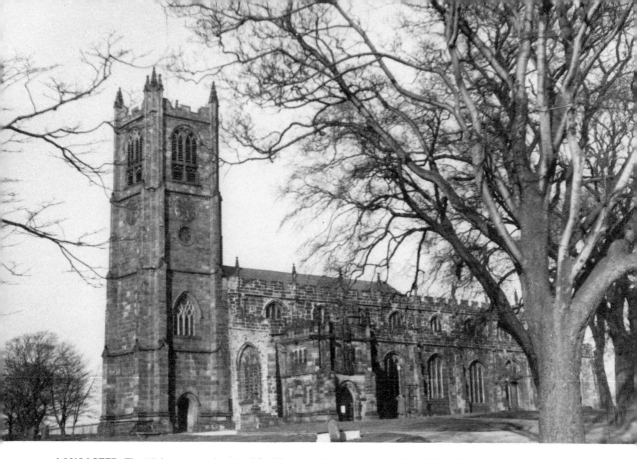

LANCASTER: The 15th century church of St. Mary the Virgin largely built *c.* 1430, adjoins the Castle standing high above the River Lune. The tower was built by 1760. The carved and canopied choir stalls, early 14th century and brought here either from Cockersand or Furness Abbeys after the Dissolution, are among the best you will ever see, displaying English medieval craftsmanship of a high order and a flair for rich and flamboyant design.

Uncle George Eyre, one of the pioneers, and directly afterwards Lord Ashton larded his beneficence, one of many, with monies to purchase extra land adjoining.

For forty years he dominated the Lancaster scene, being twice returned to Parliament on a Liberal ticket, providing homes and employment for thousands. He was lavish in charities, tight-fisted about wages and when the First World War reduced his profits he became progressively reclusive, suspicious of his fellow-men and at odds with Party colleagues, including Lloyd George. He died in 1930, this public benefactor who "acquired" a peerage in 1895, whose linoleum factory along St. George's Quay produced trainloads of floor-coverings for the Balkans, the Far East and South America, and whose exuberant memorial, perched on a moor top with views over six counties, puts life's petty irritations into perspective when you stroll in the gardens, visit the palmhouse or dawdle by the lake.

So much to be seen in Lancaster! St. Mary's Church, early 15th century with an 18th century tower, has canopied choir stalls, c. 1340, gloriously carved, some of the nation's finest. Whether they came from Cockersand Abbey on the coast seven miles to the south-west, or from Furness Abey across Morecambe Bay, those designs lovingly chiselled by monkish hands are breathtaking, though sometimes thirsty for linseed oil.

Did George Fox's lip curl contemptuously at these venerable works of hand and eye, for he was a plain man who despised ornamentation? From Pendle Hill, after his revelation there in 1652, he came from Ulverston and Swarthmoor to Lancaster and preached in the church here until the congregation turned suddenly to anger. They drove him bodily forth, stoned him along the street, and kind John Lawson, shop-keeper, sheltered him within doors. Fox, his future wife Margaret Fell, and many steadfast Friends endured much. Indeed, in those days, almost every Quaker "spent at least weeks, if not months or years, in dark and filthy gaols". Assembled worshippers "in some farmhouse or barn would be dragged away to Lancaster by the constables and all its members imprisoned".

Yet, a brave spirit prevailed here and in 1677 the Quakers erected a centre in Meeting House Lane. Dear old William Stout who joined the movement recorded in his Journal that in 1708 the building was too small to accommodate the Northern Counties General Meetings and he opened his own home for the purpose for six months until, at a cost of £180, a replacement building was completed. It is still there, quiet, sober and unassuming, in keeping with the spirit of the Friends who stood firm for conscience, braved savage persecutions, carried their message to distant places and even crossed the wild Atlantic to meet the challenge of the New World. The original dated doorhead is preserved in the Meeting House porch, along with John Lawson's gravestone. In the 1690's, the Society founded, and used the premises, for the Lancaster Friends' School which still flourishes, having spilled over into premises elsewhere.

With me, photography is a complete hit-and-miss affair with an occasional brilliant effort popping up out of a mediocre or totally disastrous batch of transparencies. Some years ago when I was conducting a W.E.A. course entitled "In the Footsteps of the Quakers", beginning with Pendle, Brigflatts and Swarthmoor, I and my exuberant party fell entirely under the spell of these lovely serene folk whose Godliness overflowed like soothing balm, whose genuine kindness shone forth in a darkling world. We came to know those Friends' Meeting Houses within easy reach of Lancaster – Yealand Conyers, Quernmore, Calder Bridge, near Garstang, Wray. As we stood in the garden at Lancaster where clumps of golden daffodils nodded in sprightly fashion among the ranks of modest rounded headstones, I was tempted to chance a shot of the Castle which, in the distance, looked almost benign, bathed in Spring sunshine and gentled by the finest of pale grey mists. The result was a little masterpiece, a study in delicate water-colours, with no hint of the anguish of those quietly determined Quakers who, all around us, in that unostentatious plot, lay sleeping.

To get the feel of Old Lancaster, first read William Stout's Journal. He is buried here. Most of his life was spent in the town after being sent to work for a Quaker grocer and ironmonger, Henry Coward, "on a month's liking" and serving for nine years before branching out on his own account. Later, he speculated in ships trading with the West Indies, losing a good deal more than would suit his provident nature. In 1699 he was purchasing masts, sails and tackle for "the ship building at Warton". It was named "Employment", had a disappointing career and after its earliest voyages had made little or "gained nothing", was taken prize by French privateers, ransomed for £1,100 and released only to run aground "in a very foul strong place where she beat till she was full of water" beneath the Red Banks between Bispham and Rossall. That was in October 1702 and Stout's heart must have sunk into his boots when the news was brought quickly to Lancaster, whereupon horses and carts with empty casks rattled with all speed to collect the sugar from Squire Fleetwood's barn and the cotton wool from Bispham Church. His sixth share in that ship and voyage had lost him well over £300, but he had many more years to live and much to record in his comprehensive account of regional life in the 17th and 18th centuries.

By 1750 the navigation of the Lune had been greatly improved and Lancaster enjoyed the principal share of trade with the West Indies, but three decades later the Lune had silting problems, Liverpool drew ahead, and Glasson Dock was built to serve Lancaster in 1787. From that time only vessels of shallow draught could sail up to St. George's Quay where today you will still see the shrimpers and small boats.

Lancaster is a glorious mixture of gracious Georgian architecture and gloomy ginnels, of quaintly named streets and narrow alleys leading to the covered Market. It is a town with a heart. The Westfield War Memorial Village, first of its type designed for disabled ex-sevicemen opened in 1927. Along King Street, tucked shyly behind an arched entrance, are almshouses grouped round a quadrangle and generously provided by a good Christian Alderman, William Penny in 1720, and a little further along, at the corner of Common Garden Street is Gillison's Hospital, another 18th century charitable foundation.

If stones could speak, the old King's Arms, rebuilt a lifetime ago, could tell some fine old tales of hi-jinks during the Assizes when jolly customers like Thomas Tyldesley and his cronies got together with "the best in ye county" and made inroads into the hostelry's cellars. Charles Dickens figures among the list of illustrious patrons. Where Penny Street, Cheapside, St. Nicholas Street and Market Street form a junction known as Horseshoe Corner, look for a horse-shoe (replaced whenever necessary) shed, legend likes to think, by John o' Gaunt's charger. At the foot of Cheapside stands St. John's Church, Italianate in style, like the Old Town Hall, and opened in 1754, with a Classic Tower and spire added by Thomas Harrison thirty years later. Harrison, a Yorkshireman, left his indelible imprint on Lancaster in his five-arched Skerton Bridge over the Lune (1788) and extensive work on the Castle and Shire Hall. The town lost St. Anne's Church (1796) when it gained The Duke's Playhouse in Moor Lane, a Civic Theatre which has become a modern Mecca for lovers of first-class productions. In Moor Lane Thomas Edmondson was born who devised the railway ticket system.

Not far from the Town Hall, in East Road, stands the Roman Catholic Cathedral of St. Peter, built in 1859 and containing brilliant frescoes, stone vaulting, beautifully decorated altars, good stained glass and a memorable figure of St. Peter. On a stiff pull-up to the Ashton Memorial stands the Royal Grammar School founded in 1472 which makes it one of Lancashire's oldest. John Gardiner of Bailrigg endowed this "free grammar school" after leasing a site from the Priory in 1469.

When the authorities were prospecting for a new university site in 1961, the City of Lancaster weighed in with the offer of 200 acres at Bailrigg, three miles south of the city centre and high above the ceaseless roar of the M.6, with panoramic views sweeping across Wyresdale to the east and from Lakeland peaks across Morecambe Bay to the heights of North Wales, to the west. The University of Lancaster was founded in 1964 by royal charter naming H.R.H. Princess Alexandra as first Chancellor, functioning in a variety of make-shift premises in the embryo years but now highly successful and impressively equipped with college buildings, halls of residence, shops, squares, chapel, car parks, colonnaded walks and assembly areas. In the same year St. Martin's College was founded for teacher training within the city on the site of the old garrison headquarters.

Among Lancaster's famous sons and daughters, one stands out as "The Father of the Iron Trade". Henry Cort (1740-1800), the ambitious son of a Lancaster mason and brickmaker, was working in London as a Navy Agent at the age of 25 when Russian iron was considered superior to that produced in Britain. When the price shot up, Cort began experimenting, invented the "puddling" process in 1784, reduced production costs, secured Government contracts and died in penury due to the dishonesty of a business colleague. The old, old story of unrequited genius which so often befell clever Lancashire lads!

8. TIDES, MISTS AND TRAGEDIES

WHEN some wild-fowler is plucked, in the nick of time, from the misty marshes off Warton, or a tide-trapped motorist is rescued after a night of roof-top terror along Pilling Sands, we are reminded of perils stalking the careless or foolhardy. The Lancashire coast from Liverpool to Furness had its tragic records of lives lost, of wayfarers succumbing to rushing tides, sinking sands or treacherous gullies.

In ancient times, when every journey was a harrowing adventure, few travelled more than twenty miles from home. But, for ecclesiastical, military, commercial or social reasons, some always had to be on the move and they came up the old Magnum Stratum from Chester, across the Mersey, then overland to the Ribble, with fords at Penwortham or Warton, through Amounderness to Lancaster and finally over Morecambe Bay to Furness and Scotland. The alternative, by way of Milnthorpe and Newby Bridge, involved mosses as dangerous as quicksands and evil characters lying in wait to rob travellers.

The ingenious Romans are thought to have slung causeways roughly along the present railway routes across the Kent, Leven and Duddon rivers emptying from Lakeland into the sea. In which case, later generations would think kindly of the departed conquerors, none more so than Christian missionaries who came south to convert the Romano-British. In the 6th century Bishop Kentigern of Glasgow strode into Lancashire and Wales, gathering "a fertile harvest for the Lord" and avoiding a watery death, by sheer good fortune! In the 14th century, after many drownings, the Abbot of Furness was authorised by the king to keep an eye on the treacherous Leven Sands. While Furness monks prayed in the chapel on a mid-estuary island, brethren guided travellers to safety. A light gleaming from the chapel preserved foot-sloggers and seafarers alike, before the Dissolution. In 1820 the Leven Sands guide received £22 a year from the Duchy and the use of three acres of land. When the railway opened there was an extra £20 in compensation for lost gratuities from grateful clients.

The longer, more dangerous crossing from Kent's Bank to Hest Bank came under Cartmel Priory and after the Dissolution the Duchy paid a salary to some local fellow, a fisherman, very likely, referred to as the "Carter over the Kent". He would know the moods and caprices of these tidal waters which still race in at the speed of a galloping horse. Morecambe Bay is no place for novices, what with 120 miles of open water between Lancashire and Ireland, and strong sou'westers ripping across, churning up foul seas too ugly for small boats to contend with. Not that you could ever frighten the Bay fishermen whose skill and courage are a byword among the piscatorial fraternity of our island.

There was a deal of smuggling once, when the Isle of Man belonged to the Earls of Derby and goods could be off-loaded there, duty free. Tea, rum, brandy, silks and fine cottons from the Indies came over under cover of darkness and found ready markets along the Lancashire coast. Storms, drownings and Excise-men only increased the excitement!

Locals and strangers alike perished along the Morecambe Bay sands, and we read of cocklers sucked down by quicksands and a coach passenger plucked with a resounding g-g-glug and not a second to spare, by a resolute coachguard. The poet Gray, on a Lakeland tour in 1769, heard of a cockler and his wife on horseback, with two grown daughters following in a cart, being caught by mists halfway across the sands. The channels had shifted. The head of the family set off to find a way out and was never again seen alive. The distraught wife refused to budge without her man and was swept away by rising waters and the daughters, by wading, swimming and hanging on to the horses, were miraculously cast up on the shore, deeply distressed but still alive. Their parents' bodies were recovered on the reflux of the tide.

From the 1780's a daily coach service plied across the sands between Lancaster and Ulverston. "The Carter" led, on horseback, and straggling behind were all manner of carts and country characters. They derived confidence from the jovial carter, mounted upon "a good horse which appeared to have been up to the ribs in water" and clad in jackboots and a rough great coat. After negotiating two deep channels, a line of rods indicated the safe track where, with expressions of gratitude, the travellers rewarded the guide, to whom they owed their lives, no less.

The Cartmel registers contain a grim record of disasters down the ages, averaging between two and three a year, interspersed with long lulls and mass drownings. In 1811, the oversands coach overturned, two dogs drowned, luggage was lost, the vehicle disappeared and the passengers were barely rescued on the backs of the horses. A coach-horse was lost in 1825, a vehicle in 1828, and in 1846 nine young people from Cartmel perished while returning from Ulverston Fair. Similarly, in 1857, farm-hands heading for the hiring fair were found drowned the following day. There is truth in the saying:

> The Kent and the Keer
> Have parted many a man and mare!

Nowadays, in the footsteps of the saints and sinners and circuit judges, the monks and merchants, tradesmen and travelling preachers, the prelates and post-boys of long ago, stride armies of old and young, hundreds at a time, prepared to tackle the ten-mile curving route purely as a novelty and a recreation.

They are led by a husky guide who knows his job, a bare-foot fresh-faced strapping fellow with a cheerful countenance and a pronounced Cumbrian burr which falls delightfully on the ears. He carries a long rod and is continually "brodding" in search of a solid footing. Such scenes, on many a summer Sunday, would have delighted William Wordsworth who had watched similar happenings from afar off and found himself longing "for the skill to paint a scene so bright". David Cox, a splendid artist, went one better and actually painted "Crossing Lancaster Sands" in 1841, and Turner was busy in these parts, while Ruskin stated boldly that "Lake scenery begins at Lancaster". From Camden's time, they looked across the sweep of Morecambe Bay towards the Lakeland mountains, in all their glory; their hearts were moved, and they marvelled. Mrs. Fiennes, Daniel Defoe, and later, de Quincey, all felt the sweet and subtle fascination of the prospect beyond the bay which to-day's tripper all but destroys in his mad determination to congregate with his own kind in great numbers in the wrong places and at the wrong times of the year. How much sweeter, to my mind, are those portions of the Lancashire coast that have no connections with summer crowds and crimsoned visitors packed like sardines in the sunshine. There is a quietude in tracts of cool mud and misty melancholy, where the wind carps, and sea-birds call, where the tide circles and creeps along gullies, as menacingly as a shifty-eyed mongrel intent upon nipping the unwary in the ankles. But then, true romance was ever spiced with danger.

In 1858 Mrs. Elizabeth Gaskell, novelist and original biographer of Charlotte Brontë, stopped writing for a few moments and watched the "slow moving train of crossers, led over the treacherous sands by the Guide, a square man sitting stern on his white horse, the better to be seen when daylight ebbs . . . " This clever lady, a Unitarian minister's wife, regularly fled from Manchester's dusty streets with her children and took refuge in Lindeth Tower at a place quaintly named Gibraltar, overlooking Morecambe Bay. She made the top room her special place where, between the scratching of goose-quill on paper, she could rest her eyes on the distant hills. The peace and inspiration she discovered in this picturesque retreat are reflected again and again in her writings; and the distant sound of a ram's horn being blown by the guide when a mist threatened must often have fallen upon her ears and drawn her perhaps, with anxious looks, to the windows.

9. MORECAMBE BAY

St. Peter's Church, Heysham.

PRACTICALLY all the English resorts developed out of hamlets where coast dwellers had fished the waters from time out of mind. They had been born by the sea; they took it for granted. Inlanders were different. Most of them lived and died without once setting eyes on the ocean. Remember how Charlotte Brontë reacted at Bridlington, at the age of twenty-three when, in all its majesty she first beheld the sea? Her poetic soul was stirred by its grandeur and, until the relieving tears had gushed, her tongue was silenced. That was in 1839. A hundred years earlier all the health resorts were inland and the coast was the fringe, the waste edge of the country. So it might have remained but for that curious 18th century health craze which captured the popular imagination, swept through every stratum of society and impelled increasing numbers, like lemmings, towards the coast.

Scarborough was the first sea-bathing resort to be mentioned in the 1730's for the simple reason that it possessed a mineral spring and had already developed into a popular Spa. By complete accident, it happened to be on the sea-coast. The sudden emphasis on the efficacy of sea-water gave Scarborough, with all its accommodations and provisions for Spa patrons, a head-start at a time when most maritime hamlets were primitive in the extreme. Sleeping space was prevailed upon in farmers' barns or in over-crowded, stinking and bug-ridden beds shared with the natives. Communal sleeping was deemed a reasonable enough price to pay for improved health through drinking gallons of sea-water, a pint at a time, of course and submitting, in a state of almost cataleptic terror, to the embraces of Old Father Neptune. The sufferer was guaranteed a purging and a thorough cleansing, inside and out, probably for the first time since the midwife packed up her traps. Assuming that his ills were caused by excesses, to which the 18th century socialite was prone, there was a degree of truth in the claims made for the treatment. The paunchy purple-nosed squire with a bleary eye and crippling gout would prance home, spry and rejuvenated, ready to resume the old rakish life after a few weeks of sea-bathing. Eventually, even the ditherers gave it a try and by the 1770's numerous resorts were doing good business, including Blackpool and Lytham. Southport did not exist; nor did Morecambe which, in 1928, was incorporated with Heysham into a Municipal Borough, and in 1974, along with Carnforth U.D.C., and Lancaster and Lunesdale R.D.C's, was swept under the wing of the Lancaster City Council.

Early last century, next door to Heysham, were three fishing communities of Torrisholme, Bare and Poulton-le-Sands. (This last-named caused such confusion in the delivery of mail that, to distinguish it, the old Fylde market town of the same name was designated "Poulton-le-Fylde"). Poulton-le-Sands was administered by Lancaster. It had less than four hundred souls until 1820 when some bright spark advertised a furnished cottage to let and called it "Morecambe Cottage".

What followed is another Lancastrian example of a bouncing daughter resort springing from, and eventually overshadowing, the original mother village, as in the case of Blackpool and Bispham, Southport and Churchtown, St. Annes-on-Sea and Lytham. It is still possible to winkle out the nucleus of the place around the church, Lord Street and Poulton Square; and the fishermen, the genuine native stock, who are part of the scene without being seduced by it. As at Lytham, these blue-jerseyed patriarchs push the boat out, gather in groups, see to their gear, bring home the shrimps. They have an instinct for the sea in all its shifting moods, and a capacity for fine judgment and endurance which men need in the Lifeboat. And make no mistake about it! There is no breed of men more heroic than the R.N.L.I. chaps who hazard their lives every time they answer a distress call, but who would never, for a King's ransom, renege on a duty! Their modesty, their courage and their confidences have immeasurably ennobled my existence; and by all contemporary standards they are rewarded with a pittance! "Why don't they pay them what they are worth?", a young student once asked me. The answer was simple. "BECAUSE, laddie! There isn't enough money in THE WORLD!" And that's how it is and, please God, for ever will be. The R.N.L.I. would be ill served by men doing it simply for the money.

To serve the Poulton fisherfolk a Chapel of Ease attached to Lancaster was built in 1745 and replaced on the same site in 1841. By then the populaton had risen to seven hundred and a spirit of improvement was stalking the village. The North West Hotel was begun in 1847; the sea wall two years later, and a Railway Company, opened in 1850. Steamer services to Belfast started up in 1851 and a strong Yorkshire connection, still prevalent, earned the nick-name of "Bradford-on-Sea" until 1870 when the name of "Morecambe" was officially adopted.

In the middle of last century there was no certainty about which way Morecambe would develop. Industry could have taken over. Pig iron came in from Furness. A stone jetty replaced an earlier wooden one and there were hopes of turning this into a great shipping centre. Instead, many noble vessels came here to die in the ship breaker's yard. The clang of hammers echoed metallically over the waters and there were relics and items of furniture to be snapped up for a song; but there were also good pickings from the more pleasurable side of life and visitors continued to pour in.

A stretch of promenade about 200 yards long in the early 1860's, daily steamer sailings to Grange, Barrow and Furness Abbey, thrice weekly crossings to Ireland, the busyness and fascination of the fishing boats coming and going, bathing machines, shrimp sellers, horse wagonette trips to Strawberry Gardens at Heysham, hawkers of turf for the fires, or butterscotch to keep the kiddies quiet, created an interesting scene and ensured Morecambe's future as a holiday resort with the supreme advantage of glorious sunsets and dramatic views across the bay to the mountains of Lakeland.

In Victorian times, of course, there had to be a pier and Morecambe acquired two. Central Pier, built 1869, improved 1897, and still going strong though fire gutted its beautiful Indian Theatre in 1933, is still a popular venue for the May festivals and seasonal productions; and the usual conglomeration of slot machines at the pier head helps to keep the old structure going. Less fortunate was West End Pier (1896), famous for orchestral concerts until the pavilion burned down in 1915, remembered for the "West End Follies" and roller skating and open air dancing . . . until disaster struck on 11th November 1977. "Heavy seas and gale force winds" were announced and sea-front residents began sand-bagging doorways and windows. By nightfall, the promenade had turned into a foaming river; planks, debris, maplewood blocks were swept along like discarded bus tickets. The great iron supports which had defied the elements for a lifetime finally buckled and dawn broke on a scene of dismal destruction. Up-ended fruit machines tossed on the sands were already being rifled by young treasure-hunters; elderly residents wept; photographers took pictures. Ornamental railings and other relics were bought, gilded and shipped across the Atlantic by a Brighouse dealer who caters to the American weakness for good old British junk.

There is something distinctly reminiscent of Blackpool about Morecambe which stages its seasonal Illuminations; promotes the Miss Great Britain National Bathing Beauty Contest; has a Marineland with performing dolphins and other delights; and an impressive Leisure Centre complex opened officially in July 1981. Yet, the Baxters are still in the fish business, as they were long ago, still famous for shrimps which are potted and sent all over the country. Look out for the Royal Warrant on the front of a cottage, and date-stones going back to 1675; and sturdy walls built of sea cobbles; and blue-jerseyed senators sunning themselves, puffing on pipes, discussing boats and tides and gear and currents, and skeers and sand-banks, and the state of the market.

Heysham

In the early days, visitors scrambled along a cliff path towards a rocky promontory with a ruined chapel overlooking a wide sweep of the bay. Heysham, a very different place, settlement of Anglian Chief Hesse, founded c. 700, referred to in Domesday as "Hessam".

There is an atmosphere of extreme old age hereabouts but, if you cannot feel it, do not worry. There are enough antiquities to put all doubts to flight! From remote times the Druids performed their peculiar rites in a grove behind the present Vicarage gardens, the Chief Druid standing before the Divine Water Stone, observers on the opposite slope. There is a mysterious area known locally as "The Barrows" (burial mounds) where, long before William conquered, human corpses were interred. Foliage has since overgrown the Druids' semi-circular floor, and children laugh and play here, insensitive to the mystical element which prevails still.

Nearby, on a rocky headland above the churchyard, are some of the earliest signs of Christianity in the north-west of England, six lid-less coffins hewn out of a great solid rock, each grooved to receive a stone lid, each having a sunken hollow at its head to accommodate a standing cross. Lengths vary but I have watched a rugged six-footer, in a somewhat macabre experiment, trying one out for size and cheerfully declaring it "a good fit!" Nearer the chapel ruins are two more similar graves, smaller, for children, perhaps, or for sacred relics. Who can say now? There are no other rock graves precisely like Heysham's and antiquarians may speculate and argue for ever, or until a systematic excavation is carried out . . . and only then will the full truth become known. The rock coffins could be contemporaneous with St. Patrick's Chapel of which enough survives to give a plan 27ft. by 9ft., and a style which is a mixture of Northumbrian-Saxon and Irish. A doorway in the south wall suggests a period 750-800 A.D., though there could have been a wooden oratory on the site before that. Only the east gable and the south wall, 2ft. 6ins. thick, remain standing.

The whole area is rife with legends about St. Patrick and one tries to separate fact from fiction. Patrick was a Roman, grandson of a Christian priest and son of Calpurnius, a magistrate and deacon. He was born near Dumbarton on Clydeside c. 372 A.D., was captured in adolescence by Irish brigands and bought as a slave by an Irish chief. Tending sheep allowed much time for prayer and meditation and Patrick vowed, one day, to convert the Irish people. First, he escaped, took ship and headed for Scotland and a reunion with his parents. But the vessel wrecked on a skeer in the bay beneath Heysham headland. Patrick and his companions scrambled ashore where the Druids were all-powerful, to whom, some versions would have us believe, he boldly proclaimed his Christian message. Twenty-six foot-slogging days later the young saint-in-the-making was reunited with his family in Kilpatrick.

The rest of the story is a jumble of claims which may, or may not, be true. They say he studied at various Continental monasteries, was consecrated a bishop and sailed with fifteen companions from Gaul in 432 for Ireland, and was greeted with hostility. Yet in 455 he founded the church and see of Armagh and in 462 he died at Saul in County Down, having spent his later years in Ulster. His "Confessio", written in Latin in extreme old age, when memory was probably confused, is preserved in the library of Trinity College, Dublin. We cannot even be sure that he came to Britain to preach though he is commemorated in place names.

Time passed, and they built St. Patrick's Chapel at Heysham. You will hear talk of raiding Vikings contemptuously unroofing the building, leaving wind and weather to carry on the destruction. A later church, St. Peter's, was built on a less obvious site beneath the shadow of St. Patrick's. Quite possibly, both existed at the same time and certainly pre-Conquest. Older portions of St. Peter's date back to the 10th century and the millenium was celebrated in 1967 with a programme of events which opened on St. Patrick's Day (17th March) and special services on St. Peter's Day (29th June). All that summer, this ancient and greatly loved church, which in normal times welcomes up to 20,000 every month, was deluged with visitors from all over the world.

Do visit! This is one of very few survivals of Early Christianity in west Britain. The setting is attractive, sheltering headland to the west, the bay to the north, the mountains of Lakeland in the distance. There are some rare antiquities including the famous Hog-Back Stone, kept in the church now though, for centuries, buried in the churchyard and discovered with a rusty spearhead nearby in 1800. Hog-backs are rare. Long interment preserved Heysham's splendidly, its curious carvings concealing a story, perhaps the Christianised version of a pagan legend from Scandinavia. The tale goes that Torrig (hence "Torrisholme"), the local leader, slew a worthy Saxon adversary, Chief Eagle (hence Eccleston in South Lancashire) and placed this mark of distincton over his grave. There are plenty of bygones in the churchyard, including part of a Saxon cross with scrollwork on one side and the raising of Lazarus on the other, 8th century perhaps, though some say earlier.

The Old Hall at Heysham, an attractive Elizabethan mullioned and transomed house completed about 1598 was purchased by a brewery in 1956 and transformed into an Old English Inn. Its original appearance has been preserved and there can be no objection to the kind of commercialisation which at the same time ensures perpetual preservation.

Manor House, Slyne.

Bolton-le-Sands, Hest Bank and Slyne.

Travelling north from Bare into William Stout's territory, take time off to explore these three attractive villages on the fringe of Morecambe Bay. But, as a preparation, dip into that celebrated autobiography of a worthy old Quaker who was laid to rest in the Friends' Burial Ground at Lancaster in 1752, having reached the age of eighty-seven. William Stout, born in 1665, prospered as a grocer and wholesale ironmonger in the county town. He was devoted to his sister Elin but never seriously thought of marrying, being a somewhat sober fellow and as industrious as his parents before him. They farmed along the bay, grazed sheep on a vast marsh now covered by tides and sands. In 1677, when William was about thirteen years old, he tells us "the sea began to break into our marsh at the south end, next Bare . . . and made it soft or quicksands . . . so that most of our stock of sheep was lost". A tidal wave, some five yards deep, had roared across like the thunder of cannon, destroying useful acres, a century's accumulation.

A worse disaster happened two years later. Farmer Stout sickened and died leaving his widow with six surviving children to care for, all boys with the exception of the first-born Elin, the dutiful drudge who waited upon her brothers, slaved at knitting, spinning and sewing, toiled in hay and corn fields and never had a moment to call her own. Nowadays we would look for the psychological origin of a recurrent condition diagnosed as the "King's Evil" which caused the poor girl to be "distempered by ulcers and breaking out her limbs and other parts of her body". She was even sent to the capital to be touched by Charles II, without benefit, which further reduced her chances of escaping family thraldom. Mercifully, she found contentment in later life with her brother William who, after attending the Bolton-le-Sands Free Grammar School founded in 1619 for the education of the children of the three villages and those of Nether Kellet, was apprenticed to a Lancaster Quaker Henry Coward, grocer, ironmonger and horse-trader.

William served his master conscientiously, worked intolerable hours, often till nine or ten at night, yet must have found time to keep diary notes from which, after retiring at a great age from business, he began, in a small neat hand, writing his life story in a small quarto volume of coarse paper. His eyesight, which had deteriorated by the age of fifty, spontaneously improved twenty years later so that he could manage without spectacles, a curious phenomenon easily explained by optical experts. This is one of the most fascinating records of economic and social life to emerge from that period. On everything from family matters to events of national import the worthy Quaker wrote his comments, giving us authentic glimpses into his training, his trading ventures, his regular business visits to London – five days each way, twelve hours at a stretch in the saddle and highwaymen lurking in lonely places, en route – the de-throning of James II in 1688, cheese-buying expeditions to Garstang or Preston, cheese being in great demand for funerals and ordered from 30 lbs. to 100 lbs., "as the deceased was of ability". He mentions the price of goods, the French wars, clipped coinage – "hammered money" – the Spanish siege of Gibraltar in 1727, and the death of the Empress of Russia at 38, "but doubted whether naturally or by violence"; piracy, inundations of the sea, pestilences and the plight of Jacobite prisoners at Lancaster Castle after the 1715 rebellion had been suppressed at Preston.

The Journal was first published in serial form in the "Manchester Guardian" in 1850, and in book form a year later. An up to date version, edited by Dr. J. D. Marshall, with annotations by a group of fellow historians, was published by Manchester University Press. Get hold of a copy. Bone up on William Stout lore. Then travel in the footsteps of the earliest tourists. At Bolton-le-Sands there are still scenes that were familiar to the diarist, picturesque 17th and 18th century cottages, some with date-stones. Last time I was there someone pointed out the quaint little library building where the young Stout brothers had their first lessons. St. Michael's Church at the south end of the village was much rebuilt during last century, but the great Perpendicular tower survived, and the nave arcade.

There was no canal in Stout's day. It borders the main street overlooked by the Packet Boat Inn and it dates back to 1817 when travellers from Lancaster to Kendal set out on the most sensuous of adventures, gliding towards Lakeland without the disagreeable accompaniment of engine fumes and vibrations and through some of the greenest and most bewitching scenery in the English countryside. Lancashire was celebrated for "its works of art in the construction of its useful and numerous canals" and even to-day cruising along still waters, miles from any town, where the cob-swan may be guarding his mate perched on her mound of twigs, and herons touch down with jerky movements, and cows gaze placidly, still chewing, and a carpet of water-iris undulates with the stirring of propellers, is still and all one of life's most voluptuous delights.

This is an area which is attractive to campers, caravanners and those who enjoy messing about in small boats. Some have been coming regularly for half a lifetime; the residents, many descended from long-time farming and fishing families, would live nowhere else. In 1900, Thomas H. Mawson, a renowned landscape architect, won a Planner of the Year Award with his design for transforming Hest Bank into a garden village. It was there centuries before that, of course! It was the terminus for a sands crossing, frequently used by the Furness Abbey Community who had possessions in the Lancaster area. Robert the Bruce and his fellow-raiders used the sands route and so did more peaceful travellers like George Fox, founder of the Quakers, and John Wesley who launched the Methodist movement. The coaches had splendid names like "Lakeland Gem", "Queen of Furness", "Whitehaven Belle", and the old Sands Inn, now renamed the Hest Bank Hotel, rigged up a lantern room to assist, not only the coach drivers, but also the rescue teams who were kept handy. They can talk for ever in these parts of tide-trapped travellers and miraculous deliverances. The coming of the railway in the 1850's put an end to the daily coach crossings.

Slyne is a village of good stone houses squatting beside the main road leading north. There are village stocks set up beside the old pinfold, and cottages with 18th century date-stones, and cramped colourful garden plots to catch the eye, and an attractive old Manor House dated 1681 at the corner of the road leading down to the shore. It has a handsome doorhead and mullioned and transomed windows. Fields nearby have ancient holy wells, one dedicated to St. Patrick supposedly being good for sore eyes.

Those indefatigable early travellers.

English tourism really began in the 18th century, coinciding with the turnpiking of roads, the improving of river navigations, the building of canals. Suddenly everyone with time and money to spare became mobile, aided by best-selling travel books which tumbled from the presses and topped the best-selling lists. From the 1760's coaches laden with passengers and mails plied regularly between Lancashire and London, three days by Flying Machine, longer by the lumbering Stage Waggons. It was expensive by contemporary standards and those jolly Christmas card scenes are ludicrously wide of the mark. Stages usually departed in the miserable light of early morning which planted a sullen scowl on the face of the landlord. Once on the road, comfort was in short supply. Outside passengers hung on in danger of being frozen alive or catapulted to certain death. Those within endured agonies of overcrowding. Joltings and the inhaling of foul air caused sickly headaches while the coachman was frequently "very much in liquor". Rabid dogs were a hazard, and highwaymen. The gentleman traveller armed himself with a veritable arsenal, from an imitation walking stick made of iron, to a brace of blunderbusses or double-barrelled pistols with spring bayonets. He was advised to afffix an emergency bolt to his bedroom door and to sleep with pistol and bayonet at hand.

Yet, early travellers were thrilled by all they saw. Every new discovery was written about and discussed – scenic delights, splendid architecture, romantic ruins and works of art were no more popular than cotton mills, coal pits, lead mines, blast furnaces and potteries. The Scottish Highlands were equally fascinating, and the wretched conditions of the barefoot natives. If it was new, it simply HAD to be seen! Tourists scaled crags, climbed mountains, wandered through cathedrals. They winced at those "horrid bagpipes" (like "pigs grunting or cats squalling"), but cheerfully wriggled down caves or had themselves lowered in buckets down perpendicular shafts to the coalface.

Before leaving Bolton-le-Sands for the English Lakes, having read West's 18th Century Guide, they pursued a climbing lane to the pleasant upland hamlet of Nether Kellet heading for Dunald Mill Hole, an underground cavern with stalactites and a stream belting along on its subterranean travels. Having descended "by means of chinks of rock", the explorer proceeded nervously through massive chambers or claustrophobically narrow passages to behold scenes of "majestic horror" heightened by ghostly echoes and glistening multi-coloured dampness on the walls revealed by lighted candles. He emerged at last marvelling at the rudeness of Nature, with another item to be enthused about in the next report home.

Over Kellet, an ancient hill-side village south of Carnforth, has a green and a village cross, and memories of St. Cuthbert in the 16th century church which has fabric from c. 1200. The Lindisfarne monks who fled with the Saint's body when Danes attacked, and wandered for years, paused at Aldingham c. 880. They crossed Morecambe Bay, rested at Over Kellet before proceeding to Lytham and over the Ribble mouth to North Meols (Churchtown) and Halsall. When churches were built later, they commemorated St. Cuthbert, the Saxon shepherd from the hills of Lammermuir.

Carnforth was obscure until coaches began trundling through to Glasgow or London. Industry gradually besmirched it, the grime of iron furnaces, the busyness of a railway junction. Nowadays, Carnforth is a place to pass through on the way to Lakeland, or a Mecca of those perpetual schoolboys who become dreamy-eyed at the sight of steam locos! A mile northwards, Warton (in Silverdale) is a very different place, a straggle of grey stone and rough cast with some grand old houses along the main street and a 14th century church with trans-Atlantic connections. The Washingtons who built the 15th century church tower and embellished it with their device of two bars and three mullets (stripes and stars) were the local big-wigs who lived at Warton for three hundred years before flitting to Sulgrave. In the mid-17th century, John Washington emigrated to America. His great-grandson, born in Virginia in 1732, became the first President of the United States and the family's device undoubtedly inspired the Stars and Stripes which Warton church proudly flies every 4th July. American servicemen made many friends here during the last war. The weathered carving is now indoors for protection, the first thing visitors ask to see before searching for Washington House in the main street, the old family home.

Warton is proud of its links with prominent figures from history. The Kitsons, a local family, married into both the Washingtons and Spencers, linking President George Washington with Sir Winston Spencer Churchill . . . and now, of course, with the Princess of Wales. George John Spencer, great-grandson of the great Duke of Marlborough, was created Viscount Althorp and Earl Spencer.

Ruins of a 14th century rectory, rare of their kind, are preserved in the grounds of St. Oswald's Vicarage. And ancient customs prevailed here until modern times – Cockpennies at Shrovetide, May-Day revelries, Rush-bearings, Arvals (burial feasts when mourners were refreshed with a small loaf and a lump of cheese), and the Feast of Dedication.

An eminent Wartonian, Matthew Hutton, Archbishop of York, gave almshouses to the village in 1594 and a school where the antiquarian, Roger Dodsworth was educated whose massive collection of "ancient evidences" is housed in the Bodleian Library, Oxford. After a period of exile school-mastering in Yorkshire, John Lucas, a Carnforth man, painted an enchanting word-picture of 18th century Warton which Leland had described as "a preti Streat for a Village". It is, indeed, a rare place for poking and browsing, soaking up atmosphere and wonderful walks.

Warton Crag, Dog Hole, Fairy Hole, Badger Hole.

The lovely coast road from Hest Bank to Silverdale slides beneath Warton Crag. For history, get behind that great mass of limestone and follow after those Friends (Quakers) who were "faithfull labourers" in the Yealand villages. Or, like Leland, who noticed "Herdes of Gotes", scramble to some rocky knoll and feast your eyes on glorious views. The crag was an Armada Beacon and hill-top fort. Caves have been discovered where Bronze Age man made his home and left evidence in the way of bones, pottery, tools, ornaments, and implements of pre-historic, Celtic or Roman origins.

There are fairy legends, too, and tales of fearsome "Three Fingered Jack", a robber who occupied one of the caves and pounced on honest travellers. In the old days newly married couples struggled up to The Bride's Chair, a limestone ledge; it determined who would be the boss for life!

10. WILDLIFE IN LANCASHIRE

LANCASHIRE is for Nature-lovers! The wild-life here is second to none in the kingdom! Huge expanses of moorland support their own life-systems. Leighton Moss, one of the best Reserves in the country, is a limestone basin of 320 acres where water is trapped and wild life flourishes. Foxes, roe deer and red deer come down in the evenings; otter can be seen playing and porpoising about; bittern, the only regular breeding colony in the north of England, settled here 40 years ago. They boom from January, can be spotted from Spring feasting on eels. There are hides and paths through acres of whispering reed beds which attract Grasshopper and Reed Warblers. The bearded tit has bred here since the 1970's. Butterflies and dragonflies are abundant and in winter ducks and waders invade the Moss. A Visitors' Centre with facilities was opened at Myers Farm, Silverdale, in 1980 (permits for parties from The Warden).

Ovangle marshes and Sunderland Point teem with bird life and coastal flora and the marshes around Preesall, Stalmine and Pilling offer sanctuary for roosting winter geese including the Barnacle, Grey Lag and Pink-foot. Tucked away behind Blackpool Zoo and of interest to ornithologists and anglers is all that remains of the once great Marton Mere (not to be confused with Martin Mere across the Ribble). Drainage operations in the 18th century reduced its size but reclaimed huge areas of glistening mosslands for argiculture and horticulture, a dramatic sight when a thousand gulls wheel and swoop after the tractor!

At St. Annes, where the builder has been encroaching for over 100 years, a stretch of the sand-dune belt along Clifton Drive North was set apart in 1968 as a Nature Reserve, nearly 39 acres of profuse growth, comparable with the Ainsdale Reserve across the water but having the odd unique feature such as a hybrid marsh plant exclusive to this area. Bird life is plentiful and varied. The goldfinch gorges on seeds of *OEnothera Lamarkiana* the blatantly yellow Evening Primrose which landed here accidentally from North America in tall masted grain ships. Skylarks nest, sea-birds wheel over, the stonechat makes the curious noise of two stones being struck together, a sparrowhawk hovers and kestrels dive after prey. Moths and butterflies, newts and lizards, many bird species and hundreds of rare sand flowerets do well under protection among the acres of marram, or starr-grass which had to be planted by coast-dwellers to stop sand over-blowing crops, by Acts of Parliament passed under Elizabeth I and again in the 18th century.

Across the Ribble, inland from Southport, The Martin Mere Wildfowl Trust opened with 260 acres in 1975. A fantastic place with facilities for visitors and school parties who find plenty to marvel at, all the year round. The shallow Mere, once covering several square miles and dotted with marsh-girt islands, was reputedly the place where young Sir Lancelot grew up before joining Arthur's Knights of the Round Table.

The Formby, Ainsdale and Freshfield dunelands, like their counterparts at St. Annes, are rich in rare flora. The dewberry flourishes, juicier than the bramble, with a bloom like blue grapes. There are clumps of sea buckthorn, wild orchids including the Bee Orchis, delight of my childhood; helleborines, the rare Grass of Parnassus. In marshy "slacks" plants like marigold, pennywort and orchid grow. Formby also has the bog-bean. At the Point you can spot wintering grebe, eider, razorbill, guillemot and snowbunting. Ainsdale dunes are a summer paradise and Freshfield pinewoods harbour foxes and fungi, owls, spotted woodpecker and nightjar. The Continental Red Squirrel, descended from escaped pets, has bred in the Formby National Trust Reserve for 40 years, integrating with the engaging non-hibernating Common Reds. There are bats, too, Pipistrelle and long-eared varieties. At night they head for St. Luke's Church and hang and sleep there until dawn. School parties come for field studies, guide books are available, footpaths are clearly marked.

The heron jerkily touches down in fields along the canals or on mosslands south of the Ribble where the Reed Warbler breeds and hares abound. The Scarisbrick heronry was decimated by tree-felling; the nearest is at Ince Blundell. Common Tern still attempt to breed along Hesketh marsh and in the Altcar dunes; and the wildfowler finds plenty to take a pot shot at on both sides of the Ribble Estuary.

The Red Squirrel can still be found in Croston woods, Worden Park, Leyland, Duxbury Wood, Chorley, and in Lunesdale, around Caton.

Melling village.

11. LANCASHIRE RIVERS

LANCASHIRE is a land of many waters. Moist Atlantics collide with the Pennines and the violent union forms great rivers flowing westward. The little heron-haunted Keer spills into Morecambe Bay near Carnforth. The lovely Lune, born in Ravenstonedale amid "the mountains rude of Yorkshire" and fed by Leck, Greta, Wenning, Hindburn and Roeburn, enters Lancashire near Kirkby Lonsdale.

The Leck tumbles below that sad little Cowan Bridge School forever linked with the Brontës. Homesick and half starved, they dreaded those detestable Sundays at St. John's Church, Tunstall ("Brocklebridge" of "Jane Eyre"), setting out chilled, "colder" still after a two mile trudge and "almost paralysed" before morning service ended. A frugal dole of bread and cold meat was nibbled in an upstairs room between devotions. The staircase has vanished but a vertical ladder gives access to that joyless chamber. The Vicar here, the Rev. William Carus-Wilson, founded the low-cost Clergy Daughters' School in 1824, doubtless from the worthiest of motives. But Charlotte was revolted by the heartless discipline, nauseating food, the omnipresent "Mr. Brocklehurst" who, in real life, wearied himself with niggling details instead of delegating responsibility, sure sign of a poor administrator.

The Lune is an angler's paradise, second only to the Dee in the north-west for salmon. Lunesdale is most beauteous and teeming with history, the very place for lovers of little old country churches. Roman veterans settled here and bred horses for the Roman cavalry. Agriculture is all important. British Freisians graze the lower pastures and black-faced ewes and grey-faced half-breds crop the higher ground. This is hunting country, Vale of Lune Harriers from Hornby and Lunesdale foxhounds yelping over from the old Westmorland fells in the season. Watch out for Lune bridges, too few of them, you might think; only one between the M.6 and Hornby.

On the southern banks, two miles along the 683 Tunstall-Lancaster road, look for Melling, a charming village of mellowed stone houses and a late Perpendicular church, built c. 1490. St. Wilfrid's has a stout porch, a buttressed tower sturdy enough to withstand the batterings of marauders, and a roof that replaced the old thatch in the 1760's. It sags beautifully, has numerous mural tablets, a built-in Roman Votive Stone, an effigy of Sir Thomas Tunstall of Thurland (1415), a hagioscope, an ancient pike chest and a chancel floor rising by groups of steps to the altar, man-high above the nave.

Over the river, an old ferry-crossing away at Arkholme ("Arkhum") another late Perpendicular church stands within an earthwork above the Lune. It was repaired in 1788 according to the testimony of John Wilson "Curet" and John Smith "Chappel Warden", extended in the 1890's, and a famous 14th century inscribed bell hangs in the bell-cote over the west gable. On the Arkholme side, two miles downstream, the Gernetts kept the royal goshawks in the time of King John. They were buried at Gressingham, another "Best Kept" village with delightful nooks and a beck bustling Lunewards, best seen in daffodil time, if it can be managed. The quaint church of St. John the Evangelist has, among many curios, pre-Conquest carved crosses, 12th century door with cable and chevron mouldings, ancient box pews and an oak pulpit of 1714.

Loyn Bridge links Gressingham with Hornby, Queen of the Lune villages, dominated by Castle and keep. Views from that lofty Eagle tower are utterly superb. It was added by Edward Stanley ("Ho! My Soldier!") who had the wit to marry the Harrington heiress and the luck to lead Lancashire bowmen to victory at Flodden in 1513. Henry VIII loved him for that, created him Lord Monteagle. He added tower and chancel to the old church but died before the work was finished. According to his wishes, they buried him temporarily in the Priory Church, at a site marked "Castlestede" on the Ordnance Map, where the

TOP:

THE LUNE AT KIRKBY LONS-DALE (left), an old border market town with the famous and much used Devil's Bridge which was built either by the monks of St. Mary's Abbey, York, or by the Prince of Evil who bargained to construct it in return for the first soul to cross over. A local woman, awaiting the return of her husband and his dog, had the presence of mind to tempt the animal to cross first by holding out a meaty bone. Whereupon the Evil One stormed off in a huff leaving behind this grand old bridge over the Lune.

MELLING IN THE LUNE VALLEY (right) — St. Wilfrid's Church, mainly Perpendicular, with a stepped chancel rising to an altar six feet above the nave.

ABOVE: HORNBY CASTLE, perched high above the River Wenning just before it joins the Lune, was built soon after Flodden by the first Lord Monteagle. The tall keep sur-vives. A house portion added in Georgian times was replaced in the middle of last century.

LEFT: WRAY. A quiet Sunday afternoon not long before the floods.

original motte and bailey once stood. Somehow, they forgot to shift him and there he still lies, the hero of Flodden, somewhere on the Priory Farm estate.

St. Margaret's, Hornby, has an octagonal tower, a "Loaves and Fishes" cross unique in England, more than 1,000 years old; exquisite stained glass and a memorial to a noted Roman Catholic. Priest-historian, Dr. John Lingard, spurned advancement, preferred his tiny flock at Hornby and laboured for forty years on his "History of England" in St. Mary's Presbytery across the road. He died in 1851, sincerely mourned by his Protestant neighbours.

Near Hornby the Yorkshire-born Wenning brings tribute from the Hindburn and Roeburn rivers. They merge at Wray (from the Old Norse "Vra", meaning "obscure nook"), a sweetly sleepy village once busy with silk weaving, making top hats, bobbin-making or fashioning swill baskets. The Quakers communed quietly in an early 18th century Meeting House, no longer in use, and life was serene for the occupants of those riverside cottages, high up, out of harm's way, until disaster struck on 8th August 1967. I was on holiday in Warwickshire at the time. My sister rushed upstairs with the news that "the river had burst its banks at Wrea Green, in Lancashire, and washed away a lot of houses!" I assured her there was no river at Wrea Green when suddenly she mentioned "Hindburn" and "Roeburn" and I thought of Wray, where I had been with a large W.E.A. party a week or two before. It emerged later that a cloud-burst had raised the Roeburn twenty feet in half as many minutes, smashing down the bridge, destroying or damaging beyond repair thirteen houses leaving as many families homeless, and littering farmers' fields with debris. In this bizarre situation, a 74-year old chap was rescued in the nick of time by the village Bobby who reached him when water was lapping round his mattress, when one wall had been ripped away and another was about to slide into the river.

Two miles below Hornby, only a Decorated east window survives from the ancient fabric of St. Chad's Church, Claughton ("Clafton") which was rebuilt in 1815 and subsequently enlarged. Its sweet-toned bell, dated A.D. 1296, is thought to be the oldest in the country. At the highway side stands a fragment of Claughton Hall (1615), a mullioned and transomed house of considerable size until a chunk was carved off, a few years ago, and rebuilt on an elevated site with superb views half a mile away.

Still on Lune's southern bank, in an area well wooded and watered by many becks, are two more valley villages, Brookhouse and Caton. St. Paul's Church, Brookhouse, serves the two communities, goes back certainly to Norman times and, though rebuilt last century, keeps its Perpendicular tower. Roman legions marched through Brookhouse and left a milestone, now in Lancaster Museum, to prove it. The village is a charmer for winklers-out of bygones, houses from William and Mary's day, a scooped-out stone on the bridge (hark for several explanations!), colourful cottage gardens and an amazing doorway near the massive 500-year old church-tower. The space between two orders of sculptured capitals has been patched up with carved stones, ancient grave slabs and fascinating fragments.

Artle Beck flows close to Caton, founded by Katti the Norseman, where fish were laid out for sale on a half-hoop of weathered stones in the Middle Ages. Cotton manufactures began in the 1780's, the beck providing the power. Soon, the river swoops sharply through woodlands, forms that breathtaking bend, "Crook of Lune", admired by monarchs and artists. A welcome bridge leads to Aughton ("Afton") across the water, famous for gigantic plum puddings dragged on a processional cart with bands blaring, a Pudding Queen in attendance, and crowds swarming in for this occasional feast which used to be held every twenty-one years.

In the time-honoured village of Halton, three miles south-west, another St. Wilfrid's church, many times reconstructed since its 7th century foundation, stands loftily with a 500-year old tower. There are scattered ancient stones and a churchyard mound indicates a Roman camp-site adopted by Anglo-Saxons. Chief attractions are the antique crosses, particularly the tall tapering shaft with a restored head, where antiquarians from all over the world have speculated on the combination of Christian and pagan symbolism and evidence of Scandinavian influences. There are two further cross-shafts within the church which has a pseudo-Tudor gable over the porch and probably lost much of antiquarian interest when it was rebuilt in the 1870's.

While travelling around the lovely Luneside churches, it will have occurred to those of us who step with awe into hallowed places that destructive forces at work in these affluent times make it necessary for church doors to be kept locked. How sad to reflect that when people were never so well educated, fed, informed, housed and entertained, far too many are only thrilled by acts of vandalism and desecrations to which their remote and supposedly "ignorant" ancestors would never have stooped! Let us hope they may come to feel the Near Presence and learn to hallow old stones steeped in the beauty of holiness.

Lancaster is near, and upstream as far as Skerton Weir the river is tidal. A fish pass placed there in 1862 made thirty-odd miles accessible to spawning salmon. The last little ancient Luneside church is St. Helen's at Overton, near the river mouth. This is a dear little village of fishermen's cottages huddled on the right-hand bank after a perilous crossing of the Ovangle marshes. A mark painted in the car park of the "Golden Ball', locally called "Snatchems" from the days when press-men pounced on unwary tipplers and hauled them aboard ships about to weigh anchor, is a daunting reminder of how high the tides can creep. There is a lovely sense of "other-worldliness" about this place which leads to another, fascinating and eerily quiet, at Sunderland Point. St. Helen's Church is tiny, less than 50 feet long, and its history goes back three centuries before the Conquest. There are still some Anglo-Saxon stones in the west end. The rest is a variety of styles reaching back to Norman and the 12th century doorway with moulded arch is one of the best you will ever see, though much weathered by rain and sea-winds. The churchyard commands arresting views across the Lune mouth.

Sunderland Point and Glasson Dock.

I was entranced the first time a friend from Heysham took me across the marshes to Overton and from there, by tide-washed macadam road winding between mudbanks and menacing gullies, to Sunderland Point, a lonely community cut off twice a day by the tides and haunted by thousands of sea-birds. It lies near the tip of a peninsula between the Lune mouth and Morecambe Bay and though you will more often than not find it deserted, it was an exciting, bustling port once, serving Lancaster which enjoyed a booming trade with the New World and the West Indies in the 18th century until silting choked the Lune mouth and Glasson Dock, which can be seen clear across the water, was built in 1787 to accommodate five-and-twenty merchantmen, and linked later with the canal system. As Glasson prospered, Sunderland Point fell into decline, and there is still, I fancy, a haunting sadness about the place where once tall-masted ships tied up, and cargoes were carried off and deposited in the warehouses along the front; and sailors were hustled into the little de-lousing centre before being let loose among unsuspecting landlubbers. They will tell you that the first cargo of cotton wool was brought ashore here; and no-one knew what it was or what it could be good for and it lay ignored for a twelvemonth until someone, a shrewd Lancastrian, you can bet your last farthing, snapped it up and got to work. The importer, Robert Lawson, a Quaker merchant, is said to have made a fortune. It enabled him to build an attractive villa, balconied, beyond the famous "Cotton Tree" (which isn't one, but it makes a good story!)

OVERTON, an old fishing community of quaint stone cottages near the Lune mouth, has this delightful little Norman church dedicated to St. Helen with a fine arched doorway, gabled belfry and squared-headed windows added c. 1770 when the chancel was widened.

Check tide tables carefully before proceeding to the Point and leave time to strike out along the only lane which dissolves into a field path and takes you to the other side of the peninsula. Here is quietude indeed, where cattle graze, and flowerets I have known all my life flourish, that like to plunge roots into the sand and be set dancing by the sea-winds. Turn to the left here for Sambo's Grave which attracts thousands every year and recalls a tragedy of 1736 when a negro slave, of whom there were many at that time, accompanied his master to Sunderland Point and, thinking he had been abandoned when the chap made a business trip to Lancaster, pined and sickened and died of heartbreak. The good Christians, now totally forgotten, who could not tolerate the idea of a "black heathen" being buried in consecrated ground, were the cause of Black Sambo being laid to rest on this lonely shore; curiously, he, the despised one, is remembered the year round, with flowers in summer, twigs or a small heap of stones, in the winter, memorials left by visitors and local children.

Sunderland Point worked magically on the young Angela Brazil's imagination. The Brazil family always spent their holidays on the fringe of Morecambe Bay and for the school girl the sea always had a special fascination. During one holiday, she was stranded for a short time on a sandbank at Sunderland. The incident, greatly embroidered, turned up in "the School by the Sea", "the Madcap of the School" and several other best-selling schoolgirl stories which kept me and my generation rooted to our seats and which are still, I am happy to notice, being reissued. On another occasion she visited Cockersand Abbey on the coast near Cockerham, overlooking the Lune waters. Cockersand Abbey, dedicated to God and St. Mary, was founded by William, the lord of Thurnham, c. 1186 after "a pious hermit named Hugh de garth" had established a hermitage and hospital for lepers in that bleak and lonely situation. By 1190 the Premonstratensian Canons arrived and the Abbot of Cockersand prevailed in power even over the earlier neighbouring abbey at Cockerham which had been operating since 1153/4. There was a good deal of jealous rivalry between the two religious establishments and litigation over boundaries, trespassing, tithes and such-like, crops up time and time again in the records. Angela Brazil remembered the fish balk which the Vicar of Cockerham had as a "perk" long after the Premonstratensian brethren had used it to supply their tables and inevitably it cropped up in "Bosom Friends", one of her earlier sprightlier works before long usage had dulled her splendid style.

The Ribble is another "come-over" from Yorkshire, rising in an eerie wilderness of moorland around Wold Fell and Ingleborough. Springs tumble into Gale Beck near Gearstones and "Little Ribble", joined by Cam Beck three miles above Horton, cascades off towards Settle, Gisburn and Sawley, entering the Old Lancashire near Chatburn and flowing south-west towards the sea. When it receives the Hodder at Great Mitton and becomes "Big Ribble", the river is still sweet and pure, as God intended; but the Calder, pouring in its poisoned waters west of Whalley, is an indictment of Man's rapacity and exploitation; and the Darwen, which joined Ribble at Walton-le-Dale, was no better until recent years, though once it "teemed" with trout when the Ribble was "solid" with salmon. In June 1768 they recorded 3,384 salmon and salmon trout taken at a single draught from the river near Penwortham; and Preston apprentices were so surfeited with salmon that a clause in their indentures protected them from having it dumped on their plates oftener than three times a week!

The authorities were busy during the 1970's improving 100 miles of the worst waters in the north-west while admitting that it would cost £1,000M. to clean up all the rivers. Pollution of the Mersey, for instance, has been halved though untreated sewage is still discharged along the Wirral coastline. Industry has much to answer for; mercantile activities at the mouths of industrial rivers cannot have helped; rising population and the growth of great resorts on both sides of the Ribble estuary have obviously aggravated a serious situation, fortunately now recognised and being tackled; so perhaps there is hope for Lancashire's rivers.

Hodder, Calder, Douglas and Yarrow.

Planners, meddlers and boundary shifters have made it hard to distinguish Lancashire from Yorkshire! Once upon a time, Hodder ("tranquil water") born in the wild grouse moors of Bowland Forest, was a boundary between the two whereas the revised map puts it in Lancashire. I can only commiserate with the good Yorkshirefolk if they are still smarting over the loss of the infant Hodder which is a healthy river for fish, all twenty-five miles of it, scenically as bonny as you could wish for, and absolutely breath-taking in that dramatic wooded gorge below Whitewell, a small place with a scattered population and a wayside inn, an old church and a little school building close together, providing instant "Salvation, Damnation and Education", as the locals told me.

Foot travellers long ago, daunted by the perilous journey along the lonely Trough road linking Clitheroe with Lancaster, would seek Dutch courage at the inn and spiritual fortification in the Forest Chapel before setting forth. Many perished, lost in mists, trapped in snowdrifts, attacked by robbers, but Quakers were not prevented from penetrating as far as Newton where a Friends' Meeting House was established in 1767. Ten years earlier John Brabbin left twenty guineas to start a school for the children of Quakers or otherwise. It was here that John Bright, the future great reformer, was sent for education and it was the making of the frail Rochdale youngster. Bracing air, country rambles and plashings in the sparkling Hodder gave him stamina enough to face life in his father's manufactory and Manchester Cotton Exchange until politics gave him his true vocation.

Hodder's chief feeder is the River Loud which rises among Fairsnape fells and drains the bonny Vale of Chipping. Chipping ("Cheapings") was a little market centre surrounded by fells north of Longridge, before Domesday. Its ancient Church of St. Bartholomew, rebuilt in 1506 and restored in the 1870's, has fragments of every period from the last 700 years. The attractive stone village has dated and mullioned 17th century properties, some with studded doors, including the Post Office (1668) and the Brabbin School building (1684). Craftsmen still make chairs here and the place stirs with life on fine weekends when you can get into the church and browse among its many bygones. You may hear the tale of the love-lorn maidservant from the Sun Inn across the road. They say she took her life after watching from an upstairs window as her faithless sweetheart stood on the churchyard steps with a brand new bride on his arm. According to custom, they buried her in the unconsecrated plot in the shadow of an ancient yew tree.

Did brave Ann Cutler stroll in the bonny Vale of Loud, I wonder? Or was she forever chained to her hand-loom at Thornley where she was born in 1759? It was grim drudgery for a miserable pittance, with actual starvation never more than a hair's breadth away. Her bare food was of the plainest order, she had received little education and faced a life without hopes or prospects . . . until that momentous revelation when good William Bramwell, a young Methodist from the hamlet of Copp, near Elswick, came to preach at Longridge and stirred Ann to the depths of her being. She joined the Methodist movement when women preachers were not exactly encouraged and by conquering a natural reticence, and by sheer power of her prayers, she became responsible for many conversions, some among the hooligans who had turned up to ridicule and disrupt the meetings. When societies floundered, they sent for "Praying Nanny" and she filled their meeting places. Her piety, her austere way of life, her hourly resort to prayer, were impressive, and everywhere she stirred cold hearts and saved sinners. She died far from Thornley, at the age of 35, after conducting a religious revival at Macclesfield where they buried her, at Christ Church.

Where Loud and Hodder meet at Doeford Bridge, the old Roman road from Ribchester to Overborough in the Lune Valley once crossed the river. In preparation for its union with the Ribble, the Hodder then sweeps round the back of Stonyhurst and heads for Mitton where history and geography combine to bless the wanderer with abundant joys. There are two Hodder bridges, not far apart. They say Cromwell crossed the lower bridge in mid-August 1648 when hastening to trounce the Royalists at the Battle of Preston. He had spent an uneasy night sleeping upon a table under the roof of a hostile host, "Mr. Sherburne . . . of Stanihurst Hall", a known malignant and papist. Old Noll, suspicious of strange beds and bedchambers, tossed all night with swords and pistols at the ready and left next morning declaring Stonyhurst to be "the finest half-house" he had come across. After his victory, he called and demanded further hospitality on the return journey into Yorkshire.

The de Bayleys had the estate from the 13th century. One was so honoured by marriage with the Shireburne heiress in 1377 that he adopted his bride's family name; the Shireburnes thus became paramount in the area for 400 years. Sir Richard Shireburne began rebuilding on a magnificent scale in 1592

View over the river (opposite, top) to the ancient hall of Great Mitton, where Cockersand Abbey priests lodged when they officiated at All Hallows' Church. Nave and chancel are both 13th century. Tower is early 14th century.

MITTON CHURCH (bottom), the alabaster tomb of "Sr. Ricrd. Sherburne Knight mast Forster of ye forrest of Bowland . . . And Dame Maude his wif daught' of Sr. Ricrd Bold Knight . . ." who died in 1594 and 1588 respectively.

when Father Robert Persons, S.J., was founding an English College at St. Omers, to provide education for privileged Catholics, including the Shireburnes. One of them built the little village school "upon Hurst Green" in 1686; his son, Sir Nicholas, who added those twin cupolas to the Stonyhurst frontage, built the Shireburne Almshouse in 1707, a handsome building, but he placed it on Kemple End, which might as well have been The World's End for the aged locals! No wonder it fell into disuse a long lifetime ago! Then in 1946 they stripped it down, carried the pieces to a site at Hurst Green near the College gates and faithfully rebuilt it. Sir Nicholas was the last of the male Shireburnes. His young son died in 1702 after eating poisonous berries, it was rumoured, and the estate passed in 1717 to his widowed and childless daughter Mary, Duchess of Norfolk, who bequeathed Stonyhurst to a nephew, one of the Welds of Lulworth Castle, Dorset. Weld sons had always been educated at St. Omers or Bruges or Liege, to which the College had been driven by various troubles. The French Revolution of 1794 caused them to flee back over the Channel, with no home in prospect until Thomas Weld offered them Stonyhurst. The hall had been deserted for fifty years, near derelict and open to the wild birds and the weather. At the end of August, after forty-six days on the move, an advance party of masters and twelve pupils first set eyes on their new quarters and George Lambert Clifford raced ahead to be the first to enter. Among the pupils enrolled that October were two young Derbyshire Eyres, distant kinsmen; another, Father William Eyre, was Rector here (1879-1885). He left his mark. The new south front was erected by his patrimony and during his Rectorate the great bronze statue, brought from Rome, was placed overlooking the Avenue in 1882.

Stonyhurst is recognised to-day as one of the finest Roman Catholic educational establishments in the world, turning out leaders, scholars and heroes. Rare and exquisite treasures repose in its museum and libraries, including Caxton's early works, a 7th century copy of St. John's Gospel retrieved from St. Cuthbert's coffin, the prayer book that was in the hand of Mary Queen of Scots when the axe fell, Sir Thomas More's embroidered cap, paintings by Reubens and Michaelangelo, and the natural history collection of a former pupil, the eccentric Squire Charles Waterton. By application to the Rector, permission to visit may be granted at certain times of the year.

In the whole of Ribble Valley there is not a church more fascinating than that ancient edifice of Edward III's time at Great Mitton. In the Shireburne chapel beneath a wealth of wonderfully carved alabaster effigies and mural tablets lie the family from Stonyhurst including the doomed youngster who ate the berries and his father, Sir Nicholas, who must have been an imaginative and warm-hearted fellow. Besides "many good charitable things", when times were bad, he allocated several rooms in his mansion to the use of neighbours who came daily for tuition in the art of spinning and each, when proficient, received a wheel and a pound of wool "which did a vast amount of good". Great and Little Mitton were once divided by the county boundary. Now they are in Lancashire, which seems logical enough, and each has a fine old hall, Great Mitton's in Tudor or early Stuart style, Little Mitton hall going back to c. 1500. This area calls for macs, brollies and wellies – anglers please enquire at the village post office about permits to fish – because the local saying is all too true:

" Hodder, Calder, Ribble . . . and rain.
All meet together in Mitton desmesne! "

The Ribble Valley authority has charge of the largest area, with the smallest population, in Lancashire. At Clitheroe, midway between Longridge Fell and Pendle, town and country come together; markets once cluttered up the steeply rising, winding main street, designed long before the internal combustion engine, and overshadowed by the romantic ruins of the oldest stone structure in the county. Clitheroe Castle, with walls nine feet thick, is said to have the smallest keep in England. It stands upon a lofty limestone knoll, a superb defensive position chosen by Roger of Poitou soon after the Conquest to keep the peace within the great territories given to him by William. The timber huts of Anglo-Saxon settlers had been there long before the Norman castle which, after Roger's banishment, became a temporary, and not particularly comfortable, home of the de Lacys until the last of them died in 1311. The Honour of Clitheroe is now held by the Assheton family of Downham whose representative, upon receiving a Barony in 1955, took the title of Lord Clitheroe of Downham. In 1644 the castle was siezed by Royalists whose night-time forays after food scarcely endeared them to the countryfolk thereabouts; but after the Roundheads' victory at Preston in 1648 Cromwell instructed his troops to reduce the castle and put it out of business. The damage was pretty thorough but the castle, which has an interesting Museum and public gardens laid out in 1920 as a

War Memorial, is well worth visiting.

On a lesser knoll stands the ancient church of St. Mary Magdalene which originally belonged to Pontefract Priory, then to Stanlaw Abbey and thence to Whalley. The church goes back more than 800 years but was entirely rebuilt in the 1820's. Boys were taught within the medieval church until Queen Mary Tudor founded a free grammar school in 1554, housed in a post and plaster building erected in the churchyard. It lasted for 200 years and was then replaced in stone; and in 1829 that little schoolhouse was dismantled, carted or trundled in wheelbarrows to the present site and rebuilt, the more modern buildings being constructed as the First World War broke out.

We think of two young Lancashire men connected with the voyages of Captain Cook, a North Yorkshireman born in 1728. The Transit of Venus, first discovered by Jeremiah Horrocks at Bretherton in November 1639, prompted the Royal Society to finance an expedition to Tahiti where another Transit could be studied in June 1769. As a bonus in January 1770 Captain James Cook, in the name of England, took possession of New Zealand, first noticed in 1642 by Tasman, the Dutch navigator who did not step ashore after attacks by cannibalistic natives. Cook next sailed to south-east Australia, discovered kangaroos and Botany Bay and planted the English flag. During the second voyage some of his men were eaten by New Zealanders; the rest returned by 1775 in good health and free from scurvy due to an improved diet.

The third and fateful expedition set out in "Discovery", under Captain Clerke, and "Resolution" in July 1776. Cook was adored by the Hawaiian natives who were continually pilfering and when a cutter from "Discovery" went missing, Cook tried to take King Terreeoboo hostage against its safe return. Emotions ran high, the Captain fired his musket, the islanders attacked in earnest. Several seamen were killed or injured, Cook was stabbed in the back and dragged off by the natives. His partial remains were eventually recovered and given a sailor's burial, whereupon Captain Clerke took command of the "Resolution" and Lieutenant Gore of the "Discovery", and the expedition sailed away from the Sandwich Islands. Tragedy still stalked. Captain Charles Clerke, aged only 37, a brave cheerful fellow dogged by tuberculosis, went into a decline which ended his life in August 1779 and Lieutenant James King, son of the Clitheroe parson and old boy of the Grammar School, took command of the "Discovery" and brought the expedition safely home in October 1780. King, by this time, had worked systematically on Captain Cook's journals; and we have him to thank for the splendid records of great exploits at sea which were published subsequently at the expense of the British Government. He was very different in temperament from his austere leader and idol, being of a mild and equable disposition upon whom responsibilities weighed heavy, causing his hair to turn grey almost overnight in his late twenties. He died in 1784, aged thirty-one, at Nice where he was buried, and a memorial in Clitheroe church recalls this sad event. A wall plaque commemorates Clitheroe schoolmaster, John Webster, who died in 1682, being a dabbler in mystical matters, astrologer and investigator of witchcraft.

In complete contrast, by the way, Clitheroe was a spa three hundred years ago. It was also the gateway to some attractive places to visit – Waddington, an enchanting "Best Kept" village with a stream babbling through beneath St. Helen's Church, and glorious old cottages, pubs and almshouses; the fragmentary ruins of Sawley Abbey, tended by the Ministry of Works, in the valley below Pendle – brought into Lancashire by the boundary re-shuffle of 1974. And Downham! . . . a delightful place without telegraph wires or pylons, with a compact cluster of Elizabethan stone cottages running down to a brook with a little bridge and Old Pendle brooding in the background; and a church of St. Leonard, centuries old and once subject to Whalley Abbey, but rebuilt before the First World War though its tower has been there for 500 years, and contains three ancient bells. The Asshetons were the Lords of Downham from 1558 when they bought the Manor, and Whalley Abbey. They have kept a fatherly eye on the place, have preserved it from uglification. Their home, Downham Hall, rebuilt in the 1830's and discreetly hidden behind the park walls, is a repository for old books and family records, Nicholas Assheton the diarist being among the company surrounding James I at Hoghton Tower in 1617. Harrison Ainsworth consulted his writings whilst working on his novel, "The Lancashire Witches" which, though a best-seller in its day, must be regarded as fiction! The stark facts are, to my mind, far more enthralling and are told in detail in my "Witchcraft in Lancashire".

At Bashall, north-west of Clitheroe, the Talbots, favoured by the de Lacys, settled c.1250, adding to

WHALLEY ABBEY, the Warden's House.

WHALLEY ABBEY after the Dissolution was acquired by the Assheton family who allowed much of it to become a ruin though they adapted and greatly rebuilt the abbot's house which survives in this attractive Conference House and retreat centre. Asshetons and their descendants occupied the property well into the last century. Whalley Abbey is governed by a committee under the chairmanship of the Bishop of Blackburn.

their holdings by force of arms or subtle means. Perhaps it was a king's curse that wiped them out in nine generations after an unforgivable act of treachery against a half-witted monarch, Henry VI, who took refuge in the Ribble Valley after his defeat at Hexham in Northumberland by Yorkist supporters of Edward IV, the man who had branded Henry V's pathetic pup as an imbecile, snatched the throne, and had himself proclaimed king in London. Poor Henry, weak in mind and body, sheltered with friends until he was betrayed by the Talbots of Bashall, captured near the site of Brungerley bridge and handed over to the enemy. After that, years in the Tower, his wife, Queen Margaret, imprisoned, his only son probably murdered, another attempt to place him on the throne, and merciful death, at last, probably by foul means. Perhaps in retribution, the Talbots ran out of male heirs over three hundred years ago.

Whalley Abbey Gateway.

Downstream towards Whalley and the Calder.

If I could be prised from the sea, I sometimes fancy I could settle in Whalley which is somewhere between a large village and small township, with a heritage that would not disgrace a proud city. Former Vicar, Dr. Thomas D. Whitaker, completed a prodigious history of the place, illustrated by the young Turner, in 1801.

Whalley, nestling beneath a well wooded Nab, has another bonus, the River Calder belting through beside which, in the 1290's, Cistercians settled, migrants from Stanlaw on the Mersey after calamities by storm, flood and fire. From upstream came drinking water, downstream they tippled the waste. Fishing was always a desideratum. Normally they would have avoided the temptations of a neighbouring township, preferring a secluded site with wastelands crying out for improvement. Nor, by the rule of their Order, should they have settled within seven miles of the Cistercian house at Sawley. It was to cause rivalry between the two abbeys for years on end!

St. Mary's Church, Whalley, had been in existence for centuries when Henry de Lacy, Earl of Lincoln, gave the Stanlaw monks the Rectory of Whalley, presided over by Deans whose authority covered half the county, in 1283. Papal consent was a long time a-coming, the monks kicked sulky heels in frustration, and Peter de Cestria, Rector for fifty years, dug in and presented an obdurate front. He was a pluralist, an administrator, a remarkable fellow and, moreover, a de Lacy from the wrong side of the blanket. Linked to the church by right of way was his manor house with private chapel, built c. 1250, of which ruins survive adjoining the Warden's house.

Peter clung to life until January 1295 and, without waiting for Papal sanction, Abbot Gregory and twenty three Stanlaw monks, leaving a handful behind, rolled up at Whalley and moved into the Manor House. Quarrels broke out immediately with Sawley whose food supplies would be threatened. Rows also developed over the Rectory of Whalley which Pontefract Priory claimed as theirs since 1122. In addition, the neighbourhood offered little shelter or timber for kindling or building. The brethren would gladly have moved but the Pope withheld permission and they were forced to dig in. A plot was consecrated in 1306 but a dozen years passed before monastic masons made determined raids on Billington stone quarry and began building the Abbey, starting with the gateway not far from the railway arches, with a chapel above and a guesthouse adjoining. The Abbey Church (1330-80) preceded domestic quarters, cloisters, chapter house, library, parlour, monks' day room, Abbot's house, dormitory and infirmary block, all complete c. 1425.

Meantime, the Black Death had decimated the population. Serfs of earlier years had disappeared. Lay brethren no longer volunteered to work for bare board and lodging and outside labour had to be paid for. The magnificent and original north-east gateway (c. 1480) is a reminder of the many distinguished personages and their retinues who came to enjoy lavish hospitality at Whalley.

About this time, 1487, young John Paslew of Wiswell Hall (now a farmhouse) entered the Abbey as a novice and between studies at Oxford for a Divinity Degree, spent his vacations with the brethren. He was a warm, clever, ambitious chap, zealous for the dignity of Whalley. They elected him Abbot in 1507, the local boy who made good, and halcyon years passed before the Dissolution. Paslew progressed around the countryside like a Nabob, returning visits and earning the respect of rival Abbots. Were his stars afflicted, one wonders, when the northern rising known as the Pilgrimage of Grace fell apart within five days in October 1536? Paslew's marginal involvement with the ill-fated scheme had direct consequences for Whalley. He was offered a free pardon but could not bring himself to swear loyalty to Henry VIII and for that he was tried at Lancaster for treason in March 1537 and executed on the day following. The Earl of Sussex immediately seized the Abbey, ejected the monks, grabbed the valuables and sold land and buildings to the Bradylls and the Asshetons for just over £2,000.

The Abbey Church, so long in building, was dismantled, stone by stone, and used in erecting the present Conference House, originally the mansion of the Asshetons. Further fragments were loaded on to carts and bounced all the way to Old Langho where the quaint little St. Leonard's Church was built in 1557. Some days after locating it for the first time down a lane winding down from the main highway, and talking to a cheery-faced farmer's wife who told me that the old place had been cleaned up and was being used regularly for monthly services, my guide sent me newspaper cuttings recording the first wedding ceremony to be conducted there in eighty-odd years! The daughter of the landlord of the Black Bull nearby had applied to the Archbishop of Canterbury for special permission. The old stones had been accustomed to solemn funeral rites but on that September afternoon in 1981 they echoed to the happier sounds of nuptials.

Apart from the Lay Brothers' Quarters which the Catholics acquired, first Manchester Diocese in 1923, then Blackburn Diocese in 1929 purchased the property, uncovered the foundations of the Abbey Church (site of the altar marked by a plain stone table), the octagonal Chapter House, an unusual feature for the Cistercians, and the Abbot's original residence. Among fascinating bygones unearthed were grave slabs, skeletons, old coins and floor tiles. A Service of Re-dedication was held, in the rain and before a great congregation, in June 1936. The old Abbey Fields have been developed into a pleasant estate of modern bungalows and houses where the older generation boast of going to church, doing their shopping and changing their library books, "all on the flat!"

The Church of St. Mary and All Saints plunges back to the Anglo-Saxons. Whalley (meadow with wells) was not particularly important to the Romans but coins of that era have turned up in the churchyard. Domesday records the existence of a church before the Conquest but the 14th century Statutes of Blackburnshire claim that St. Augustine founded it in the early 7th century. Incumbents at the original wooden "white church under the hill", were styled "Deans", ruling over a widely scattered flock. The Normans replaced wood with stone c. 1080, and some major disaster caused a re-build c. 1200. The

Old Langho Church.

THE FAMOUS WHALLEY VIADUCT spans the Calder valley to the west of the Abbey ruins. It carries the Blackburn and Clitheroe railway, opened in 1850.

church's oldest relics, three Celtic crosses, are much older, some say as early as St. Augustine's mission (597) though others plump for the 10th century. The tallest is the oldest. Commonwealth vandals flung all three into a ditch from which they were rescued and returned to their bases by an 18th century Vicar. The churchyard is a rare place for sunny afternoon browsing, or for sitting and watching the world ambling by.

The church is glorious, a veritable repository of history and human interest. The massive buttressed tower is 15th century, similar in age to the canopied choir stalls with intriguing misericords, carved c. 1430 and brought over from the Abbey church. There is Abbot Paslew's gravestone, carved with cross and chalice, but it is debatable if he is buried here, and though it makes a good story, he was never brought to Whalley for his hanging! Look for the Nowell family's "Kage" pew, elaborately carved and quite startling, with dates from 1534 and 1610 to 1830, reminders of ownership disputes which flared up down the generations. There are treasures galore here – chained books, ancient pews, a 14th century screen and Peter de Cestria's tombstone. Retreating Jacobite rebels heard this organ in 1745 in Lancaster's Priory Church for which it was created in 1727; and perhaps the most famous curio is the Catterall brass of 1515 showing "Raffe Catterall esquyer and Elizabeth hys wyfe" and "all ther Chylder", full twenty of them, and all piously at prayer. There is a recument effigy of the Vicar-Historian and the east window is a glowing tableau of Lancashire heraldry.

Bronze Age artefacts excavated at Portfield in 1966 prove human occupation in this area 800 B.C. But the great viaduct of 49 arches carrying the railway from Blackburn to Chatburn and opened in 1850 with a celebration run, a coachload of musicians and a Grand Dinner and Ball and a treat for the work-force, was a superb Victorian achievement for which 7,000,000 bricks were produced in the locality.

Yes, I fancy Whalley would keep me entranced for the rest of a lifetime. Besides which, it is familiar. I have known it from those weekly trans-Pennine trips to the coast when I was a saucery-eyed youngster with a headful of curls and irritating bouts of travel sickness, before windscreeen wipers, traffic lights, Highway Codes or cats' eyes had been invented; when our strong-minded Yorkshire mother insisted on keeping homes in both counties. Almost invariably, when she spotted a row of pea-green young faces, she would announce with a sigh: "It's no good! You'll have to pull up, Dad!" An irritable haul on the hand-brake and we would clamber stiffly out and stumble about in the fresh air until we had either parted, or come to terms, with whatever happened to be troubling us at the time. We braced ourselves for the remainder of the journey, but spirits always lifted at Whalley's T-junction for within thirty miles lay "our other", and my real

HACKING HALL by the Ribble banks not far from the time-honoured ferry crossing which survived until modern times. Perfect of its kind, this house of many gables presented on a doubly-recessed frontage, was built by the famous Judge, Sir Thomas Walmesley, in 1607. A handsome oak staircase and 17th century panelling were later removed to Dunkenhalgh, once the home of the Walmesleys.

home and earthly paradise by the sea. To the left, near the oddly angled bridge over the Calder, Harrison Ainsworth stayed in one of the stone houses while preparing his "Lancashire Witches". Then off to the right, past the balconied Terrace Row, our silver-coloured Cubitt tourer with running boards and a pull-over hood labouring up Billington Brow past the "Judge Walmesley", half a century before the bypass.

This jolly fellow was an honest Judge of the Northern Circuit and a trusty servant of Elizabeth I. He was a Catholic turned Nonconformist who married the heiress of Hacking (Haakon's ing, or settlement) in the flat peaceful pastures where Calder joins Ribble west of Whalley. His family were the Walmesleys of Dunkenhalgh, near Clayton-le-Moors, whose 16th century seat was rebuilt c. 1800 in stone, a low handsome battlemented building, now a hotel and popular venue for functions, which incorporates portions of the old place. The Walmesleys suffered for their stubborn Popery, particularly during the Civil War when Dunkenhalgh was ransacked by Roundheads. Protestant Thomas Walmesley escaped such tribulations, marrying into a Puritan family, prospering, acquiring lands in the Ribble Valley and amassing wealth. His best memorial is Hacking Hall which he rebuilt in 1607, near a former ferry crossing. It is a splendid example of its period, three-storeyed, with five gables presented on its doubly recessed frontage, and a special charm washed into the stonework by the weathering of many years.

Gawthorpe Hall.

Calder risings and valley towns.

The Ribble Calder, perhaps eighteen miles of it, rises sweet and sparkling in the heights near Holme in Cliviger but industry in its valley townships have caused heavy pollution. After collecting Colne, Wycoller and Pendle Waters near Nelson, Calder "goeth by Burneley", is joined by the Brun and flows towards Padiham ("abode of the sons of Padd", according to the worthy Dr. Whitaker), an old village developing into a cotton town in Napoleonic times.

Padiham came under Whalley Abbey whose last Abbot (Paslew) donated a replacement font sculpted with his arms in 1525. There was a chantry priest here in monastic times but a mutilated cross indicates Christian worship long before the Conquest. With funds raised by a brief of 1763, the body of the old St. Leonard's Church was rebuilt "entirely out of character", says Baines, in 1776. Within fifty years the population had leapt and a new church rose in "modern 15th century Gothic" in the 1860's. There are memorials of the Starkies of Huntroyde, and the Shuttleworths of Gawthorpe who arrived at "Goukr", named by Norsemen, c. 1300. In Ughtred's time (c. 1390) a four-storey pele tower with walls 8ft. thick was protection against enemies or plundering Scots, and a parcel of good farmland provided food. Ughtred steered clear of trouble, married wisely, absorbed ancient deer grazings and common field. Fortunes were consolidated and in 1599 Sir Richard Shuttleworth, Chief Justice of Chester, sent his bachelor brother, the Rev. Laurence Shuttleworth, to build him a fine house around the pele tower which could house the staircase. In seven years the job was done, largely in local materials, and the sons of Gawthorpe, ardent anti-Papists, began a long and distinguished tradition of public service, producing M.P's, Sheriffs and heroes in both World Wars.

Though some members actually died for the Stuarts, Shuttleworths largely sided with Parliament during the Civil War and their Hall became an unofficial Roundhead headquarters. Good marriages increased their holdings and they shuttled between their estates, London and an elegant townhouse in Winckley Square, Preston. Heiress Janet Shuttleworth, born in 1817, married the future baronet, Dr. James Phillips Kay (1804-1877), a Manchester doctor and first Secretary of the Board of Education. This brilliant and compassionate fellow, who assumed the name and arms of his wife's family, toiled lifelong for the betterment of the poor, but he becomes very real to me when he acts the host to Charlotte Brontë, and takes her on "quiet drives to old ruins and old halls, situated among the older hills and woods". In great trepidation, the trembling genius visited Gawthorpe, finding it "much to my taste; near three centuries old, grey, stately, and picturesque"; and later in the year, 1850, and "chiefly to please Papa", she visited the Shuttleworths' Lakeland home, Briery Close, at Low-wood not far from Bowness. There she met her future friend and biographer, the talented Mrs. Gaskell, to whom Brontë devotees will ever be indebted. Soon after Charlotte's tragically brief marriage, Sir James offered Curate Nicholls a much more lucrative living at Habergham. It had to be declined on account of old Mr. Brontë's increasing frailty but the graceful gesture must have pleased Charlotte who, so soon, was to leave this world for ever.

Writing this, reflecting on past visits when I was shown "Miss Brontë's little sofa", revives fragrant memories of the last gracious chatelaine of Gawthorpe, the Hon. Rachel Kay-Shuttleworth who, after a lifetime of good works and public service, set about with unquenchable cheerfulness to raise £100,000 with which to endow Gawthorpe when her nephew offered it to the nation. It now belongs to the National Trust, is administered by Lancashire County Council, and operates as a Crafts Centre where ancient fabrics and finest examples of embroidery can be studied from the Honourable Rachel's collection, she being a superb needlewoman and of great artistic talent.

Altham comes next, pylons, cables and a mess of industrial activity having approached as near as they dare. The village on Calder banks south west of Padiham was "Alvetham" when Hugh, son of Leofwine the Saxon, had it by grant from the de Lacy's of Clitheroe, along with Clayton and "Akerington". Years before Whalley Abbey was thought of, Hugh founded St. James' Church here, intending it for a Parish Church. He met with formidable opposition from Peter de Cestria, Rector of Whalley, who appealed to Rome, claimed Altham to be a dependent chapelry, and so it remained until the 19th century.

The church stands apart, challenging good Christians to make the journey, and its "front garden" is a forest of tasteless Victorian and later monuments which almost mask a view of this venerable structure. I recorded a broadcast from here some years ago, loved the place, felt its extreme age and could have spent days poking around. In the porch, carved from a huge block of stone and made into a seat now, is a font which must be one of the oldest in Lancashire. Many an early Lord of Altham must have been baptised here. They lived at Altham Hall for centuries, a moderately grand moated manor house which gradually relapsed into farm use. They coped with Scottish raiders who were here in 1316 and 1322 and were a great nuisance after Bannockburn; they were sucked into local squabbles, including the Banastre Rebellion against the Earl of Lancaster in 1315; and when males petered out, their heiress Johanna took Altham to her marriage with Richard Banastre of Walton-le-Dale in 1386.

The church was rebuilt in that century, the Perpendicular nave some two hundred years later, the chancel and tower added in 1859. There is a fine Decorated east window in the north aisle and in the chancel an ancient piscina and two "witches' stones", actually 13th century grave slabs, found in the churchyard. One has a cross on one side and a circle on the other, a double protection against evil spirits! There are the "chevron between 3 mullets pierced" (stars or spur-wheels with holes in the middle) of the Althams, memorials of the Banastres whose males also faded out in 1694, and brasses of the Cunliffes with their "punny" coat of arms, three rabbits (coneys) impaled with those of Chetham.

Jennet Cunliffe was excommunicated in 1655 "for keeping company with a Papist" – whom she later married – and the chap who threw her out was the famous ejected Minister, the Rev. Thomas Jollie. He came fresh from Trinity College, Cambridge, to Altham at the age of 21, a stern Puritan and sturdy champion of Independency which demanded unqualified support of set forms of service. In fact, one of the Banastres ejected him from his benefice but that didn't stop him preaching in contravention of the Five Mile Act (1665) and, several times, landing up in gaol in Lancaster or York.

Poor Thomas Jollie, a lovable bigot and a lusty fellow – he put four wives down – was savagely persecuted until the Toleration Act of 1689 and by then he had bought Wymondhouses, near Pendleton, where he built a small chapel in 1688. He denounced Popery, tobacco-smoking, "lewd carriage, ill behaviour, pride, self-conceit and ill temper" and in 1654 he "cast forth Prudence Riley out of the church" and delivered her up "to Satan . . . until she repent", though mercifully she was re-admitted five years later. In 1689 he achieved unwelcome notoriety by figuring in a case of supposed Daemonianism when Richard Dugdale, a young groundsman-servant of Surey, near Whalley, behaved in a strange manner, capering, leaping, pulling faces, spitting up stones, rolling his eyes and generally drawing attention to himself. Suspecting Satanic possession through witchcraft, Jollie and his colleagues fought the Evil One by weekly prayers and fastings which, eight months later, had accomplished nothing! By that time, Dugdale had emerged as an incorrigible exhibitionist since childhood and an old school-fellow had dismissed his antics as "Nothing Else but a Cheat!" The Divines withdrew from the business leaving Jollie sticking to his guns but probably feeling rather foolish.

Near Great Harwood (locally, "Gret Arrod", "Arrod" or "Snuffy Arrod") where snuff taking was a popular habit with the old weavers, the Hyndburn Brook joins the Calder, the two bordering the Manor which the de Lacy's granted to Richard de Fitton, along with Martholme, in return for Knight's Service, in 1177. Once, there were approximately 60,000 Knights' Fees in the kingdom, each worth £20 p.a., and in time of war, title-holders had to support the king, in person, and take tentants and vassals along equipped for military action. William de Fitton died in 1289 without male heir and Great Harwood was divided between three daughters who married into the Leghs of Hapton, the Nowells of Read and the Heskeths of

Rufford. The Leghs sold their portion to the Heskeths which set them above the Nowells and created bad blood between them until 1390 when John Nowell', in church, solemnly swore fealty to Thomas Hesketh and that settled the matter for ever. The two ownerships continued until the Nowells sold out in 1773 and the Lomax family bought the Hesketh holdings in 1819 for £75,000. Lomax descendants sold portions a lifetime later and the remainder was auctioned in 1925, ending a Lordship which had survived for nearly 900 years.

Martholme, once moated and protected on two sides by a loop in the Calder, is still there. Upon marriage into the Fitton family, Sir Thomas Hesketh left Rufford and settled here, partly rebuilding the manor house (now a farm) and adding a gatehouse, 1561, which can be viewed on several days a week or by appointment.

. St. Bartholomew's Church, Great Harwood, began as St. Laurence's Chapel attached to the Mother Church at Blackburn, as early as 1335. Whalley monks often cast acquisitive eyes on the estate but never owned it though there were perpetual law-suits and squabbles between them and the Heskeths. The battlemented buttressed tower is solid 15th century Perpendicular and the 16th century body of the church remained unchanged until the 1880's when the nave was extended and the chancel was rebuilt. A good deal of secular business was conducted in the south porch which has a stone bench on either side, in the old days. Beside a grand old four-plank Tudor style oak door is a pre-Reformation holy water stoup where hard-working fingers would be dipped, Romanist fashion, on entering the building before Henry VIII caused the great upheaval.

There is a piscina in St. Bartholomew's Chantry (1521) founded by the Heskeths in this lovely old country church. For that is just what it was, the House of God at the heart of a hillside community with marshes all around, ministering down the generations to textile workers long before the Industrial Revolution. It was hard to keep the church going after the Civil Wars and the devotion of a small population was sorely tried by a chill and cheerless church and the musty odour of graves rising from a damp and greasy beaten earth floor. Only the better off could afford the 12 pence to be buried inside and, inside or out, few could pay for headstones.

Lifelong handloom weavers were in distress when the new machine age dawned and the population doubled to about 4,000. The railway, arriving in 1877, brought in even more . . . hence the church extensions! Until 1952 they maintained a kindly old custom and distributed a Dole of Bread to needy parishioners attending church, fourteen 2d. wheaten loaves every Sunday. What a pity to let it lapse! This was another in the "Country Churches" series in the days of Radio Blackburn and I have never forgotten this splendid old church with so many features of interest, from an ancient oak poppy head bench and a carved octagonal font of 1662, to the parish chest, 8'6" long, knocked up by some local craftsman while the village blacksmith supplied three hinged iron straps fitted with padlocks. There were box pews here, too, before the "improvements"! But modern heating was infinitely preferable to strewn straw which, as late as 1820, was supposed to keep worshippers' feet warm!

Buried here is John Mercer of Dean, Fellow of the Royal Society, (1791-1866) who introduced a new word into the language, "mercerising" by which cotton fabrics acquired a silk-like sheen. He was a weaver at ten, a warper later, worked 12 hours a day, studied at nights and spent his "leisure" experimenting with dyes. An early industrial chemist, in fact, though blessed with multifarious talents, music being one – he founded a choir and is thought to have invented parchment paper. A French firm offered him £40,000, a fortune in those days, for his "mercerising" patent, but he declined it, being patriotic. This township commemorated his genius in June 1903 by unveiling the handsome Mercer Memorial Clock Tower which stands in the town square. His daughters left money for the Mercer Hall, built in 1921.

"Big Ribble" – Ribchester to the sea

"BIG RIBBLE" heading towards Ribchester has a sprinkling of ancient halls along its banks, Dinckley perhaps oldest and bonniest, with cruck timbers and two massive stone chimneys. Here lived the Talbots whose male line was petering out before the 1715 Rebellion. Otherwise they may have paid dearly, like many a neighbour, the valley being rife with recusants who, after punitive fines and persecutions, paid lip service only to the '45. Glorious walks lead to the bluebell woods of Sale Wheel.

From Bailey Hall, a farmhouse now with a dry moat, came that de Bayley who married a Shireburne daughter. Dutton Old Hall, handsome and full of character, is late 17th century with mullions, a courtyard and lovely views. Towneleys had it. Jacobites plotted here. Gallows Lane, Gallows Brow, the names tell all, not places to be dawdling on moonless nights when winds whine and naked trees set up weird creakings and groanings.

Ribchester village has a grand old pub, a fine Early English church, attractive dated cottages and total identification with "Bremetennacum" of the Romans. They were here soon after AD.78. established a large cavalry station, accommodated many en route to and from Hadrian's Wall. The village was so backward last century that strangers were pursued by ignorant country lads in clogs and precocious females who tormented the horses with mops and brushes, uncouth behaviour due more to "pressing poverty and continued neglect" than to outright malice.

For centuries, scholars and historians had wandered here in the footsteps of the Romans. John Leland considered the place "a poore thing" adding that "It hath beene an Ancient Towne, Great Squarid Stones, Voultes & antique coynes be founde ther; and ther is a place wher that the People did fable that the Jues had a Temple" (for "Jues" substitute "heathens"). Camden came twice, noting "many signs of Roman antiquity" and Defoe included Ribchester in his "Tour". When Dr. Wm. Stukeley came in 1724 the shifting Ribble had destroyed one third of the station site. Leisured gentlemen had made off with carved stones to adorn their Lancashire mansions.

The greatest excitement occurred in 1796 when Joseph Walton's lad unearthed a miscellaneous collection of metal objects packed in sand, deliberately hidden. Servicemen approaching retirement often stashed away bits of metalware, intending later to trade it in for cash. But sudden death occasionally intervened and hoards lay undiscovered until modern times, puzzling archaeologists until they fathomed it out. Among this cache was an incredibly beautiful ceremonial parade helmet with face mask, the finest specimen from Roman Britain. Hot-foot came Charles Towneley whose collection adorns the British Museum; and Ribchester, when it acquired a museum in 1914 (National Trust property now) only had a replica. The great Dr. Whitaker was searching and conserving in 1813 and excavations have continued, particularly during church restorations of 1924-5 and through the Ribble Archaeological Society, founded 1967.

A clear picture has emerged of an important rectangular station crammed with buildings (wooden originally, replaced later in stone), covering the best part of 6 acres. It was 12 miles upstream from the sea. It protected important crossroads to Carlisle, Clitheroe and York, Manchester, Preston and Fylde. Gravelled roads linked four gateways. There were turrets on rampart corners, a wharf on the river-front. Besides the central Principia, Commandant's house, sick bay and two granaries each 103ft. long, there were orderly rows of barracks and stables. The whole densely populated place would be as bustling as any modern Army base and outside the fort walls was another hive of activity, a civilian settlement with huts and tradesmen's workshops. The Brigantes may not have welcomed their conquerors in the first place but would soon recognise the benefits of trading and intermarriage.

Asturians from northern Spain, here for about 50 years, were replaced by Sarmations from the lower

Ribchester Parish Church.

ALMSHOUSES AT STYDD near Ribchester.

Danube area. They were brilliant horse-breeders and as veterans with Romano-British offspring many settled in the Lune and Ribble Valleys, supplying mounts to the cavalry, all beautifully matched for size and colour. What a glorious spectacle they must have presented. Small wonder that local maidens voted wholeheartedly for fraternisation!

Behind the village inn, which is older than the date suggests, the Romans built a stone bath-house with a tiled floor and a hypocaust beneath warm and hot rooms. Pillars in the porch of the White Bull and a couple under the singing gallery in the church come from that bath-house. Church and churchyard, Rectory and grounds, and Churchgates cover what survived from the fort site. Sacellum and strong room were located beneath the sun-dial in 1925 and mementoes have been rescued from the river or unearthed during grave-diggings.

St. Wilfrid's Church is a gem, half of its stones and much of the village of Roman origins. There may have been a Celtic mission here 200 years after the Romans departed for St. Kentigern, the Culdee, laboured in the north-west and St. Wilfrid, Archbishop of York, the church-builder, had lands "juxta Ripple". The Early English style is clearly visible in this lovely House of God; the tower is late 15th century Perpendicular and there are many treasures – a medieval wall painting of St. Christopher and the Holy Child, triple sedilia, hagioscope, Jacobean pulpit and dormer windows, 1680-1712.

Half a mile away, Stydd has the quaintest almshouses you are likely to see – five arranged on two floors, built by Shireburnes in the 1720's for "5 poor persons to live separately therein". Weathered stone steps lead to a triple-arched arcade with a parapet supported on two pillars, (almost certainly Roman; the stones, too, if the truth be known!) Across the fields the tiny 12th century Chapel of St. Saviour is all that survived from the considerable estate of the Knights of St. John of Jerusalem, a Crusading Order. They were here for 200 years and their chapel, unashamedly Norman, with stone floor, chevron mouldings and round headed windows, has an ancient door, an octagonal font, an old carved pulpit and a floor slab with two floreated crosses. Here lie Sir Adam de Cliderhowe and his lady, Alicia, whose home, Salesbury Hall, occupied a Ribble Valley beauty spot. The chapel key, as weighty as it is antique, is kept at the Rectory.

From Ribchester, the Ribble gurgles along to Samlesbury, Cuerdale, and Walton-le-Dale, broad now where it collects the Darwen, flows through Preston, heads for the sea; one more tributary to merge at Freckleton Naze, the Astland (Douglas) composed of two rivers, Yarrow and Douglas, which share neighbouring nurseries in the windlashed heights above Rivington, not far from Winter Hill. They join forces near Bretherton, collect the little Lostock and rush on towards the Ribble, no longer as important as in the days of the flourishing Wigan coalfields, and laden barges making for the newly prosperous Fylde coast resorts and discharging on slades, at the cliff edge, in inlets among the dunes.

Stydd Chapel.

Journey down the Wyre.

Not the best-known, not the largest, but a sweet-tempered, living and lovely river that empties into the sea at Fleetwood. It was noted, once, for "trout, chub, gudgeon and smelts", for cockles and mussel beds near Knott End, for "Hambleton Hookings" that occasionally contained pearls. It rises in the fells of Tarnbrook and Marshaw, streamlets spilling down and meeting at Emmotts, near Abbeystead, then capering off towards a man-made lake created in the 1850's to accommodate water for Lancaster.

A few monks from Furness Abbey arrived at Abbeystead, centuries ago, to found a daughter house near a river, a Cistercian tradition. It was too harsh, too cold. They cleared off to Ireland in the 12th century when St. Mary's Priory took over, then the Duchy. A chaplain was sent to serve the isolated shepherds and cattle farmers of Over Wyresdale where there were a dozen "Vaccaries" or dairy pastures. At this point, the sprightly prattling Wyre is as beautiful as the village deserves and, truly, Abbeystead is a little paradise, a fairyland, a sylvan nook with a cluster of ancient properties, renewed and lovingly tended. The pinfold is still there. The 17th century Post Office stands among the flowers of a cottage garden. Three hundred years ago the village belonged to the Cawthornes, an eccentric bunch of country squires who ruled the roost, founded Cawthorne's Endowed School in 1674 and appointed masters only "of sound religion, grave behaviour". John Fenton Cawthorne was the last of them. He went bankrupt after planting many trees around Marshaw and building a great mansion, and after long Squire-less years, the Earl of Sefton purchased Abbeystead and 13,000 acres, restored the village and built a magnificent shooting lodge for his guests, in the 1880's.

A mile down the road, beside sheep pastures and a lake that could be Nature's own, is Christ Church, "The Shepherds' Church", they call it, built in 1733 around a prevailing theme of shepherds and sheep . . . in stained glass, in the inscription over the entrance. Here is a tranquillity which is a rare tonic for town-jaded nerves. Across fields, the Wyre bustles along with many a flash of leaping salmon and lesser waters

HACKENSALL HALL (opposite, top), built in 1656 by a branch of the Fleetwoods of Rossall, stands on the northern bank of the Wyre near the golf links at Knott End. The house is famous for its legendary horse-boggart which, in return for a cosy place at the fireside, helped during the night with the farm-work.

PARROX HALL, PREESALL (bottom), from the rear, the charming home of the Elletson family for 300 years, dates back to the Tudor period and has a handsome early 18th century staircase and panelled hall.

tippling in on either bank until Dolphinholme is reached where the wool-workers always celebrated the Feast of St. Blaize on 3rd of February. Romans put Bishop Blaize (Blasius) of Cappadocia to death in 316 after raking his naked flesh with iron combs. Medieval woolcombers adopted him as their patron saint and commemorated his martyrdom with feastings, bonfires, wearing woollens and even trimming horses with fleeces.

Even this quiet place, improbably named after "Dolphin", the Norseman, did not avoid the Industrial Revolution and by 1800 a warehouse and a mill employing thousands soared above the waters, the one still usefully serving as a village social centre. There is a bridge now where straining horses lugged their loads across the ford, and the Wyre henceforth does venturesome things like passing under Street bridge, diving under a main London/Scotland railway, performing the Limbo under a motorway and cheekily flowing beneath the Preston/Lancaster Canal. Scorton comes next, a village popular with getting-away-from-it-allers, good food hounds and ramblers heading for Nickey Nook, particularly in bluebell time. It even attracted factory bosses, the Fishwick's of Burnley in 1809.

The Wyre flutters a languid hand at Garstang where there is a salmon ladder by the bridge and street markets held since 1288. Garstang's interest in manufactures was short-lived; the old market town preferred agriculture, livestock trading, clog-making, shire-horses and such-like. The gaunt ruin of Greenhalgh Castle . . . "this prety castle of the Lords of Derbys" . . . is a reminder of Royalists beseiged for months on end by Cromwell's forces. Henry VII gave the estate to his stepfather, the first Earl of Derby, after his victory on Bosworth Field in 1485, and allowed him to proceed with fortifications.

Near Catterall comes the Calder ("frothing, rushing water") which rises on Calder Fell, comes by Oakenclough and Calder Vale. This is the Wyre-Calder as distinct from the Ribble-Calder. Not so odd, really! There are two others in the kingdom, four Derwents, several Aires and a whole batch of Avons! Calder Vale reminds me of Lakeland in miniature. From Wyresdale in 1835 came the Jackson brothers, honest Quakers who built a couple of mills and workers' cottages. The hard-working community has won "Best-Kept" awards and is always worth wandering through though, a dozen years ago, slump followed the boom-time.

The Wyre swerves sharply west, ducks behind St. Helen's churchyard at Churchtown (Kirkland). The church is incredibly old, "The Cathedral of the Fylde", they sometimes call it, though other descriptions were probably applied when corpses had to be carried from Garstang, on shoulders, in all weathers! The one and only village street shoots off the highway near the "Horns Inn", passes the old market cross, some bonny old houses and a pub called "The Punch Bowl" . . . formerly the "Covered Cup" because of the Butlers who lived at Kirkland Hall across the highway. Their device was a chevron and three covered cups or chalices and if you search diligently you will find it carved and much weathered on the copings of the churchyard wall.

St. Michael's next and a watery embrace with the River Brock which forms from waters on Fairsnape Fell. St. Michael's is a little love of a country church, mostly Perpendicular with a low tower of 1611, with fragments of ancient glass and memorials of old Fylde Families. Its predecessor, mentioned in Domesday, was possibly founded by Paulinus c. 640. A 14th century mural was uncovered in the Sanctuary in 1956 and there are indications that a grammar school was conducted in the south aisle. The Wyre is embanked in these parts for, like any lady, when unduly provoked, she can occasionally "go over the top!"

A mile away, where there had been a "cart ford", they built a toll bridge, not to be compared with the 325 yard structure that spanned the Wyre downstream on the site of the historic Aldwath-ford. "Safe and easy as Wyre water" . . . the old saying generally applies in the Shard Bridge area, and the broadening mouth is busy with weekend sailors. On the northern bank, near Knott End Golf Links, stand two more historic Lancashire halls, Hackensall, built in 1656 by a branch of the Fleetwoods, Parrox Hall, centuries-old seat of the Elletsons, Squires of Preesall. Somewhere in this region, though never located, the Romans operated from "Portus Setantiorum". Sub-aquarists have often gone searching, for what? . . . they know not! They have always concerned themselves with the broad river mouth where salt and fresh waters mingle. I suspect the Romans would have placed their "Portus" as far up-river as was navigable by decent sized vessels; and there is a point, near Preesall, where Roman shipping might have tied up and unloaded. But that presumes the river has kept a constant course for nineteen hundred years; and one must never be presumptuous about moving waters, not even those of the serene and silvery Wyre!

12.   A GALLERY OF MINSTRELS

LANCASHIRE was never short of songsters to hymn her praises. Her bards and rhymesters down the centuries would pack a cathedral. Long before the commonalty could read or write, some balladier composed "Warrikin Fair", a broad dialect account of a Warrington con-man acquiring Gilbert Scott's mare without paying. Gilbert's wife lambasted her "udgit" (idiot) spouse when he returned with this lame tale and for five market days waited for "th'mon a ridin' th'mare into th'town". Whereupon, she "poo'd an' thrumpered him" and caused such a stir that Randle Shay stepped in as peacemaker, offering Grace "th'mare or th'money". She took the cash, kept it and taught her simpleton husband a lesson . . . a tale that goes back to 1548 when Randle Shay was bailiff to Sir Thomas Butler. It was probably handed down orally for long enough, altering in the process but using words still familiar in the county, like "gradely", "gloppen" (surprised) and "swat" (struck).

In an area like Lancashire where the dialect is still mouthed with gusto, we know that the versifying did not cease in the mid-16th century. Two hundred years later John Byrom of Kersal (1692–1763), Jacobite poet and composer of the hymn "Christians Awake" tried to write the dialect only to have it dismissed as "unintelligible to readers in general". But he enjoyed writing, whether hymns, contributions to the "Spectator" or verses in pleasant pastoral style. He lived in London for a while, devising and teaching a system of shorthand, but his inheritance of the family estate at Kersal brought him back to Lancashire where he lived to a contented old age.

It was John Collier (1709–1786), however, who took the folkspeech at its broadest and crudest and turned it into an art form. By many he is regarded as the Rabbie Burns of Lancashire and, like the Scot, he was fond of roystering in taverns. His best known work "Tummus and Meary" appears, at first sight, as incomprehensible as Welsh or Chinese shorthand and even the exponent needs a glossary at his elbow. But it enjoyed an immediate success when it appeared under the pseudonym of "Tim Bobbin" in 1750 and placed him permanently in the front rank of dialect writers.

"Tim's" own story, a gift to biographers, is as rumbustious as anything he wrote. Having been born into the large family of a poor struggling curate at Urmston, he began working on the Dutch loom at twelve, gave it up at sixteen and became an unqualified itinerant teacher trudging between Rochdale, Oldham and Bury for rewards that barely kept body and soul together. At the same time he was picking up and noting down quaint snatches of dialect transmitted in purest form through centuries of time. They became his idiom, his stock in trade.

When he was offered an assistant's post at a Free School at Milnrow, near Rochdale, he was fain and glad to settle for the unprincely sum of £10 p.a. The headship, twelve years later, doubled his salary. He was in his mid-thirties, a bachelor comfortably off, an attractive proposition. To the chagrin of local maidens, he married Mary Clay (21), a socialite from Flockton in the West Riding. She had a lick of London polish, a dowry of £300 and plenty of common sense, all very appealing to the fun-loving, musical, tavern-haunting schoolmaster whose verses and caricatures found a ready market with their subjects.

Within two years, to his shame and repentance, "Tim" had dissipated Mary's fortune and, with a family springing up, he was obliged to turn his talents to profit. Altar pieces, inn signs, etchings and crude cartoons brought in a few extras, while dialect satires, coarse and primitive to some, tumbled from his goose-quill. For a year he was tempted away to Halifax to a life of desk slavery for twice his Milnrow salary. It bowed his spirit, nearly broke his heart and he was thankful to get his old job back and return to that grand little cottage near the school at Milnrow. He was never again lured away, but scribbled poetry and prose, feasted on mulled ale and toast, entertained his taproom cronies or sat in his garden beside the River Beal. He came more to appreciate Mary whose death he did not long survive and their grave at St. Chad's, Rochdale, has been a literary shrine ever since.

In honour of the bicentenary of his birth, a few ardent spirits devoted to the dialect met spontaneously in April 1909 at Rochdale. In the course of that convivial meeting, Allen Clarke proposed that an association

THREE WHO WROTE AND SANG FOR LANCASHIRE. Samuel Laycock (top left), Edwin Waugh (top right) and Joseph Cronshaw (below).

be formed of writers and lovers of Lancashire literature and history and at another meeting at Rochdale, in the November, when fewer than twenty attended, rules were agreed and subscriptions were fixed at — Gentlemen half a crown (12½p), Ladies one shilling (5p) per annum. The fees have risen since but the Lancashire Authors' Association flourishes and is motivated by the same warmth and friendliness that launched it in the first place. Quarterly meetings move round the county but Rochdale is always the venue for major milestones, like the 21st birthday in 1930 and the Golden Jubilee in 1959.

In addition, the Lancashire Dialect Society and the Edwin Waugh Dialect Society work to keep the old folkspeech "wick" (alive and kicking) "Tim Bobbin's" work continues and the old roysterer could return to any of these meetings and feel completely "at home".

Samuel Bamford, born at Middleton, two years after "Tim's" death, was a muslin weaver's son who went to Manchester Grammar School, drifted for a year or two, then settled to weaving. He dabbled in politics, led a contingent to the tragic Peterloo affair in 1819, was gaoled for that and later published an account of his arrest and imprisonment. His homely rhymes were well received and presently he left the loom, took up the pen, wrote for a London newspaper, reminisced about his early days and his Radicalism. He was briefly a messenger at Somerset House, but London palled and Lancashire pulled, and back he came to the weaving, achieving a fine old age and a niche in the Hall of Fame. There is a memorial monument at Middleton Church where thousands attended his funeral in 1872.

Meantime, Edwin Waugh, the "Laureate of Lancashire", another home-spun genius, had been born in 1817 in a cottage at the foot of Toad Lane, Rochdale. Life was comfortable until his father, a flourishing clog-maker, died at 37 of a brain fever. Edwin was seven, with two years' schooling behind him and years of penury ahead. His adored mother was his rock. She shaped his impressions of the outside world, gave him an education, conveyed the kind of thoughts and feelings which had uplifted her through many pressing cares and fostered the seeds of his intellectual life. Mary Waugh, a devout Methodist and a fine singer, was remarkably gifted and her clever son spoke of her tenderly to the end of his life.

At a young age he became errand lad to Thomas Holden, bookseller and printer, then shop-boy, then apprentice with seven years to serve, starting at half a crown a week (12½p) rising gradually to 11/6d (57½p). But he was surrounded by books, could read and absorb much about his beloved Lancashire, her literature, her history. Literary ambitions were born of this atmosphere. His pen was rarely inactive. He loved the works of Robert Burns and, using the same homely and heart-tugging themes, wrote movingly of the hills and moors about Rochdale, and the country folk whose anecdotes he savoured. "Come Whoam to thi Childer an' Me", his most celebrated poem, was published in the "Manchester Examiner" in 1856 and brought instant recognition.

Whether Waugh excelled in Standard English or the Lancashire Dialect is difficult to determine. He had few equals in either. Indeed, his eye-witness accounts of the "Factory Folk" during the great Cotton Famine of the 1860's are deeply moving. It pained him to watch helplessly while honest folk starved to death because of a trans-Atlantic Civil War. He accomplished more then he knew, however, for those comments, published in 1862, had more effect than a ton of dry official reports.

Waugh was a prolific writer, a popular performer on the concert platform and an honoured member of Literary Societies. He was rich in quality of life, this cheery, homely, well-favoured north countryman who had a natural gift for making himself agreeable; and he entertained many with racy tales of bygone friends and fellow scribblers. Manchester threw him a celebration dinner on his 70th birthday. His noble brow was crowned with a fine crop of silvery hair, his expression was most benign. Latterly he received a Civil List pension of £90 a year . . . not exactly a fortune but his days were crammed with interest. Mortal illness was already upon him. The pen dropped from his fingers. The tongue that had delighted in the dialect was soon to be silenced by cancer. He died, universally lamented, in 1890 and was buried at Kersal Moor. Fame and honours had come in the lifetime of this lovely man who was industrious, sweet natured, eminently sane, acutely observant and full of fun. His very wholesomeness reproaches those who, in more modern times, cannot amuse without resorting to salacity.

Willing disciples were ready to take up the torch, two of his contemporaries, both surviving him briefly. Ben Brierley of Failsworth (1824–1897) was born into a poor family, was a bobbin winder at six, advancing to piecer and handloom weaver, which absorbed most of the hours God sent. At Sunday School and night-school he learned how to read and write, began contributing to the "Manchester Spectator", published two books before 1860, took a pseudonym "Ab-o-th'Yate", spent a few months in London. Was a founder-member of the Manchester Literary Club in 1862, secured a job on the "Oldham Times" shortly after, published several books and launched "Ben Brierley's Journal", monthly first, then weekly. It flourished for two decades.

Like Charles Dickens, Brierley had a flair for dramatic renderings of his writings from the concert platform. He would have made a first class actor. Instead, he entered local politics, served on Manchester City Council for six years, visited America twice — most unusual in those days, and continued writing to the end, his best work appearing in his tales and sketches. He was buried at Harpurhey and a memorial statue stands in Queens Park, Manchester.

When the late Wilfred Pickles read his favourite dialect poems on the wireless, he often included "Bonny Brid", a poignant piece by that frail little genius, Samuel Laycock. It was written during the Cotton Famine, when Lancashire's looms were starved of raw materials and operatives were laid off in their thousands. Another mouth to feed would cause anxiety, not rejoicing. Sitting by the empty grate, Laycock imagined that the expected child was already here on his knee, a welcome little lad . . . "but shouldn't ha' coom just when tha did!", the worried young father ruminates into that soft little ear.

> *We're short o' pobbies for eawr Joe . . .*
> *But that, of course, tha didn't knaw . . . Did-ta, lad?*

He sighs, remembering the other "childer" upstairs asleep in bed and wonders how on earth they will manage. Then, tenderness wells up, and fatherly pride, and he snuggles the babe to his bosom and, with a love that will not be smothered, goes on:

> *But, tho' we've childer two or three*
> *We'll mak a bit o' reawm fer thee; Bless thee, lad.*
> *Tha'rt prattiest brid we have i'th' nest,*
> *So hutch up closer to mi breast . . . Ah'm thi dad!*

The "Bonny Brid", in fact, turned out to be a daughter who grew up, married Sim Schofield, another dialect writer from the Failsworth school. He contributed to the "Fleetwood Chronicle" after they moved to Thornton-le-Fylde, and memories of his father-in-law appear in his "Recollections". For instance Laycock, who had a bookstall on Oldham Market, would stand all day without selling a single volume, reflecting that he would have been better off selling quack pills or black puddings. He would labour for hours over a poem for some public gathering and after journeying miles at his own expense, or on shanks' pony, would barely receive a vote of thanks.

His head seemed over-large for his body, probably due to malnutrition in childhood, and he looked as though a puff of wind would blow him over. Yet, he once walked in pouring rain to recite a specially written piece which was rapturously received by the audience, but returned home remembering that everyone else had been thanked — chairman, performers, caterers, caretakers probably — but not the poet who paid his own cab fare home!

Today's "What's in it for me?" attitude was unknown to Laycock. He was born at Marsden, near Oldham, in 1826, a handloom weaver's son who, at nine, was working fourteen hours a day in a woollen mill for two shillings (10p) a week. Apart from Sunday School (God bless Gloucester-born Robert Raikes whose movement released so many humble geniuses from intellectual imprisonment last century), he was self educated, always hungry for knowledge. He moved to Stalybridge at eleven, tended a power loom, became a cloth looker. He read and was inspired by Waugh's works, began writing verses, tasted the bitterness of unemployment, began printing broadsheets to encourage and uplift down-hearted comrades. They called him the "Laureate of the Cotton Famine".

His works appeared in book form in the 1860's and brought fame to their creator. He forsook mill life, moved to Fleetwood on the Fylde coast, became curator of the Whitworth Institute, then opened a small business in Blackpool. In the 1870's both he and Ben Brierley contributed pieces to the "Blackpool Gazette", and Laycock was now the recognised voice of working Lancashire. He received honorary membership of the Manchester Literary Club. The rich and scholarly sought him out. Two more collections of his works were published before his death in December 1893, but seventeen years elapsed before his worth was truly assessed. In 1910 great literary figures assembled in Blackpool to pay homage to his genius and to unveil a full length portrait now in the Grundy Art Gallery. He is still one of the best known and best loved of all the Lanky Songsters and every "Lonkysheer Neet" contains something from Laycock.

Collier, Waugh, Laycock, Brierley . . . they set standards which later bards have striven to uphold. No-one outclassed Ammon Wrigley (1862–1946) for instance, in the portrayal of the moors around Oldham and the countryfolk from those "cold grey hills" . . .

> *In the days when life was stern,*
> *When work had left the old hand-loom*
> *And wages were hard to earn.*

He wrote with lyrical affection of the Friezland area and its home-brewed ale spiced with country herbs and rustic know-how.

> *A pint of sunshine at a draught,*
> *All sparkles, grip and mettle.*
> *There never is a cloudy day*
> *When Friezland ale's in fettle.*

As an amateur archaeologist, Wrigley toiled for twenty years to uncover prehistoric remains, and he recorded much local history from the Saddleworth area, retiring from writing in his sixties and enjoying long years among the hill folk he had always loved.

Joseph Cronshaw, born eleven years before Wrigley, was a Lancashire minstrel who stuck to homely themes, courting, the domestic hearth, the loss of "precious little bairns", so constant a sadness last century, and a childlike love of Nature.

> *Ther's a bonnie little dingle*
> *Abeawt a mile fro' here,*
> *An' when mi wark an baggin's o'er*
> *Ah'm welly allus theer;*
> *Ther's a summat seems to draw me*
> *Wheer owd Nature weaves her spell,*
> *That's why Ah like to wander in*
> *Yon bonnie little dell.*

The limpid sweetness of his countryside pieces contrasts sharply with the harshness of the poet's early circumstances. He had a rough and ready upbringing, went into business on his own on a capital of 1s.9d., hawking salt from a hand-cart; saved up for a donkey, invested in a stud of donkeys on Blackpool sands but specialised in grease refining and salt-trading; spent his life among the roughest types on Salt Wharf, Ancoats, an unsavoury place in those days — yet, loved the theatre, and amateur acting, and reciting the prose and verse which he wrote in both dialect and Standard English. He was a great humorist, convulsed his audiences, loved meeting fellow scribblers and helped to found the Lancashire Authors' Association in 1909, having earned recognition for his works in the Waugh/Brierley/Laycock tradition. His "Dingle Cottage" (published 1908 and 1911) was dedicated to "Loving Parents" who, all their lives, conversed in the beloved Lanky twang.

These are a few of Lancashire's minstrels. My good friend and President of the L.A.A., Lionel Angus-Butterworth, M.A., has recalled a hundred in "Lancashire Literary Worthies" (1980). The list is nowhere near exhausted. This project, indeed, is like an exercise in chasing after a disappearing bus because, as old and honoured voices are stilled, sprightly pipings are heard from a new generation of Lancastrians who have been touched by the magic of the Muse, and who have every intention of singing proudly for their county.

13. TOWERS, MOORS AND OLD MILL TOWNS

STRETCHING EAST from the M61 to the Yorkshire border, you may wander the "silent mystical moors", an infinity of bracken and heather and, like Ammon Wrigley, experience that "loneliness . . . which is the most exquisite companionship". The very silence is a misnomer. All the year round, Nature is about her business and her music plays without ceasing. Far from the klaxon cacophony of civilisation, the pressures subside, the inner ear becomes attuned and the released spirit enters "a kind of converse of which not a syllable is heard, but much felt".

These wild spaces between hard-working towns are a reproach to those misguided ones who regard Lancashire as one vast dingy urban sprawl inhabited by third-rate characters communicating in an incomprehensible tongue and clattering about in clogs, cloth caps or Hilda Ogden curlers. What nonsense! As if everything and everyone north of a mythical line can be dismissed as dismal and of no account, whereas — and every northerner worth his salt knows it! — it was HIS cleverness, HIS energy that put our nation on the road to undreamed-of prosperity and influence, and HIS gusto and sense of comedy that brought us through the bad times!

The ignorance of the average Southerner about the north in general has to be experienced to be believed! Often, he cannot distinguish between those two great counties separated by the Pennines, a situation calculated to make any self-respecting Yorkshireman flare up and bluster. His Lancastrian neighbour would more likely grin slyly and shrug off the ramblings of "know-alls-and-know-nowts!" Yet many Londoners, whose posting to Lancashire was as welcome as a death sentence, have quickly felt so "at home" in the place that the capital has become a place for holiday visits and family reunions, and warm-hearted Lancashire has become "home".

It would be odd if it were not so. For this is a brave and beautiful county whose genuine warmth of heart, I think, cannot be matched anywhere on earth, except perhaps in the western area of Scotland. Lancashire's ties are not easily broken. She binds her children, and her foster-children, in silken cords of affection; and a whole lifetime will not exhaust her treasures and little hidden delights.

Take that fascinating area east of the A666, starting north-east of Bolton, at Bradshaw, a village connected with John Bradshaw, the "Regicide" whose signature headed the death warrant of Charles I and whose hectoring bullying behaviour towards the luckless monarch rendered his name odious to honest men on both sides of the conflict. Bradshaw was not Lancashire-born but his family's old home, Bradshaw Hall, survived until the 1950's. The village pub was a brewhouse long before it was recorded as "House Without a Name" by magistrates who granted the first licence in 1832. The church is the only one in England dedicated to St. Maxentius, an obscure French saint who trained at Poitou, became Abbot there in the time of Clovis I (481–511). The church is towerless but in the graveyard stands a churchless tower! Back in the 1820's when the previous structure, c.1560, was decrepit and in in need of rebuilding, the parishioners put the work in hand, took fifty years over it and either couldn't agree, or ran out of cash! There it is, a curious phenomenon which adds interest to a journey.

Two or three miles northwards, Turton Tower, an embattled medieval pele, was turned into a home in 1596 by William Orrell. At that time a Crumpsall youth was apprenticed to a Mancunian linen-draper, a first step towards that fortune which established Chetham's Hospital and Library (now Chetham's School of Music) in the city. Humphrey Chetham acquired Turton Tower from the debt-ridden Orrells in 1628 and bequeathed it to a nephew, George, whose descendants in 1835 sold it to James Kay. If the good Turton folk had had their way, the beneficent Humphrey would have been commemorated in a tower similar to the one at Holcombe. Alas for good intentions! They ran out of funds! Turton Tower, immensely popular with visitors, has half-timbered domestic quarters, a collection of armoury, a resident "black lady" — the Catholic Orrells once harboured priests — and the legendary Timberbottom skulls. A large 17th century barn connected with the Tower has been converted into a luxury mansion near the entrance gates; and when I last visited in the company of a radio producer, a great water wheel, rescued and restored by enthusiasts, was waiting to be set up over a nearby stream.

Bromley Cross has shown the world what can be done with old stone houses, and a short trip to Old Turton village (otherwise "Chapeltown") is like travelling back in time. Nothing can have changed much in a hundred years or more and while poking around after delicious pub–grub under the scrutiny of a very senior citizen sheltering beneath a projecting stone porch, it occurred to me that the identical scene was probably witnessed by intrepid travellers in Georgian times! Jumbles Valley Country Park, sylvan and flower-besprinkled, attracts the crowds, particularly on Bank Holidays. An area was flooded a few years ago to make a reservoir for Bolton.

The Edgworth–Blackburn road via Wayoh Fold strikes an old Roman route linking Bolton and Ribchester, long before the lower road was cut. In the old days men and horses struggled up steep gradients but to-day's motorist discovers a splendid getting-away-from-it-all area with heights of over 1,000 feet near Hoddlesden and Blacksnape and glorious views over Darwen, pronounced "Darren", where they built impressive mill chimneys, the best known, at India Mill, soaring to 303 feet and being likened to the Campanile in Venice. But the most arresting landmark, perched on a moorland summit, resembles an inter-planetary rocket poised for take-off, Darwen Tower, built in 1897 in double celebration of Victoria's Jubilee and the citizens' right of free access to the moors after years of campaigning.

Building presented a fearful challenge. The stone came from Red Delph nearby. The weather deteriorated. Gale force winds actually blew over horse and cart conveying rubble for foundations and the two stone-masons, toiling at 1285 feet above sea level, faced a daily walk of ten miles to and from work. The tower is a monument also to their craftsmanship and fortitude. I struggled up to it on one occasion, gasping like a grounded whale and suspecting that the Angel of Death might beat me to the top while my young companion bounded effortlessly ahead with all the agility of a mountain goat. But it was all worth it for the superlative views over darkling moors and sparkling reservoirs and huddled townships and the structure itself is a beauty, costing originally about £700 whereas the fund raised £2,000, so the "Darreners" got a District Nurses' Home thrown in for good measure! The first glass and teak cupola blew away in a storm in 1947. It was replaced in the 1960's when the grime-blackened stone was cleaned up like new. They predicted that the tower would "draw people out of the streets into the glorious heather" and it has been doing that since its completion in 1898.

Over to the east, dominated by the tall spire of its church rebuilt last century, Holcombe clings to a hillside overlooking the Vale of Irwell. "Th'Owd Doctor", William P. Woodcock (1796–1884) snoozes among the saints and sinners, many of whom he delivered. They reckon he brought 10,000 into this harassed world, this shopkeeper's lad from Moor Bottom Road, who knew the Cheeryble Grants, lived at "Woodside", later the Rectory, and turned out in all weathers to attend patients who would likely never pay. In an age of "characters", the silver-maned bearded patriarch was a genuine one-off, forthright in speech, niggardly with money . . . he once even swopped hats with a scarecrow because his was shabbier . . . and let fly with a fowling piece when sparrows raided his seed beds. He was in practice during the Chatterton Riots, the Plug Riots of 1842, and troubles with Irish labourers when the Bury–Manchester Railway was built in 1846.

A steep track leads to "Holcombe Tower", a memorial to Sir Robert Peel, financed by admirers in the 1850's and built at 1,100 feet on a blustery site which commands breathtaking views. Again, one feels sympathy for those old-time masons who constructed the 120ft. high tower with a projecting base. A mile northwards, a memorial marks the site of a 12th century cross where pilgrims rested and Whalley Abbey monks paused for prayer on their weary travels. Long before that, the Ancient Briton pounded his trackways, hunted deer and wild boar and lost many a flint arrowhead in the soggy peat!

Old-time sports around here were as violent as the weather. A great deal of money changed hands during cock-fighting, clog-purring and brutish bare-knuckle bouts. Fifty pounds would seem a fortune in 1839 but did it compensate Charley Jones, victor of a 30-round contest on a bitter November day, up there on Holcombe Hill? And what of the loser, poor Sam Paxton? The Holcombe Harriers have survived, still going after hares. They were formed (it is said!) after James I hunted with the local hounds during that memorable stay at Hoghton Tower (1617) and graciously authorised the Holcombe huntsmen to wear the royal insignia on their jackets, which they do, to this day. More easterly, over by Whitworth, even as late as the 1880's, enormous crowds turned up for naked racing across the moors, contestants wearing only belts worn round the loins.

Helmshore is the place for Industrial Archaeology. When Higher Mill was threatened with closure in 1967, local enthusiasts formed a group to work for its preservation and achieved their objective with massive help from mill owners who donated manufacturing bygones. The 1789 mill started in woollens. The fulling stocks are still there, giant wooden hammers used to beat and thicken cloth brought in by handloom weavers. The teazle gig raises the nap. Motivation is by a 18ft. diameter water wheel. Here, Arkwright's Water Frame and Hargreaves' Spinning Jenny can be seen working and you can discover what it means to be "on tenterhooks". Millowner's house and workers' cottages have scarcely changed in 200 years and human nature remains constant! Helmshore folk, last century, hid their illicit stills in lonely places. They suffered at the hands of the machine wreckers. Higher Mill had 106 looms smashed to fragments in 1826, a sorry business, spreading through Rossendale. Next day, five men and a woman were killed when soldiers opened fire!

Between A666 and M61 spreads a glorious expanse of heathered wastes and dreamy solitudes, of hills brooding over dimly remembered secrets, of little wayside ruins . . . how did folk survive, long ago, in such splendid isolation? . . . of time honoured villages, of reservoirs and ancient legends.

Start at Rivington Pike, that assertive, eye-catching beacon site where flames flashed a warning of the Spanish Armada on 19th July, 1588. Ancient heart-flutterings matched by modern heart-poundings on Easter Saturdays when the traditional Fell Pike Race is held and eager athletes explode into action along a 3¼ mile course up to the Tower and back, a lung-bursting muscle-screaming haul to the 1,192 ft. summit, followed by the excruciating descent, egged on by well-wishers who turn up in their hundreds, and dreaming always of cracking the 15-minute barrier. It hasn't been done, yet, but the hopefuls keep at it!

Squire John Andrews built the tower, with single chamber, fireplace and cellar beneath, in 1773 to assert his ownership of the moor. Rival families had argued for ever about who owned what, a situation resolved by costly law-suit a year or two after Henry Lathom, mason, had completed his work in durable gritstone. The weathered base-stones probably belonged to the ancient beacon. The Pike, popular with picnic parties, hikers and motor-bike scramblers, affords fantastic views over half the county and a fine Country Park has resulted from reclamation of the late Lord Leverhulme's Rivington estate.

Back in the days when the millionaire soap-manufacturer was plain William Hesketh Lever, he purchased 2,100 acres of moorland, laid roads, built a large wooden bungalow, "Roynton Cottage", and indulged his fancy for landscaping and laying out gardens. The rest was for public enjoyment, a proposal welcomed in 1901 but challenged by Liverpool Corporation a year later in a bid to protect the watershed of their reservoirs which formed part of Lever's Rivington Hall estate. They had reckoned without the little man's genius for getting his own way and, in fact, he retained his bungalow site and 45 acres, received compensation amounting to double the total purchase price and an undertaking to preserve 400 acres to be known as Lever Park. With bold ideas and lofty motives, he developed an open-air zoo at the approach to Rivington Hall, planted an avenue of trees down to the reservoir and built that romantic replica of ruined Liverpool Castle overlooking Cross's Creek.

In the bungalow grounds, Lever created a Japanese fantasy of caves, waterfalls, lagoons, stairways, temples, bridges, archways and walks. From a dreary hillside sprang the magic of foliage and flora and Lancashire acquired another landmark when a tall summer-house, always known as the "Pigeon Tower", soared up giving fabulous views. Sir William, a Baronet by now, was riding high in 1913. On that July evening, he and Lady Lever dined with King George V and Queen Mary at Knowsley, as guests of the Earl

Lord Leverhulme's "Pigeon Tower", Rivington.

RIVINGTON's two grand old Saxon cruck barns, unique in the north, have survived largely through the generosity of the first Lord Leverhulme. The larger structure, the Hall Barn, measures over 105ft. by 57ft. Great House Barn, pictured above, is only 42ft. by 48ft. It belonged to Great House farm, many of whose acres lie submerged under the waters of the Lower Rivington Reservoir. The barns offer refreshments to the many visitors to this lovely part of Lancashire.

RIVINGTON. This lovely little Unitarian Chapel (1703) overlooks the village green and retains its ancient box pews and an atmosphere of the unspoilt past.

and Countess of Derby when word came through that their Rivington home, filled with tapestries and art treasures, had been burned to the ground. That very date had been fixed by Edith Rigby, a militant suffragette, to hump a can of paraffin up that steep hill to "Roynton Cottage", a story graphically told in "My Aunt Edith" by Phoebe Hesketh who lived at Rivington for a number of years. Three weeks later, Lady Lever was dead. The sorrowing widower replaced the bungalow in more durable materials, adding a splendid circular ballroom and a telescope swivelling clear across seven counties. But that, too, vanished completely and after Lord Leverhulme's death in 1925 Nature over-ran the once immaculate grounds and a tangle of undergrowth gradually obliterated terrace and staircase alike.

All that has been cleared and nowadays the Country Park attracts greater numbers than ever, though Rivington has always been popular, particularly with antiquarians. The hall is still there, 18th century with older bits behind. The huge Hall barn, a Saxon cruck structure supported by six pairs of enormous oaks, and the lesser Great House Barn, must be unique of their kind in the north of England, the former being a popular venue for receptions and dances, the latter, less than half its size, offering refreshments. Lord Leverhulme paid for their restoration. Rivington Grammar School, founded in Tudor times by a Bishop Pilkington, is now reserved for the juniors, the older pupils sharing a more modern building nearer Horwich with scholars from Blackrod. Another Pilkington, Richard, rebuilt the church in 1541, the origins of the first being lost in the mists of time. Both church and grounds have many curios. A mural tablet bearing a recumbent skeleton reminds: "As I am, thou shall be!" Another recalls "John Shawe, seconde sonne of Lawrence Shaw of High Bullough in Anglezarke . . . by whose guift and provision out of lands the yearly summe of Ten Shillinges is to be payed yearly for ever, towards the repayre of this church . . . and also the yearly summe of Twenty nobles to be distributed yearly for ever unto the poore people inhabitinge in Ryvington, Anglezarke, Heath Churnocke and Anderton . . . the one moytie on Good Friday & the other moytie on the 1st Sunday in Advent". Kindly John died on 12th November 1627 at the age of 55 years. Do they still distribute his "nobles", each worth half a mark, or 6/8d., in old money?

Overlooking the tiny village green is the grand little Unitarian chapel of 1703, one of the earliest nonconformist places of worship in Lancashire. It has a splendid pulpit, a quaint collection of box pews and a fulsome memorial to the Lords Willoughby of Parham, benefactors and dissenters. There are bygones hereabouts — village stocks; a tethering post at the old school; a carved head from the Black Boy Inn of the pre-reservoir era, set into a barn wall; and legends — of a spectral horseman whose head only materialises near the vicarage garden; of the "Twa Lads" memorial out on Wilders' Moor, on Winter Hill, recalling two young shepherd lads who became mesmerised during a snow-storm and perished together in this inhospitable place, popular among sportsmen and ramblers; two cairns were raised there but only one remains.

Winter Hill, looking mountainous from some angles, but rising 1500 ft., has its weird collection of masts and Scotsman's Stump, a monument to an unsolved murder. This dome-like bump midway between Rivington Pike and Belmont lay on George Henderson's route on that foggy night of 9th November 1838. Before daylight broke, he met his death, perhaps from a poacher's stray bullet, though a man was charged with his murder and found not guilty. There is a distinctly weird feeling in this wild sort of moorland and in the dim mist-shrouded bulk of Noon Hill it is not difficult to believe that the place is haunted. Bronze Age relics were excavated in 1958 and are now exhibited in Bolton Museum. And the legend persists that a dreadful apparition, mounted on a beast capable of treading the bog without wetting a hair of its foot, hovers about here waiting to waylay the unsuspecting traveller. Timorous souls are happy to leave this brooding place to the curlews and the sheep!

All around Rivington, lonely paths strike out past sad ruins, tumbled stones of homes once dear to now-forgotten characters like "Old Rachel", "Old Will", "Old Kate", "Stoops", "Simms" or "Henshaw". Who were these ghost-people who lived and loved and laboured hereabouts, and slid off, at last, into the silence of the forgotten? And Moses Cocker . . . did he really try out his home-made wings from a barn-top, only to land in the midden? They were telling the same tale about Dick o'Joshua's over at Goodshawfold a couple of lifetimes ago!

You won't catch me wasting time on motorways when it is possible to drive over Belmont moors and recapture a feeling of infinite space and glorious freedom. I would always take that route towards Bolton, passing through Belmont village that developed out of steads straddling an ancient track that was turn-piked early last century and that burgeoned when Bolton took to bleaching and dyeing in a big way around 1820. By mid-century Belmont had enjoyed a boom-time, had grown, had purloined water for its industrial processes, which swans now frequent and Sunday afternoon yachtsmen. Angela Brazil's family settled here while the author-in-the-making was still at school, a weekly boarder! She became the idol of half the gym-slipped young hoydens of the nation and I must have devoured every word she wrote, a dozen times over!

Over to the west, where Chorley's own Healey Nab stares across Anglezarke's stark moors and silent waters towards Rivington's lofty pike, I think of the Angles whose "airgh" this was centuries before the Conquest, of the wild cattle that grazed here, of early man patiently fashioning his arrow-heads of flint and, much more irritably, losing them out here by the hundred. A chum of mine spent years of his life roaming these moors, rarely returned without two or three arrow-heads in his pocket — all found on the surface — and boasted an accumulated sack-ful at home! The bonny face of White Coppice, more hamlet than village, has decorated many a picture postcard and colour calendar. Two mills were once powered by a brook babbling in front of a handful of weavers' cottages lovingly tended by house-and-garden-proud owners. A place to visit when spring flowers bloom or, better still, when a rose display proclaims the cricket season!

Abbey Village, along the old Preston–Bolton Turnpike, has also had a face-lift following the closure of its main source of livelihood. The village sprang up beside the mill in the 1840's, all its eggs in one basket and smashed, it seemed, beyond repair when the premises were offered for sale, rendering a large work-force idle. Hearts were troubled in the early 1970's but after diversification, and a complete modernisation of all the early Victorian terraced properties, the village looks good and feels hopeful.

Where Darwen Moor dips towards Blackburn you will find Tockholes, "Toki's Hollow", where handlooms clattered before the Industrial Revolution, where machine-minders' clogs kicked up a commotion on the way to the mills in later years. But the mills died and the commuters arrived, young couples with growing families and a fondness for giving decaying properties a new look. They have re-animated an area that might have become moribund, useful only for farming. The long low-roofed National School, mid 19th century but looking a good deal older, spills forth youngsters with the bloom of health on their cheeks. It is fresh up here, all the year round, a perfect joy in summer. The school stands in the churchyard where there is an open-air pulpit for fine-weather sermons. There was a Chapel of St. Michael here, no-one quite knows how long ago, and a preaching cross that was old before the Conquest. A fragment of it survives, along with the Toch, or Magic Stone, beside St. Stephen the Martyr's Church door — there was a re-dedication following a total rebuilding on a barn-like scale in 1833 to accommodate a swelling industrial population. In the declining years, a dwindling congregation rattled about like a handful of peas in a drum until a new, cheerful and much smaller church was erected covering only half the old site.

Because Tockholes was remote from civilisation, the illegal distilling of spirits was a lucrative pastime. Presbyterianism was strong, dissent flourished causing acrimonious schisms in the 1660's. Tockholes parishioners broke away, refusing to adopt the prayer book, and chapels came into being. One was built in 1710, replaced in 1880. Another, small and ruinous within a burial ground was built in 1803 by followers of Selina, the Countess of Huntingdon, who promoted an 18th century religious revival based on Whitfield's Calvinistic Methodism and who devoted her life, wealth, connections and considerable intellect, to religious concernments.

Like all old places, Tockholes is rife with folk-lore and legend . . . of an 18th century forger busily counterfeiting in a workshop at Fine Peters, a house built by the prosperous, strait-laced chapel-going Marsdens in 1757.

He was fortunate only to languish in Preston Jail for that; he might so easily have hanged! . . . of "Owd Aggie", who lived alone and was murdered when ruffians with blackened faces broke in demanding her savings . . . of a faithful dog who used to accompany his mistress eight miles across the moors to Tockholes Chapel and after her death still turned up Sunday by Sunday . . . of Treacle Mines and a Tripe Delph! . . . of a Wishing Well with magic properties near the ruins of Hollinshead Hall and fine old farmhouses with centuries of time on their backs — like Ryal House, 1676, once the home of the Walmsleys . . . and 17th century Higher Hill with projecting gable, stone mullions, gabled porch, and jutting from an outside wall an upstairs lavatory with a stone seat and a free fall into a cesspit below! . . . of stonework rescued a lifetime ago and re-erected over a spring near the Vicarage when Garstang Hall was demolished. Garstangs took Walmsley brides from whom the Walmsleys of Dunkenhalgh are thought to have sprung . . . of another Winter Hill, without those famous masts, rising over 900 ft., opposite the Rock Inn at Tockholes . . . of a tradition that Oliver Cromwell fought a battle here in 1642 in Kill Field, near the Church . . . of the parson who shocked dozy congregations to attention by shouting: "Wake up!" and reminding them there was "plenty of time for sleeping . . . in Hell!"

Tockholes boasts one home-grown genius, John Osbaldeston, who sleeps in the churchyard. He invented the weft-fork, a valuable device that halted the loom when the thread broke; and who should have made a fortune — which he probably did — for other people! "Smart as paint and daft as a brush", just about sums up poor John who was frequently in his cups and babbled all his secrets. Drink was his downfall, drove him to the workhouse where he died in 1862, confessedly "A Dupe of False Friends and the Victim of Misplaced Confidence".

Blackburn

"Grim" . . "drab" . . "down at heel" . . . that is perhaps how Blackburn first strikes the stranger. Hills soar up on all sides, a barrier at one time to advancement. Domesday's "Blackborne" had a square mile of woodland, an "aerie of hawks", and St. Mary's Church serving an old Anglian settlement near a ford over Blakewater. The Whalley Abbey monks took it in hand later.

PLEASINGTON OLD HALL (above), a charming 16th century mullioned house across the fields from the meandering River Darwen. The Ainsworths moved in after John de Aynesworth married the de Plessington heiress, the families having lived as neighbours from time out of mind.

PLEASINGTON R.C. CHURCH (left) designed in 1818 by John Palmer who was determined to incorporate every architectural style in the kingdom from Ethelbert to Henry VIII.

Until cotton crossed the Atlantic, farming and weaving of woollens occupied whole families. Babyhood was brief. Infants learned to strip seeds from raw cotton which their elder siblings carded and passed to the spinsters. The yarns were devoured by the master of the house toiling on the handloom. John Kay's Fly-Shuttle (1733) speeded weaving, created an imbalance until James Hargreaves, a "Gobbin-lander" from Oswaldtwistle invented the Spinning Jenny, c. 1764 while he was working at a cotton factory near Blackburn and living at "Rose Cottage", now the village Post Office, at Stanhill. He had been puzzling how to spin several threads simultaneously and inspiration came when a child in the family knocked over the spinning wheel which kept turning while in a horizontal position. He developed the new principle and found himself in a storm-centre attracting the hostility and suspicions of his neighbours who feared these new machines. Simultaneously, Sir Robert Peel's grandfather "Owd Parsley" Peel who had been born at Peel Fold near Stanhill, was experimenting with calico printing. He and Hargreaves were neighbours and near enough in age to give mutual encouragement and perhaps it was Peel, knowing the climate, who advised Hargreaves to work secretly on his Jenny in the remoter area of Ramsclough. Even so, angry spinners burst in and broke up Hargreaves' machines. Dragoons rushed from Manchester to quell riots and "two wicked and dangerous persons" were charged.

Following Arkwright's example, Hargreaves packed his traps and flitted to Nottingham and, even there, found opposition to the "Jenny". It must be remembered however, that life was unbelievably harsh, with scant comfort, plainest fare, poverty, superstition and premature death producing a "dour and forbidding people". Between 1747 and 1761, Wesley encountered "a mob savage as wild beasts", ruffians stopping just short of murder while indulging in "all manner of wickedness" and barbaric recreations for which the moorland communities were notorious. Even last century, the Blackburn operatives were no more enlightened than to react violently against newly installed dandy looms. Soldiers could not prevent a rampaging mob of 10,000 wielding sledge-hammers from smashing looms to fragments in 1826. St. Mary's Church, nucleus of the Cathedral and designed by John Palmer, was completed about that time. The railway and Borough status came in 1850–1.

From King Street, once the fashionable area, the voice of B.B.C. Radio Lancashire speaks to the county. Here, the forward-looking families like the Liveseys, the Hornbys, and the Sudells, forsook farming and trading as chapmen and concentrated on manufactures, while the Feilden brothers settled at Feniscowles, beside the Darwen. At Pleasington, which has a 19th century Hall and a mullioned Old Hall of the 16th century, John Palmer designed the R.C. Church in 1818 incorporating all the architectural styles from Ethelbert's time to Henry VIII. It is strikingly poised above the Darwen, wonderfully ornate and eminently photogenic.

Accrington

Like Preston, once a linen centre; now famous for carpet sweepers, Terylene, and those superb bricks with an intense redness and a slight sheen; and much, much more . . . brushes of all sorts, baseballs for the Americans, billiard tables, glassware, machinery and textiles. Accrington lay in a hollow near the central Lancashire moors, a large village of colliers and weavers last century, hard-working and intensely house-proud. The 1974 boundary revision drew it into Hyndburn Borough, along with Church, Clayton-le-Moors, Great Harwood, Oswaldtwistle and Rishton.

The town centre has a dignified Town Hall and street stalls vie with the multi-arched Market building of the 1950's, and there is "character", still, in the rising Hollins Lane. Young Richard Kenyon, an apprentice in his father's jobbing shop at Ewbank in the 1860's, put a new word into general usage by developing a carpet sweeper and calling it "Ewbank". During World War II the factory switched to producing bomber and glider parts. Accringtonians were always patriotic, raising a battalion of 1100 "Pals" in eight days in the First World War and losing 150 in one day on the Somme in 1916.

Accrington once belonged to Kirkstall Abbey whence came lay brethren to establish a monastic grange. Whereupon previous owners, according to Baines, set about and slew "Norman, Umphrey and Robert" and attacked the property which "fell into a heap". A weeping Abbot reported the matter to the de Lacys who took revenge on the malefactors and extorted damages, when rebuilding proceeded. When confiscated monastic estates were sold for a pittance at the Dissolution, the townsfolk bought the ancient chapel, which may have been an oratory for monks, for £2.6s.8d. The present St. James' Church was built in 1763, the tower added forty years later.

The Art Gallery's outstanding collection of Tiffany glass attracts thousands every year and the new Sports Centre, one of the best and biggest in the north-west, was built by the new Hyndburn Borough Council — as you would expect — entirely of best Accrington bricks!

Burnley

In recent years the Burnley authority have taken their run-down smokey old mill town by the scruff of the neck, shaken out the bad bits, kept the best of the old, and transformed the place into an exciting and pleasant place to live in. I did not consider it odd, but James Cobbledick, a Plymouth octogenarian, caused a sensation in the national press when it was revealed that he always spent his holidays in Burnley! Except that I would forever be pining for the sea, I could settle here happily now that you can see clear across to old Pendle in the north, the bump of Boulsworth and fells leading to the Pennines in the east, and in the distance between, only a few miles from the Yorkshire border, the clustered dwellings and three mill chimneys of Briercliffe. Before the Clean Air Campaign that was not possible except during Burnley Fair Week when the mills shut down and all who could afford it went to Blackpool. The rest stayed at home and enjoyed the fun of the fairground amusements. The Fair still comes but what happens now is a poor substitute for the old days.

With his totally false impression of industrial Lancashire, the stranger cannot believe that the area around Burnley is transcendently lovely, that some of the finest countryside in the kingdom lies within walking distance. Talk to people like local artist David Wild whose passion for the place stirs all his conversations. "Burnley is set in a bowl-like valley created by glacial water melting and rushing down to form a lake between Pendle and Cliviger Gorge. It is rich in stone buildings and industrial archaeology and, since smoking abatement, has become environmentally exciting because, at last, everything is visible! It has great tourist potential. Height apart, John Ruskin compared Cliviger Gorge with anything in Switzerland for dramatic effect. Go up to the village of Shore, between Cliviger and Todmorden, a magical little place with fantastic views! Stride out in any direction. Every path opens up exquisite landscapes!"

When he is not rhapsodising about Nature, or painting or roaming the hills, David Wild ardently supports the Friends of "The Weavers' Triangle" which, he insists, is NOT a slum but "a record in bricks and mortar and machinery" lying along the canal bank, "a marvellous area, untouched, which says everything"; and he reminds me (as if I were a southerner and didn't know any better) that the Industrial Revolution which hit this place like a tornado led to Man going to the moon! His artist's soul is, however, sensitively aware that things are subtly changing. In the beginning, Lancashire allowed itself to be put down. The working man did not benefit from the wealth he created. Now, he yearns after middle-class status. So, the Burnley folk get out of the place as soon as they can. The girls dress up like London models. Even the cooking has altered from the traditional cheap cuts, which were appetising and wholesome, to the more exotic convenience stuff, which means that the southerners' image of Lancashire folk being "good sensible people eating good nourishing food" is gradually disappearing. All inevitable, of course, in these days of powerful media advertising, conveyor belt education and almost obligatory package holidays abroad. But it is sad, because the East Lancashire character is special and Burnley's contribution to the great world of commerce, paid for with human sweat and tears, is beyond calculation.

Talk to Roger Frost, teacher and local historian. He has studied Burnley's past in depth and is devoted to the famous "Triangle". He recalls the days when Burnley was the great cotton weaving centre of the world, with more factories than anywhere else, specialising in calico printing. Now there are only two cotton weaving firms left and 2,000 looms operating compared with 100,000 in 1913. A sad decline but, fortunately, the canal is still there and will remain if the "Friends" have anything to do with it. The Canal Tollhouse Museum opens up on Wednesdays and at weekends, and my young companion, who might have stepped out of pages by Dickens, was kind enough to escort me along the towpath, pointing out Queen Street Mill, now a workers' co-operative, the last steam-driven mill with Lancashire looms in the county. Co-operation is nothing new in Burnley. During the 19th century periods of depression, workers clubbed together from 1855 onwards, emptying their pockets and starting one mill with as little as 15/- (75p). It became one of the largest cotton concerns in the district. Altogether, twenty two mills in Burnley were run by families, and the village of Harlsyke, meaning "flax ditch", grew up around the original mill.

Along this stretch are canopied wharfs, a mule-spinning shed, still in operation, a throstle-spinning mill begun in the 1850's, and Slater Terrace, a range of stone buildings with balconied workers' maisonettes on top of an old cotton warehouse on the canal bank. Unique of its kind, its condition to-day is pretty dismal but not beyond restoration and it would certainly feature in some future Heritage Holiday programme as a prime example of industrial archaeology. Canals, in any case, are utterly fascinating and "away from it all" retreats. A lone angler plucked out a roach popped it into a keep-net, sighing: "The only one to-day. Yesterday, I got 22!" A long boat chugged placidly by, with hubby at the tiller, the Missus on a canvas chair in the prow and a resigned-looking shaggy dog with his chin draped on the bows. There are many canal bygones, iron rings set into the towpath every few yards, bridge uprights chafed with ropes or scarred by chains, a horse-slade for recovering horses that happened to fall in. There were always accidents in such a busy, bustling place.

They still argue hereabouts as to whether it is a Paulinus cross or a 13th century market cross which stands in the old Grammar School gardens up Bank Parade, near the River Brun (from which the town is named) which has a weir close by and at this point swirls and swoops through a perfect "S", enclosing St. Peter's churchyard in its tail. Burnley Grammar School is an Elizabethan foundation of 1559 and there has been a school in "Top o'th' Town" area for five centuries and more. St. Peter's Church, even older, goes back to 1122 but was rebuilt in 1532 and again in 1790. Much has been altered since; the 15th century tower, for instance, was heightened in 1803. Nevertheless, there are many ancientries including a medieval cross slab, a 16th century font and a curious carving on the tower, which may represent a pig — in which case it commemorates supposed goblin activity when the site was chosen elsewhere and masons and craftsmen were confounded by demon pigs undoing their work during the night and moving the stones to the present location. In the end, the superstitious townsfolk took the hint and settled for this present site of St. Peter's. Lancashire has quite a tradition of "goblin" work during the building of churches.

Markets have been held in Burnley since Edward I granted the right to Henry de Lacy in 1294. I talked to Bill Kippax, stallholder in the fourth generation from 1898. He operates in the palatial Market Hall, on first floor level, created c. 1970 on the original site when, after hundreds of years, food stalls were banned from open market trading. He has seen many changes, blocks of flats rising in place of old back-to-back terraces, clogs and shawls disappearing about twenty five years ago, bus fares discouraging outliers who would come in once or twice daily but now limit their visits to once a week. Bill admits that the loose biscuit trade is now "a nostalgia business", very popular with outside visitors who are accustomed to buying in packets. He sells pikelets (crumpets) and Scotch pancakes also, and the biscuits are made by a family connection who started in a back kitchen, moved to an old chapel and thence to an abandoned market hall, now employing fifty girls and distributing between Glasgow and London. The market stall has virtually become the last bastion of the family business in the town centre, but it isn't like the old days, when some old dear in curlers would ask for "a bob fer t'leet" (a shilling for the gas-meter), when succulent genoa cake sold for 1/4d. a lb., and mixed biscuits were half a pound for 9d. He remembers post-war rationing, and scissors on a string for cutting out coupons, and Penguin biscuits coming as a luxury (you could buy two with every ½lb. of cream crackers), and being on the ground level. Nowadays, it is ramps, or steps, from whichever direction, and a long way indeed from super three-tier wedding cakes sold for £8.16.0! The old cloggers have been pushed into the outskirts and nowadays clogs would, more likely than not, have rubber soles, and weaving has been overtaken by diversification into aircraft, electricals, motor tyres, brushes, polishes and paper manufactures.

The scintillating jewel in Burnley's diadem is Towneley Hall, home for centuries of the great Towneley family and built for defence with walls two yards in thickness. About the year 1200 Roger de Lacy granted the estate to his son-in-law, Geoffrey, who maintained a hunting lodge there and used the common pasture. From this, developed the Towneley home which, during the persecution of the Catholics, became an important centre for harbouring missionary priests, clay and rushes sound-proofing a large secret chamber. The domestic chapel, c. 1500, has a magnificent altarpiece installed by Charles Towneley (1737–1805), the celebrated collector of art treasures (many now housed in the British Museum), while Richard Towneley's kitchen was reconstructed in 1628. The old nurseries and family bedrooms have become spacious and lofty art galleries. A once derelict Brew-house, now beautifully restored, houses a museum of industries and crafts, and in the park, first acquired along with the property by Burnley Corporation in 1900 for the perpetual enjoyment of the public, a green knoll topped with railings indicates the Ice House, the 18th century equivalent of the domestic deep-freeze. In those days, ice was collected from ponds or frozen field-waters and deposited in a subterranean chamber with several feet of earth acting as insulation. The Ice House at Towneley can be inspected, by arrangement.

Sports facilities abound here. Turf Moor is the home of football and cricket, Clowbridge Reservoir provides sailing, fell-walkers and climbers head for Thursden Valley or Cliviger Gorge; dawdlers choose one of half a dozen fine parks in the district. Padiham is nearby and 16th century Gawthorpe Hall, built round a medieval pele tower — which shows how far south the wild Scotsmen came on their raiding sortees — and Brontë territory lies within comfortable reach, while within a short journey lie the remains of Whalley Abbey.

Nip over to Briercliffe where a band of Yorkshire counterfeiters and clippers had a hide-out, the Cragg Vale Coiners led by "King David" Hartley. He was hanged at York and is "supposed" to be buried at Heptonstall. Not far away from Briercliffe, an old weaving community with double windows in many an attic, "to get the length", with floors, window mullions and even staircases made out of durable local stone, stood a former "Robin Hood's House", though now only the foundations can be seen. Another reminder that hereabouts two great rival counties rub shoulders and relapse into a common lingo.

There are signs of prehistoric occupation on the moor on top of the quarry at Rotherham Gate, near Twist Reservoir, and a Roman fort, never excavated, is still visible. Over at Castercliff, excavations have uncovered an Iron Age hill fort with Roman overtones, and Worsthorne is proud of its Ringstones.

Beneath that lonely moor that rises to the peaty plateau of Black Hameldon Hill lies the dead-end hamlet of Hurstwood, famous for its associations with Edmund Spenser, the Elizabethan courtier-poet who penned the "Faerie Queen", and the "Shepherd's Calendar", his first published work (1579). The ancient and attractive house where he spent several years with relatives, during which time he fell desperately in love with a local lady whom he lost to a rival, is still there up a farm track leading from Hurstwood Hall, another Elizabethan house built by the Towneleys. Spenser, who delighted the Virgin Queen with his readings "at timely hours", and whose works she considered of "wondrous worth", did eventually marry an Irish girl, and had by her two sons, Sylvanus and Peregrine, who were left without provision when "The prince of poets in his tyme" died penniless and "for lacke of bread" though at the height of his fame and still in his forties. They buried him close to Chaucer in Westminster Abbey, this London-born Lancastrian who grieved over-long for his Lancashire Rosalynd and could not prevent her from stealing, in all her wit and beauty, into many of his later works.

The Whitaker family's long association with Holme, set amongst trees in the most pictorial portion of the deep Calder valley, began in 1347 when Richard de Whitacre wooed and won the heiress. The original timber hall survived until 1603 when the middle portion and east wing were reconstructed in stone but the remaining wing hung together until 1717, when that too was replaced. Holme was and is an attractive house in a beautiful setting and the Whitakers were worthy custodians, producing men of ability and several with a literary bent. One, Dr. William Whitaker, D.D., born here in 1577 and first educated at Burnley, was taken to London and placed in St. Paul's School by his uncle, Alexander Nowell of Read, Dean of St. Paul's and author of several learned works on doctrinal or theological matters. The nephew also took up the pen, expressing himself and his Calvinist views most elegantly in latin and earning, at the age of 22, Queen Elizabeth's appointment as Regius Professor of Divinity at Cambridge. Even Catholics respected him as "a most learned heretic".

It was a later Whitaker who is best known in this county. Dr. Thomas Dunham Whitaker, LL.D., would have been born at Holme on 8th June, 1759, except that his father happened to be curate at Rainham in Norfolk. Nevertheless, he was Lancashire to the last fibre, and when he was seven years of age, his father, who had inherited Holme in 1760, placed him under the tutelage of the Rev. John Shaw of Rochdale, whence he proceeded to Cambridge, secured a degree, considered taking up the law, but returned instead to Holme on the death of his father and launched into a programme of improvements, including new plantations. Three years later he entered holy orders and in 1785 paid £400 to regain patronage of the living of Holme, held for so long by his ancestors who secured it after the dissolution of Whalley Abbey. The dear little church was crumbling, its grounds choked with weeds, and a congregation of rooks kicked up a perpetual cacophony from the sycamore grove. Dr. Whitaker commenced his restoration work in 1788,

HOLME IN CLIVIGER (home of the Whitaker family for generations) is an ancient house, timber originally, rebuilt in stone *c.* 1602, added to subsequently and set in the picturesque Calder ravine. The mullioned windows are particularly notable. The historian, Dr. T. D. Whitaker, planted thousands of trees in the late 18th century, providing a splendid backcloth to this comely Tudor hall.

incorporating 16th century carved panelling, adding a bell turret with an octagonal cupola, Perpendicular pulpit, oak stalls with misericords from the parish church of Blackburn and other features. His heart was in the work; his parents were buried there; and the man was a dedicated historian. On his own nomination, he was licensed to the perpetual curacy of Holme in 1797, and subsequently became Rector of Heysham, then in 1809, Vicar of Whalley until 1818 when he took the living of Blackburn.

Dr. Whitaker will forever be remembered for his "History of Whalley", his "History of Craven" and other scholarly works, and for elegance of prose and diligence in accumulating archives. The beautifully wooded area around Holme is, to a great degree, due to his landscape artist's eye; and many of the furnishings in the Hall were there in his day and long before that, used and loved and cherished, as were the books in his study, which he pored over and consulted, along with his Amanuensis who shared the labours. He married Lucy Thoresby whose ancestor, Ralph Thoresby published a topography of Leeds in 1715 and a history of the church in 1724. Dr. Whitaker corrected and extended Thoresby's work and brought out a new edition in 1816. The worthy Doctor died at the end of 1821, having left instructions, faithfully carried out, that his body be interred beneath a larch tree which he himself had planted in 1786, and having passed on to posterity, through his devotion and industry, a wealth of knowledge that might otherwise have lapsed into the silence of the forgotten.

Nelson and Colne

Fans of the "Juliet Bravo" series on B.B.C. Television will have recognised Nelson in the fictional "Hartley". Almost accidentally, Nelson grew out of two old settlements of Great and Little Marsden when they put a railway halt near a pub called the "Lord Nelson". There was human activity here in the Bronze Age, however, and coins have turned up from the Roman "Colunio". By Tudor times trade in woollen outstripped that of neighbouring Colne and in the 18th century handlooms clattered in every attic or kitchen. The Ecroyds built their Edge End factory in 1740 and Lomeshaye Mill, powered by water, in 1780, both attracting "little maisters" from their upland steads into the factory system.

Marsden had a cotton mill in 1784; others followed. There was water, coal, too, and skilled men to build steam engines for the mills. The warm out-flow kept the Leeds & Liverpool Canal from freezing over in the severest winters. The splendid Victorian Gothic Town Hall is proof of Nelson's go-ahead spirit though Pevsner sniffs at the place as "entirely inarticulate" and "depressing". The contraction of the textile industry has hit the place, but Nelson is far too intelligent and ingenious to go under, switching instead to engineering of all kinds, plastics, clothing, food, soft drinks and a variety of trades. This is a soft water area. There were two chalybeate springs in the district. The countryside for miles around, dominated by Pendle (1,831 ft.) is quite superb. To the east, moors rising to 1,110 ft. sweep over to Bronté-land and Haworth.

Music making is another surprising facet of this area where cotton and choral singing went naturally together. Nelson Civic Ladies' Choir, memorable for superb television performances and formed in 1949 as a Children's Choir by a local headmaster, now ranks among the top choirs in Europe. The perfect blending of voices produces an angelic quality of sound, justifying the claim that there is more music in Nelson than anywhere else in the world! Certainly, this choir is good to look upon, row upon row of lovely, honest, wholesome countenances rapt in the creating of that special sound which one associates with the foothills of Old Pendle; and anyone who thinks Lancashire is too hard-headed and money-grubbing to know anything about culture should buy himself a one-way ticket to the Nelson area, for a start!

One of the nation's most honoured local historians was born at Little Marsden in 1861. Dr. William Farrer, who dropped the family name of Ecroyd at the age of 35 upon inheriting a fortune from a great-uncle, was the son of Wm. Farrer Ecroyd, woollen merchant and M.P. for Preston. He wrote many learned works, was co-Editor of the "Victoria History of the County of Lancaster" in 8 volumes; purchased Hallgarth, a Georgian mansion at Over Kellet, whence hailed his maternal relatives, the Backhouses; and was awarded Honorary Degrees and appointments for a lifetime of writing and research. Manchester Public Libraries acquired his Lancashire papers in 1931.

"Bonny Colne" has a different story, of spinning and weaving going back before memory, of a Royal Charter of 1296 for markets and fairs, of links with the Romans at Castercliff and evidence of Christian missions before the Normans conquered. A lifetime later, St. Bartholomew's Church was built on a ridge between Wanless Water on one side and Colne Water on the other, a little country church of 1122 which still has original fabric. When I first saw it, the old stones were black as the fire-back with centuries of industrial grime. They smartened it up by whitewashing the outside in the 1830's. Now, after a stone-clean, it is full of charm and dignity after keeping faithful vigil for eight and a half centuries. The style is mostly late Perpendicular; the embattled tower is low and sturdy. Above the open porch is a curious cube sun-dial — I cannot recall another — and to the right-hand are three stone steps from which the parson preached in fine weather.

Stocks on wheels, a quaint mobile contraption providing for three sinners to be publicly shamed at the same time, can be found in the churchyard, a precaution against rowdies at the fairs! It was last used in June 1850. The old grammar school, founded about 1640, stands in the churchyard. What competition there would be last century for those six free, precious, coveted places for local boys!

Within, there is much to fascinate — rounded Norman pillars that could be original (they were tilting and threatening to fall down until 1815), an invocation in Latin by former Vicar, William Hyrd, to the Blessed Virgin to protect him against horrid phantoms in the hour of his passing, in 1508; Tudor screens, memorials to the Emmotts of Emmott Hall and the Parkers of Alkancoates; and hatchments, one from the Cunliffes of Wycoller Hall that now stands in ruins a few miles away, a sore point with me. The last true Cunliffe, buried at Colne, was old Squire Henry who died in 1773, twice wed but childless. He left Wycoller to another nephew, Henry Owen, on condition that he assumed the name Cunliffe, instead of to his first choice, Thomas Eyre of Sheffield, his sister Elizabeth's boy. In the days of primogeniture, younger sons of younger sons of the great landowning, freebooting Eyres, custodians of the Royal Forest of High Peak in Derbyshire from Henry III's time, had followed varying fortunes, some crossing the stark moors into Sheffield and descending into trade. Thomas's father was a Master Cutler, his offspring Catholics. Every time the youth visited Wycoller, his Uncle Henry enquired if he still had "the Pope in his belly", and when he proved steadfast to the Old Faith he was cut off with the proverbial shilling while Henry Owen inherited who, in turn, died childless in 1818, propped up in his deathbed, they said, watching cocks fighting on the floor of his chamber. This argumentative, sporting, gambling country squire, a "low life rascal" according to some, extended the hall considerably after 1774 and left mortgages and debts that caused the carve-up of the estates and the decay of Wycoller Hall. It would all have been so very different if the fecund Eyres had inherited and we would not to-day be gazing with tremendous affection, because of its Bronté associations, upon a roofless ruin that must weep for its lost splendours.

The name Hartley is significant around Colne. (Sir) William Pickles Hartley was born here in 1846, left the Grammar School at fifteen, helped in his mother's little grocery business, began jam making, prospered, sold out and invested in a fruit preserving factory at Liverpool. His name became famous at home and abroad and his wealth promoted many public benefactions. Hartley Hospital lies along the Keighley Road near Laneshaw Bridge, the gateway to romantic Wycoller where three daughters of Haworth Parsonage were wont to roam, talking if at all in subdued tones, remembering everything. Here, though she couldn't know that, was the "Ferndean Manor" of Charlotte's masterpiece, "Jane Eyre". The area is a Country Park now, and life is returning to properties which the handloom weavers abandoned when the factory life beckoned them away. It is a fascinating exercise to cross the Dene by one of the ancient bridges and strike out on foot across the moors, past ruined homesteads and the Brontë Falls, towards Haworth, though just to dawdle at Wycoller is pleasure enough.

Another Hartley from Colne perished with the "Titanic" which sank during her maiden voyage in May 1912 after striking an iceberg. Wallace Hartley, to whom there is a beautiful monument, a music-loving former bank clerk, was bandmaster on the doomed vessel and the story of those brave bandsmen playing "Nearer my God to Thee" as that floating palace tilted and slid under the icy waters, has gone into history.

Way back in July 1789 a villainous young man, Christopher Hartley of Barnside, first poisoned, then all but decapitated his pregnant sweetheart, pretty Hannah Corbridge of Laneshaw Bridge. He hid the body at home in an oaken chest for a day or two, then buried it in fields near Barnside Hall. The mystery of Hannah's disappearance was solved by a local wise-man who "sensed" what had happened. Sure enough, according to an account in Colne parish registers, she was found dead in a ditch with throat so deeply cut that her head hung on by two ligaments and in later years, when Barnside Hall was dismantled, there were rumours of stones oozing blood where the murderer had rubbed his hands clean after the awful deed. Hannah's ghost upset farmers around Barnside until a Catholic priest performed an exorcism whereby her restless spirit was released from earth bondage.

C.H.A. and Holiday Fellowship, a movement that enriched innumerable lives, was born at Colne in 1891 when a Congregational Minister, the Rev. T. A. Leonard, organised a four-day walking and climbing holiday at Ambleside for thirty young men, guaranteeing that it would cost no more than a Guinea a head! They set off on Saturday, 12th June, 1891, walked the following morning to Dungeon Ghyll, held a service within sound of the Falls. They studied Nature, gazed enraptured on lakeland scenes and came home with bodies refreshed, minds stretched, and a determination to repeat the exercise, at Keswick next time, and "other lovely places". "Food, beds and good fellowship" were at the heart of those cheap, wholesome holidays which quickly caught the popular fancy and the Association was formally established.

Mounting numbers joined. A good week's holiday would cost only 30/- (£1.50) and 12/- (60p) would buy a return train ticket. The impact was tremendous. Young Victorians enjoyed the rare opportunity of meeting the opposite sex, outside chapel or church, in an atmosphere of equality and goodwill, though perhaps females were welcomed with some reservations in the first place. Responsible hostesses were appointed to uphold virtuous standards and fears gradually subsided.

Canon Rawnsley, Vicar of Crosthwaite, supported the movement and led many an early Lakeland walk. He, Ruskin and T. A. Leonard shared the same ideals of wholesomeness, excellence and quality of life, maintaining that Man has a choice between high and low, and can never achieve true happiness until he has learnt to enjoy doing the right things and to take an elevated view of his own human nature. The underlying philosophy was inspirational:

> "Truth breathed by cheerfulness . . .
> Spontaneous wisdom breathed by health!"

The founder, T. Arthur Leonard, loyally helped by his wife, became General Secretary as the movement gathered strength and spread overseas long before popular package holidays were thought of.

14. THE ROSSENDALE VALLEY

Bacup

Beyond Haslingden spreads the ancient Forest of Rossendale, an area most beautiful and eminently favoured by Nature. There is no forest, as such, nor has there been for many a long century, but the contours soar and swoop dramatically and in the valley bottom the road winding through ancient manufacturing communities is at times reminiscent of a mountain pass in miniature.

The new Rossendale Borough, formed in 1974, took in Haslingden (town of the hazels), Bacup, Rawtenstall, Whitworth and part of Ramsbottom and the setting for miles is utterly dramatic. We may no longer hear "clogs before dawn tapping a dotted line of sound through peat and bracken" but the wild moorlands and stone quarries are not far away, and hills rising to 1300 feet. "Here English soil is more ancient than anywhere else", wrote C. E. Montague, "for here alone the edges of towns . . . are frayed against ridges of rock that were old before the site of London was made".

In this region "th'owd lingo" survives in all its richness and humour and the visitor is accorded a welcome as warm as the old gritstone houses are enduring. Long before its turgid waters separate the two cities of Manchester and Salford, the River Irwell, aided by its tributaries, drains the Rossendale Fells and proceeds through Waterfoot and Rawtenstall, having risen not far from Bacup at the head of the valley. Bacup is a smallish manufacturing town with hills rising up on three sides to 1550 feet but, whereas once there were numerous working cotton mills in the district, now there is only one and, even about that, no-one cares to give any guarantees. The manufacture of shoes and slippers has become the principal occupation with printing, felt-making and quarrying running alongside.

Incidentally, I was fortunate in Burnley to visit a gracious elderly lady who told me about her Great-Grandfather McClerie, a Scotsman from Busby, outside Glasgow, who came down to Lancashire to make his fortune. He settled in the Rossendale Valley when everything was centred on cotton and he noticed that at the end of a gruelling day in the mill the workers gratefully stepped out of their clogs and spent the evening in bare or stockinged feet. The mill-masters, by contrast, could afford comfortable slippers, and it occurred to the Scotsman that the operatives also deserved decent leisure footwear and he began experimenting with pieces of felt. As soon as sewing machines appeared on the market he bought and adapted one for slipper making and eventually he opened a factory in Rossendale. My informant firmly believes that it was her ancestor who launched the trade for which the valley and Bacup are still famous.

Bacup has a flourishing Local History Society which takes a pride in its past and supports a well-stocked museum of Local Antiquariana and Natural History, housed in a building which is not short on history, for it began as a couple of cottages, became a pub, then a common lodging house. Across the road, re-erected on the lawn in front of the modern Health Centre, are the old stocks and a hefty stone-crushing circle brought down from Guide Quarry on the moors towards Todmorden. It was operated by horse power and I reckon the most determined vandals would blunt their energies without dislodging this ponderous device for crushing lumps of rock into fragments.

Bacup's town centre is over 800 feet above sea level but Parrock Mill at Sharneyford at 1250 feet was the highest mill in the country. This is a musical area. The hymn tune "Bacup" was composed by the Rev. J. E. Roscoe, Vicar of Christ Church, and Irwell Springs Band won the Brass Band Championship of Great Britain three times at the Crystal Palace. On Easter Saturdays, the Britannia Coconutters, a unique troupe of folk dancers, famous at home and overseas, black up, put on their black velvet, clogs and fancy hats and dance all round the villages, and on Saturdays Bacup has a small open air market. You can track down bargains in footwear, poke around 19th century churches, head for the boundless desolate moors, and picture the "Plugdrawers" of 1842 setting out from here with stakes and crowbars, ransacking shops and inns for food and drink, dowsing factory fires and draining factory boilers on their way to Halifax and Bradford to demand higher wages. Times were grim, working hours had been cut back, the death rate had soared and in desperation the operatives were agitating for the People's Charter. The demonstration, resulting in riots and arrests, achieved little in August 1842 nor in the renewed Chartist surge of 1847–8 accompanied by urban violence. The Rochdale Co-operative movement was more successful in the painful evolution of the democratic system; but from to-day's comfortable viewpoint it would ill become us to look back disparagingly on the workers who became agitators during those grim Hungry Forties.

The situation of Bacup, surrounded by boundless moors and glorious open plateaus and hillsides, has great appeal for those who like to get away from it all. Thieveley Pike (1,474 ft.) is the high point of Rossendale Forest and a motorist's Mecca. Along the Burnley Road are Broadclough Dykes, a system of grass covered mounds and earthworks enwrapped in legends going back to Saxon times which appeal to the archaeologist and antiquarian. But during a recent visit, wandering among the older stone houses that must have been there during the Plug Riots, and noticing an old-timer nodding off in the sun on a bench bearing the name of Harry Craven, I was reminded of a popular L.A.A. member among whose homely masterpieces "A Draughty Heawse" and his rendering of it stand out.

Here is a short extract:

> Aw'm frozzen stiff, do wod Aw will —
> Yon heawse o' mine gets cowder still!
> It seems to goo fro' bad to worse,
> It isn't worth a tinker's curse;
> Aw'm plagued wi' every wail an' whine
> o't'boggart winds i' wintertime.
> Aw couldn't sleep a wink las' neet
> Fer chronic cramp an' deeod feet!
>
> When t'deein' fire shunts deawn in th'grate
> Aw wekken up as cowd as slate.
> My arms are numb an' on mi legs
> Ther's goose-lumps big as pigeon eggs.
> Aw poke an' prod, an' rake th'owd bars
> Still th'embers fly like shootin' stars.
> Wife drops her book an sez: "Neaw, then!
> Thee shap' fer bed, it's hofe-past TEN!

It is no better when he goes upstairs where the carpets swish and curtain swings "An' th'oilcloth flaps an' beats like wings" and his wife won't join him until he's got the place warmed up and he reckons it will be cosier, one day, down in the family vault!

> Aw've left instructions, when Aw flit —
> Thee build mi tomb o' millstone grit;
> Til that day cooms Aw'll grunt an' greawse,
> Aw'm livin' in a draughty heawse!

Harry, who had been an impressive opening bowler for Sharneyford Methodists, but whose heart and tongue and pen were devoted to Lancashire dialect, lived at Stacksteads but worked at Bacup for a printing firm whose proprietor kindly showed me the machine on which he had toiled until his death in 1971. I can scarcely believe that so many years have rolled by since his last recital at the Lancashire Authors', since his poetical sparring partner Clifford Heyworth ("Bill o' Bow's"), with whom he ever corresponded in rhyme, penned this tribute:

> Farewell, Owd Brid, thy singin's done.
> A gradely rest be thine.
> Through generations still to come —
> Thy name shall ever shine . . .

Although, too soon, tha's ta'en thi hook
    An' left this earthly wom,
May many a mon, an' mony a book
    Quote thee, fer years to com'.

Amen to that! God love thee, Owd Songster! Aw'm fain Bacup honoured thee wi' a Memorial Neet at Mechanics' Institute an' put yon gardin seeat to thy memory in t'middle o't'teawn!

Bacup has every right to hold its head up in pride, for it was visits here, the "Bacup adventure", which gave a "decisive turn to my self-development", wrote Beatrice Potter, Socialist-Author-Reformer-Bluestocking and one of the most eminent women of last century. She worked with Octavia Hill, served on Royal Commissions into capital and labour questions and the Poor Law and eventually, after keeping the poor man dangling for years, married Sidney Webb, leading Fabian and friend of G. B. Shaw. But it was Bacup that determined her future as "an investigator of social conditions", and the good mill folk who arrived home "quite worn out with the day's toil" and yet retained a simple piety, a natural refinement and a "quite classical" way of talking which charmed their listener's ear. Her cousins were among them for, though Beatrice was a leading literary figure who had grown up in a country mansion in Gloucestershire in material comfort and with the freedom to pursue an independent path among the progressives, particularly in the capital, she was as Lancashire as black puddings, on both sides! Her paternal grandfather sat as a Radical M.P. for Wigan after the Reform Act in 1832. His brother sat for Manchester. Between them, they founded "The Manchester Guardian". On the maternal side, Grandfather Lawrence Heyworth manufactured woollens, became a rich Liverpool merchant, sat as M.P. for Derby, but married a cousin from Bacup who worked in a mill. Their daughter, Lawrencina, married Beatrice's father, Richard Potter, and it was in his household that Beatrice spent much of her time up to her marriage with Sidney Webb in 1892.

In 1883 she visited Bacup incognito in the guise of "Miss Jones" from Wales, staying in Irwell Terrace at John Ashworth, the chapelkeeper's home. The haunting impression that Lancashire working folk were dominated by three influences, the mill, the co-operative society and the chapel, brought her back three years later when her first impressions were reinforced. "This is the only society I have ever lived in", she wrote, "in which religious faith really guides thought and action and forms the basis of the whole life of the individual and the community". On this occasion, in 1886, she stayed with different relatives at 5, Angel Street in Tong Lane, to whom she revealed her identity, and through whom she was able to investigate conditions of labour.

Ramsbottom

A 19th century township along the Irwell, surrounded by moors, famous for Dickensian connections. Harcles Hill (1,216 ft.) rises to the west, Whittle Hill (1,534 ft.) to the east. A range of hills commences at "Top o'th Hoof" where Grants' Tower stood, a landmark popular with generations of picnickers until it collapsed from neglect in 1943.

In 1783 William Grant from Morayshire, stood with his son, William, on that knoll, surveying that panoramic scene and wondering what the future had in store. William, Senior, carrying a letter of introduction to the famous Richard Arkwright, hoped to procure employment for himself and three sons old enough to be apprenticed. The rest of the family waited back in Scotland, unaware that Arkwright could offer nothing. However, James Dinwiddie, a Bury calico bleacher and printer, did offer work to the Grants. Grace Grant and her brood, Daniel being six months old at the time, knocked the Scottish mud from their brogues and embarked on a daunting journey into deepest Lancashire. The foundations of the Grant fortunes were laid.

At this period, cotton was burgeoning; enterprising men could get on in the world. Having mastered their trade, William Junior and Daniel prospered exceedingly and their father did well trading in fents from a shop in Bury. An older brother returned to Scotland, to calico bleaching, but William Junior, thirty years old at the dawn of a new century, headed Wm. Grant and Brothers in Cannon Street, the heart of industrial Manchester. Twenty-five years later they owned a spinning mill at Nuttall and Robert Peel Senior's bleaching works at Ramsbottom, a haphazard mess of buildings which they replaced with Square Mill, the most modern of its kind in Europe — both operated by water-power which was plentiful. A younger brother, John, farmed 300 acres at Nuttall with outstanding success and the Grants had much cause for rejoicing. Daniel's young wife died within a year from childbirth and thereafter he consoled himself with a mistress, Elizabeth Brereton, an epileptic who brought him two sons, openly acknowledged and provided for. William, who lost an eye from falling on the fire after some silly adult, who threw him up in the air, failed to catch him on the way down, never married.

The mutual devotion and inseparability of the two brothers, a legend in Mancunian business circles, came to the attention of Charles Dickens when, at the age of 27, he was writing "Nicholas Nickleby" by instalments. His friend and fellow author, Harrison Ainsworth, gave him a letter of introduction to Solicitors James Crossley and Gilbert Winter of Manchester. Winter arranged a dinner party to which Dickens, his illustrator "Phiz" (Hablot Browne) and the Grants, William (69) and Daniel (56) were invited. The Cheeryble Brothers were born that evening, noted, as were their originals, for benevolence, honest dealing, concern for their work-folk and brotherly love.

Six years before his death in 1842, out of his considerable fortune, William Grant laid the corner stone of St. Andrew's Church, Ramsbottom, with full Masonic pomp and ceremony. Daniel died in 1855 and the two inseparables share the same vault in Ramsbottom's "Cheeryble Church" where Vicar R. R. Carmyllie is an authority on the Grant family and their romantic flight from persistent floods in Scotland to wealth and immortality in Lancashire, England.

Whitworth and the famous family of doctors

One day, someone with sufficient nous will organise British Heritage Holidays based on this part of Lancashire where literally everything awaits the curious traveller, glorious views, historic halls, literary shrines, canals and all the clutter of industry, fantastic cultural and sporting amenities and a wealth of

GRANT'S TOWER near Top o'th' Hoof between Ramsbottom and Bury, c. 1900 at the height of its popularity as a picnic spot. After years of neglect, it collapsed in 1943.

Lancashire folklore and legend. Such a project would include an excursion to Whitworth, a moorland township which was little more than a hamlet lying off the Bacup–Rochdale road when medical history was being made 200 years ago and a family or gruff blacksmiths and farriers, turned bone-setters and surgeons, were actually curing cancers!

Their name was Taylor. Their origins are hazy, but they sprang from honest Lancashire stock and they were clever enough to read and write and study herb lore, handy for the treatment of animals. These astute, hard-working, straight-talking chaps were sensible enough to marry industrious helpmeets who got on well together and became dab hands at making salves, pills, potions and plasters in wholesale quantities as the fame of the Whitworth Doctors spread far beyond this hilly region. Most outstanding — and they practised with huge success through half a dozen generations — was "Dr. John" Taylor (1740–1802) who had no formal training but plenty of natural sagacity, immense moral courage and an almost womanly insight into the fleshly ills of both man and beast.

The tale goes that early in the 1760's he was returning over the hills from Halifax heading for Bacup where there were family connections, looking for somewhere to start up in the farriery business. As darkness descended, he considered it prudent to tarry overnight at Whitworth where he learned that the local blacksmith was laid aside through illness. He stayed to help out before proceeding to Bacup where he quickly decided that Whitworth offered a better opening. Soon after his return, the local blacksmith died and the smithy trade naturally came John Taylor's way. His skills commended him to all the remote hill farmers for miles around and his instinct for diagnosing and treating animals earned him the reputation of "a clever young fellow". He gathered his own herbs and simples, mixed his own concoctions and compounds. They worked well on horses, cows and dogs, and customers began to assume that John's remedies might be equally effective with humans. He also had a remarkable flair for setting fractured limbs in the days when a homely do-it-yourself job with the aid of a broom handle resulted in some hideous and permanent deformities. In such cases, John would secure the patient to the railings, back off, work up a good turn of speed, approach with a flying kick, smash the limb and start again!

Amazing queues began to form and medical matters outstripped the work at the smithy. John coped by taking his brother George and later his sons James and John into the practice, and George's two boys also joined the team. The doctors moved to Whitworth House, a gracious, double-fronted stone house which is still there, not far from the Red Lion where patients from a distance took lodgings. (During a visit a couple of years ago I was graciously invited to look round by the young owners and it was a tremendous thrill to wonder through the doctors' consulting rooms and the kitchens where their womenfolk presided over boilers, pillboards, pestles and mortars).

The fees charged were identical in all cases, 1/6d. (7½p) a week (later raised to 2/- (10p)) including all operations, applications and medicaments, and it was "first come, first served" with both peers and paupers. At the end of the stay, a whole year's specifics could be purchased and taken home for 6/- (30p). Many eminent personages, in great faith and at not a little inconvenience, headed for Whitworth and mingled with sickly beggars and whey-faced peasants who wandered up the village street in their hundreds. On Sundays, the Doctors bled their patients free of charge, one applying the ligature, another opening the vein, the third binding up. Their famous Red Rubbing Bottle was sold on markets all around; and folks swore by their digestive mixture. They boiled salves and ointments in their gallons, purchased Glauber Salts by the hogshead, thrust mis-shapen feet into metal boots and sent cripples hobbling away to exercise, willy nilly, across a moorland path known ever after as "Cripples' Walk". Treatment directed against surface cancers was as crude and direct as the others. A corrosive substance called "Keen", which must have caused excruciating agonies, was applied to the affected part for as long as the patient could bear it. Then the effect was halted by the application of a soothing substance. Some stoics bore it for an hour or two each day. Others spread the treatment over a longer period. Either way, it was pure torture . . . yet it worked (probably in a manner similar to Radium to-day).

The tale of a brave lady who had come from afar with an advanced cancer of the breast has gone into the rag bag of folk lore and legends. Dr. John weighed up the situation and asked why she had come. "To be cured, to be sure", she told him. Bluntly, he replied that she was beyond help and might as well pack up, go home again, and dee! With equal gusto, she challenged him to prove his worth, boasting that she could bear any treatment he dared to dish out! "Tha'rt a brave wooman!", he conceded at last. "Aw' reet! Aw'll try mi hond, and may God prosper us both!" After months of suffering, the cancer was completely cleared. The patient returned home, lived healthily for thirty years more and undoubtedly helped to spread the fame of the Whitworth Doctors.

Brother George specialised in bone-setting, as did John's two sons later on. When they visited patients in their homes, they charged 1/- a mile, including medical attention. Dr. John, who was slandered, resented and dismissed as a "quack" by the orthodox medics, was quick to remind them that they charged infinitely more for their killing and curing. Indeed, there was a contagious cheerfulness in his attitudes and conversations which inspired confidence in his patients. They treasured his wise and witty sayings uttered with a light unforced laugh that betokened a mind entirely at ease. "Care is an enemy to life", he would declare, or: "A light heart lives long!" Those who became too impatient were reminded that a wound never did heal "but by degrees!"

On Mondays, Dr. John held surgeries at the Angel Hotel, Lord Street, Rochdale, where he addressed the crowds in homely terms. An Irish Bishop who came over too late to consult him about an advanced cancer of the tongue died in Rochdale and was buried in the Parish Churchyard in November 1800 but there were many illustrious names on his list and his fame extended at last to the Royal Family. It happened after John had travelled to Cheltenham to attend a dying Duchess whose life he saved by lancing an abscess. The great lady, who was in waiting to Queen Charlotte, sang the praises of the straight-talking chap from the north, and King George III promptly called him in to treat the Princess Elizabeth's "head complaint" which was probably a sinus condition.

Now, in the back garden of Whitworth House grew the rare woodland plant *Asarabacca Europaeum* of which the dried leaves could be powdered into a potent stuff. Dr. John left a goodly supply with the young Princess who spent the night all but sneezing her royal head off. BUT . . . she was cured! So was a lady patient whom Catherine Hutton met at Blackpool in 1788 and who had endured the "Keen" treatment for one, two or three hours daily to eradicate cancer. "She married and has children", wrote Catherine, "but her constitution seems to have received a shock", she added, supposing that the lady might the more wisely have taken longer over the business. But then, the whole Lancashire visit came as a shock to Catherine's delicate sensibilities though she was moved to comment, in a blinding flash of enlightenment: "The people of the north are not equal to those of the south in refinement, but they surpass them in sincerity!" (And with that candid comment I would not presume to quarrel).

The doctors, who were capable, confident and maybe even a trifle eccentric, were unique in their or any other day; and their innate courage inspired them to tackle what more orthodox hands would never have attempted. They were no money-grubbers. Large rewards from rich men were diverted into the Subscription Box from which fees for the penniless were taken. No-one was turned away on account of poverty and every patient could visit the surgery as often as he liked for the same modest weekly fee. The practice brought fame and prosperity undreamed of to this obscure hillside community. Cottage lodgings and the Red Lion were perpetually full. The streets were crammed with groaning, hopeful patients, and at the front door of Whitworth House, until modern times, was a wooden contraption for securing horses during operations. The Taylors never lost their partiality for their original patients and would forsake a waiting room bulging with more than a hundred humans to go and attend "yon hoss". At other times, when the atmosphere became unendurable, they would rush out into the sweet fragrant air without explanation or apology, saddle up, summon the hounds kept at the back, and go hunting for an hour or two over the wild moors. It was all accepted with tolerance and good humour for the Taylors were the last hope of many and their fame, having spread far beyond Lancashire, ranked them amongst the most remarkable men in the kingdom.

Dr. John died in January 1802 from a stroke during a night of violent storm and was buried with due honours in the churchyard nearby. Dr. George died in 1804. Each left two sons who, between them, branched out at Todmorden, Oldfield Lane, Salford, Huddersfield, and outposts in Cheshire, in addition to the Whitworth practice and Rochdale surgeries. Later generations entered the profession by more orthodox means after training in London and when the last of them, Dr. James Taylor, died in 1876, crowds swarmed into Whitworth from miles around to pay their last respects to the most outstanding medical dynasty of all time. There was no Taylor available to take over. It was the end of an era, of a tradition which commenced in 1764 when John Taylor, Blacksmith/Farrier/Herbalist and a "reet clever young fellow" arrived in the village . . . now part of Rossendale Borough.

Whitworth House is still there, and Cripples' Walk where the halt and lame took exercise beyond the steeply rising church path paved with setts; and the Red Lion with its front square yard and the churchyard entrance leading directly to the Taylor memorials. The mischievous thought may occur to you that the burial ground rises steeply above the stream flowing behind Whitworth House from which supplies for medicines would be taken by the doctors' wives! (Plenty of body in it, you might say!) St. Bartholomew's Church has the Royal Arms of William and Mary carved on the porch. It was rebuilt (1775) while young John Taylor was still making his name, and again in 1850. There is a "Taylor Street" here; an atmosphere of the dramatic past; and evidence that sand-blasters have been busy scouring the grime from honest stone houses and revealing their biscuit-fresh and enduring beauty.

Rawtenstall

In 1891, a number of separate communities like Crawshawbooth, Goodshawfold, Constable Lee, where the Constable of the ancient forest once dwelt in a clearing, Loveclough, Lumb, Newchurch, Water, Waterfoot and Whitewell Bottom, were swept into the Borough of Rawtenstall which in turn, in 1974, was absorbed into the new Borough of Rossendale.

By its very geography, Rawtenstall (pronounced "Rott'nstall", meaning "roaring pool or stream") in the upper Vale of Irwell, gravitated towards industry. The great Forest or Royal Chase of Rossendale once had eleven vaccaries or cow pastures. It was Henry VII who authorised its disafforestation which was more or less accomplished by 1500. The soil, however, was not of the top quality for agriculture at that time and the self-employed "little Maisters" who, of necessity, grew their own food, concentrated on home production of woollens. The whole area remained pretty wild and difficult of access even into last century.

Rawtenstall's modern commercial story probably began in the 1820's when the Whitehead Brothers built the steam-powered Higher Mill. The railway came through from Manchester and Bury in 1846 and workers flooded into the Valley attracted by prospects of regular work and wages. Twenty years later there were more than 150 mills in the area, all of them badly hit by the Great Cotton Famine. Rawtenstall's "Pop-balls" take their name from the days when there were five pawn-brokers or "pop-shops" in the town. Luckily, the Lancastrians' adaptability and willingness to diversify came to the rescue and the availability of premises and idle hands combined to launch the slipper industry, an off-shoot of the felt trade. During the last war, for instance, Rawtenstall manufactured gun-cotton which helped our nation to victory but further polluted the long-suffering Irwell.

To-day, Rawtenstall has motorway links with Manchester and Hull, splendid access by roads from both sides of the Pennines and a variety of manufactories from the traditional textiles and footwear to engineering and modern science-based concerns. The area has much to fascinate the student of industrial archaeology, from Higher Mill, Helmshore and left-overs from the old lead and coal mining days to one of the best little museums in the north, in Whitaker Park, which tells you everything about clogs and how to make them. The fell walker finds his Nirvana on the breezy uplands where there are views across many miles of moorland and hill farmers tend their sheep flocks and somehow wrest a living from the steep fells and valley sides; and anyone wishing to examine 19th century church architecture can find numerous examples hereabouts to be studied. The tower of St. Mary's soaring out of the trees against a backdrop of moorland has a curious little spire on its turret and St. John's (1890) at Crawshawbooth looks solid enough to defy every blustering breeze for ever and ever.

Rawtenstall at 825 ft. above sea level is a town of stone houses, steeply rising hair-pins and the almost obligatory post-war shopping piazza. When the handsome Public Library was opened in 1907 the donor, Andrew Carnegie, came over personally to inaugurate it and for that they made him Rawtenstall's second Honorary Freeman. Over 100 years ago a chap called Poplin started from here and captured "The Champion Clog Walker of the World" Award with 20 minutes to spare! One shouldn't be surprised, therefore, to discover one of the longest artificial ski slopes in the country out at Cribden, with restaurant, 177-yard toboggan run, and all!

15. SOUTH-EAST LANCASHIRE

Bolton

Lancashire, now and for ever, though swept into Greater Manchester during the great boundary re-shuffle, Bolton, always a progressive town, was the birthplace of great men with original ideas. In every respect, it is a satisfying place to visit, having splendid shops, stirring history, handsome municipal buildings, a fine art collection and superb theatre. The standards maintained at The Octagon are consistently high and memories of performances there linger for ages.

Bolton-le-Moors, to give its correct title, was a community cradled in heathered wastes and surrounded by darkling moorlands, long before the Conquest. Its inhabitants engaged in textiles and in 1337 there was a modest influx of Flemish clothiers and weavers who clattered about in clogs but did NOT introduce the fashion! The British were wearing wooden footwear a thousand years ago.

Bolton lads were bonny fighters at Flodden Field under Sir Edward Stanley whose "high Accomplishments in the Art of War" and the valour of his archers secured a great victory for Henry VIII. John Leland, the king's antiquary, noted "Bolton apon Moore Market (which) stondith most by cottons and cowrse yarn", but he was referring to woollens. The old chronicler died in 1552, confused and worn out by prodigious travelling and recording; and it was several decades later that cotton was introduced into the county.

The Parish Church of St. Peter, rebuilt in 14th century style in the 1860's, is perched high above the Croal, once crystal clear and teeming with trout. It succeeded a more ancient edifice with Saxon fragments and its list of Vicars reaches back to the late 15th century. Three hundred years later, unlike much of the county, a strong Puritan element turned Bolton into a "Geneva of the North". During the Civil Wars the town stood for Parliament, repulsing two Royalist attacks in 1642 only to face bloody retribution in 1644. On 28th May, 12,000 Royalists headed by the King's nephew, Prince Rupert of the Rhine, stormed Bolton, defended only by 4,000 troops under Col. Rigby, and lost 200 men. Rupert's vengeful cry rang out: "No quarter!", whereupon the attackers, under the command of the Earl of Derby, surged forward, perpetrated the most terrible atrocities on helpless citizens, men, women and infants, pursued and hacked down until the waters of the Croal were stained crimson. C. Allen Clarke, the Bolton writer who flitted to the Fylde, recreates the story in every lurid detail in "The Lass at the Man and Scythe" (1891).

This blackest incident in the bitter internecine struggle had fatal repercussions for James Stanley, the 7th Earl of Derby. When the first two phases of the conflict had died down, and when the King had been executed and all seemed hopeless, he returned to the fray in 1651 from his Isle of Man Kingdom, was captured after the Battle of Worcester and sentenced by Puritan judges at Chester to be executed at Bolton where memories were still painful. On an October day, he arrived in the town before the scaffold, close to Bolton Cross, was made ready, and for his last few hours he rested at "Ye Olde Man & Scythe", chatting with friends. To the last moments, he was dignified and composed, "with a good and quiet conscience, without Malice to any". He handed over two pieces of gold to the headsman, forgave his enemies and praised his courageous wife. The axe fell as he prayed whereupon sighs and sobs burst forth from the assembled multitudes. The Earl's remains were conveyed to Ormskirk and the curtain was lowered on the Civil War.

Gazing down on these tumults from moorland slopes north-west of the town was Smithills, one of the oldest manor houses in the county. By tradition, a Chapel of the Blessed Virgin was consecrated here in 793 by the Bishop of Hexham, and at this place Egbert, father of King Alfred, held court. The 12th century Knights Hospitallers of St. John of Jersualem were followed by the Radclyffes and the Bartons, in 1485, by marriage to Cicily, the heiress. Afterwards came the Belasyses, the Byroms and the Ainsworths who sold out to Bolton Corporation in 1933.

Oldest is the Great Hall where the lord's family occupied the dais above the rest of the household though, in eating or sleeping, there was precious little comfort until Cicily's son, Andrew Barton, added the beautifully panelled Withdrawing Room with an oriel window, and a bedchamber above, c.1516. He also added the Chapel which was rebuilt in 1856 after a fire, and again restored and re-dedicated in 1957 through grants from the Ministry of Works, Pilgrim Trust, faithful Boltonians and ex-patriates.

Smithills has a fine whiff of antiquity about it and is open daily except on Thursdays in summer, and Thursdays and Sundays in winter. Senior Citizens have a home here and the Coach House is a popular restaurant. Look out for the legendary Bloody Footprint on a flagstone in the corridor where Vicar George Marsh of Deane stamped his foot in anger following the travesty of a trial at Smithills in 1554 in the reign of Mary Tudor. The Catholics were baying for blood; their taunts followed the good Vicar who had borne all with Christian forbearance and in an anguish he called upon Heaven to give some sign of the injustice. The ineradicable mark, probably a natural fault in the stone, has given rise to several legends, but remains a memorial to a Protestant Martyr who was carted off to Chester and there burned alive.

By the mid-17th century, fustians were finding their way to Bolton market, "the staple place for this commodity", according to Dr. Fuller writing in 1662. The production of woollen and cotton cloth became big business and in 1979 Bolton celebrated the bicentenary of an invention which revolutionised the textile industry throughout the English-speaking world.

Hall-i'th'-Wood and Lord Leverhulme

After Smithills, visit Hall-i'th'-Wood, off Crompton Way. It is beautiful, a jewel in Old Lancashire's crown, and when the Brownlows first built it in 1483 in black and white "magpie" style, it actually was deeply embowered in trees and a stream gurgling through the grounds came in handy for farming and processing cloth. An Elizabethan stone wing was added in 1591 and when the Norrises took over they built the most modern portion in 1648. For its own sake, it is a delight. As a shrine to slighted genius it tugs at the heart-strings. Wander through its ancient rooms among the Crompton relics and (unless you are extraordinarily insensitive) you can feel the presence of clever, gentle, dreamy Samuel, whom Destiny ill-used, and his capable and determined mother, Betsy Crompton.

The story began a mile away at Firwood Fold which lies off to the left of Crompton Way just after the traffic lights at the crossroads with Tonge Moor Road. Hidden among modern bungalows, Firwood Fold is an artist's and photographer's Arcady; it is like stepping back two hundred years in time, though some of the properties are centuries older. One or two owners have allowed me to prowl among the ancient roof timbers; that gives you the "feel" of the place like nothing else will and made it easy to picture the Cromptons living in the hamlet, in a stone cottage with a thatched roof, when Samuel was born on 3rd December, 1753.

They were small time farmers who supplemented the family income by spinning and weaving in the cottage kitchen. When the boy was five they moved into Hall i'th' Wood on a caretaker rent. Samuel's father was a talented musician but he died at thirty-seven and Betsy was left to fend and do her best for Samuel. She gave him a decent education which continued at a Bolton Evening School into his young manhood and Samuel proved an excellent scholar. Nevertheless, Betsy drove him hard and demanded a daily stint of work. Otherwise, he felt the weight of her hand about his ears, particularly when he was held up for yarn due to the inadequacies of Hargreaves' Spinning Jenny. Samuel had been trained as a weaver and was good at his job, for he had been at it since his legs had been long enough to reach the treadles. Kay's Flying Shuttle (1733) had speeded the process but the strong warp threads still had to be produced laboriously on the old fashioned wheel, Jenny-threads being sturdy enough only for weft.

Samuel began experimenting in his spare time and to procure the necessary tools he made a violin and played for 1s.6d. a night in the orchestra of the old Bolton Theatre. It took five years of his youth and "every shilling I had in the world" to perfect his famous "Mule", and the wreckers were out to smash every machine in creation. In 1779 he was offering on the market the surplus fine yarn, suitable for muslins, produced by his invention. The first profits paid for a silver watch from George Hodson of Bolton. Rival manufacturers were all agog and came, fawning and flattering, though only to plunder his brilliant ideas. "Don't bother about a patent", they said, "we will raise funds when you have made your machine public!" Alas, poor Samuel, he believed their empty promises and collected less than £80, whereas he could have expected £200 for displaying the Mule at the Manchester Exchange.

Disillusioned, he took his wife and family off to Sharples, out of the way, refusing even Sir Robert Peel's

HALL-I'TH'-WOOD, BOLTON, a famous Lancashire home with three centuries of building styles and reminders of the local genius, Samuel Crompton, inventor of The Mule.

offer of a partnership at Bury for, by now, he trusted no-one. The apprentices he trained were lured away by his competitors offering higher wages, and life struggled on until 1796, by which time the Cromptons were living in King Street, Bolton, using the attics for machines. But in that calamitous year, Samuel's wife and two of their eight children died and religion and music became his chief solace. He wrote hymn tunes, constructed a cottage organ . . . it is still there, melodious as ever, in the Museum.

In 1802 Manchester spinners opened a fund which might have raised £900 but, instead, produced only £350 with which Samuel opened a factory in St. Edmond's Street and took his sons into the business. Five years later they were in desperate straits and Samuel applied to the Royal Society (he should have approached the Society of Arts!) for a reward for his "Mule". Naturally, nothing came of it. He brooded for a while; then, when the Rev. Edmund Cartwright received £10,000 from Parliament for his Power Loom, Samuel's feckless and covetous sons hit the roof! Poor Samuel, done down by rivals, let down by his offspring, plodded round 650 cotton mills within a 60-mile radius and discovered that 4,000,000 Mule spindles were operating in 1811, almost ten times the Jenny and Throstle spindles put together.

With the backing of Lord Stanley, John Rennie, the engineer, and other notables, he went hot-foot to London in January 1812, spoke to the Prime Minister Spencer Perceval, who appointed a Select Committee, and began to hope for a national award in the region of £20,000. Then, of all things . . . and in retrospect it seems that Samuel's luck was consistently cruel . . . the Premier was actually assassinated within the very walls of Westminster as he was hurrying to propose a grant in the House of Commons. After this shattering blow and a considerable delay, Crompton's cup of bitterness spilled over when he was given a mere £5,000, the very minimum that the murdered leader had had in mind.

He dragged himself wearily back to Bolton and financed his sons in business ventures which speedily dissipated the grant until there was but £4 left. His slapdash daughter, Betty, kept house for him. Two of his sons languished in Lancaster Castle for debt, and in sorrow, the shy genius who was hopeless at business, eked out a pittance from making domestic wringers. He was rescued from desperate poverty in 1825 when conscience-stricken manufacturers raised enough to purchase an annuity worth £64 p.a., and even this, with persistent Cromptonian ill-fortune, he enjoyed for barely two years, for he departed this ungrateful world on 27th June, 1827 and was buried in the churchyard of St. Peter's.

By courtesy of Lever Brothers, an early photograph from the annals of the Sunlight Soap saga. The poster at the rear of the tilt-van refers to "The Largest Sale in the World", no mean claim! The picture was assumed to have been taken around Wigan, though "near Horwich" has been suggested more recently.

"A very quiet civil felly and a rare good fiddler", they called this man who had dreamed, and drudged, and triumphed and despaired; who enriched the world and, posthumously, reaped the reward of a monument. Withal, the Hall itself will ever be his best and most appropriate memorial.

In the late 1890's, this fascinating old house was lapsing into decrepitude and would have approached the point of no return but for decisive intervention of a more recent Bolton-born genius. He purchased the property, restored and furnished it, opened it on 23rd July, 1902 and gave it for the free and everlasting enjoyment of the citizens of Bolton . . . and anyone else who happens to pop in (open same days as Smithills).

William Hesketh Lever (1851–1925) was the longed for son of James and Eliza Lever, who had already produced six daughters and desperately wanted an heir to their wholesale grocery business. They lived in a dignified Victorian backwater at No. 16 Wood Street (now a Socialists' Club), were devout Congregationalists and were to rear, in all, ten children. William was sent to a private kindergarten when he was six, where he met his future wife, Elizabeth Ellen Hulme, and his future architect Jonathan Simpson, and at thirteen went to a Church of England Institute where he worked hard but excelled only at swimming.

At sixteen, he started work in the warehouse, tackling menial jobs like taking down shutters, sweeping up and cutting bar soap for 1s. 0d. a week. Next he went into the book-keeping section, mastered and improved on the methods, spent every moment of leisure on extending knowledge and keeping fit. From the start, he never wasted a single hour but put every conscious moment to good and profitable use . . . the kind of lesson it takes most of us half a lifetime to learn. At nineteen he begged for a job on the sales staff — a harsh option of long hours, horse-drawn gig in all weathers, evenings spent cashing up and writing out orders. In no time at all, he had doubled the turnover and started courting. He married his life's love in

1874; expanded the business and moved to Wigan; suddenly got the idea of manufacturing soap instead of buying from suppliers; took premises at Warrington, experimented for several months then launched into production . . . 20 tons a week, then 250 tons, and before the lease ended, 450 tons of soap manufactured and sold by Levers. Irish imports of farm produce, slickly organised by William, had placed Levers above all competition in the north-west, and at the age of thirty-three the thrusting young tycoon could have retired and lived in luxury.

Instead, he sought a coastal site for a new soapworks, with unlimited opportunities for expansion; found it on the Wirral Peninsula, 52 acres to start with, 230 acres later on; built the No. 1 Soapery and 28 beautiful houses for his workfolk. That was the start of Port Sunlight, that incomparably attractive model village which still astounds visitors from all over the world. It became the throbbing heart of an industrial empire that girdled the earth, with factories in Canada, Europe and Australia, palm oil plantations in the Congo.

Wm. Hesketh Lever was no mere money grubber who made his millions and finished up with his personal life in a shambles. His affectional ties were maintained intact, lifelong; I always maintain that he could have made his fortune dealing in art treasures; he was an indefatiguable collector who adored beautiful things above all; loved books and the theatre, was a genial host and an enthusiastic traveller; rose at four-thirty, used every moment to the full and retired early; built more houses, each batch more attractive than the one before, one resembling beautiful Agecroft Hall. This 14th century half timbered mansion of about fifty rooms was lapsing into decay at Pendlebury when Lever spotted and was entranced by it, and brought his architect over to take note; result, a near likeness, which must have cost the earth to build, as accommodation for employees. But the man who pays the piper has every right to call the tune, and with an instinct as unerring as Lever's, the outcome was felicitous, to say the very least. See this gem at Port Sunlight. The alternative is to cross the Atlantic and visit Richmond, Virginia, where the original Agecroft Hall which was bought, dismantled, crated up and shipped over in 1926 stands re-erected on a landscaped site overlooking the James River.

Created a Baronet of the United Kingdom at the age of sixty, Sir William enjoyed a warm relationship with the royal family. In fact, in 1913, while he and Lady Lever were dining with King George V and Queen Mary, as guests of Lord Derby at Knowsley, Suffragettes burned their Rivington bungalow to the ground. Three weeks later, Lady Lever died and was buried at Port Sunlight, a great loss to the community and to her devoted partner, who began designing the Lady Lever Memorial Art Gallery and Museum. George V laid the foundation stone and, several years later, Queen Victoria's youngest, Princess Beatrice, opened this Temple of the Arts, the ultimate ornament to the village, a perpetual monument to a treasured wife, and worthy setting for one of the finest private art collections in the whole of Europe. (Free admission week-daily 10.00 a.m.–5.00 p.m., Sundays 2.00 p.m.–5.00 p.m.). When Sir William was raised to the peerage in 1917, he added Elizabeth Ellen's name to his own and became the first Viscount Leverhulme of Bolton-le-Moors.

In every respect, his life was outstanding. He first introduced the 8-hour working day, staff canteens and the exploitation of a brand name; he befriended the Hebrideans with generous improvements, launched MacFisheries to promote fish sales; bought Lancaster House and gave it to the nation; founded Schools of Architecture, Russian Studies and Tropical Medicine; and always claimed that his success came "through plodding hard work within the reach of all who will make the necessary sacrifice". Not particularly tall, yet he was a giant among men and a brilliant all-rounder, travelling to the end and with a thousand schemes still buzzing in his lively brain. After a trip to the Congo, death came swiftly in May 1925, and his tomb at Port Sunlight is a reminder of what inspiration and human energy can accomplish in a single lifetime.

Bury

This old town in the Vale of Irwell has an excellent market and is famous for black puddings, simnel cake and outstanding sons. There was a castle here, once, but it was demolished after the Civil War. Farming and woollen textiles prevailed in Tudor times; cotton came later, followed by engineering and paper, clothing and carpet manufactures. Near the fine old parish church rises a noble bronze statue of Sir Robert Peel (1788–1850), former Prime Minister, founder of the modern Police Force, repealer of the Corn Laws and champion of Catholic Emancipation. His father, the first Baronet, who had succeeded by his own endeavours, entered Parliament for Tamworth where he had a large estate in 1790. Young Robert was dedicated to his country's service from the moment of his birth at Chamber Hall, Bury. His grandfather, Robert "Owd Parsley" Peel, a spinner and weaver, accidentally discovered a calico printing process, experimented with a sprig of parsley, introduced the method into the county. In Lancashire and the Potteries area, he prospered, survived many reverses, and his descendants inherited his cleverness and commonsense.

Before the Industrial Revolution, handloom weavers toiled in dimly lit cottages and draughty garrets and from such respectable stock sprang a Bury genius, John Kay, inventor of the Fly-Shuttle in 1733. It speeded up weaving, placed England in the forefront in textiles, brought him much tribulation and an unmarked exile's grave somewhere in France. To-day his achievement is remembered and honoured by a handsome memorial, with his portrait, in the town-centre Kay Gardens, presented to Bury by a descendant, Henry Whitehead, who also donated Tower Gardens, a tranquil triangle amid the traffic roaring in from the Manchester Road. A strikingly ornate clock-tower in light-coloured stone with a green dome, pinnacles and gargoyles, commemorates Walter Whitehead, "eminent surgeon and native of Bury" and brother of the donor. At the further end is a moving monument to Lancashire Fusiliers who fell during the Boer War, 1900–1902.

Philanthropist Thomas Wrigley, a Bury paper manufacturer and lover of the Arts, left a collection of paintings and Wedgwood ware which his family gave to the town and Bury built a gallery to house them. Bury was the birthplace in 1880 of Tommy Thompson, author of "Lancashire Mettle" and other works, contributor to the old "Manchester Guardian" and author of "Under the Barber's Pole" broadcast by the B.B.C. Tommy excelled in dialect mouthed with Chaucerian relish and peppered with penetrating wit. He was a devastating de-bunker of sentimentality, commenting about a Day in the Country . . . "If tha gooaz in Spring, th'meadows stink a mon's heyght! . . . In September, th'midges are at thee . . . thi shoon are slutched up to th'ankles! If tha gooaz o'er a style, th'owd bull's waiting on thee wi' id tail swingin' . . . If tha sits under a tree, a brid drops thee one for luck! . . . Me! . . . Ah'll sit in th'bar parlour wheer id's cool an' free frae cleggs an' muck-flees!" Tommy, a popular broadcaster, wrote film scripts, received an honorary degree from Manchester University and was writing up to his death in 1950. Not bad for a lad who left school at ten, went half-time to the mill, learned book-binding and broke into writing in his mid-thirties, using the mean streets of his Victorian childhood, the patient courage and full-blooded humour of the Bury folk as the well-spring of inspiration.

Rochdale

Boisterous mountain air sweeping down from the Pennines calls for an extra muffler and sharpens the intelligence. In this area, many a spark of genius was fanned into a blaze for the common weal, inspiration drawn, perhaps, from those breezy heights and a love of Nature. In Tudor times, the Rochdale folk were wool-workers who gradually went over to cotton. They were miners, too, long on guts and a passion for fair play. The Chartists were active. So were the Quakers. So was old Betty Brindle of Church Lane who had been "ducked" oftener than any woman of the parish for bellowing forth on behalf of her sex, long before Women's Lib. was thought of. She used the pot-house table as her pulpit, fell off after liberal potations and had to be trundled home in a wheelbarrow by her harassed spouse. Whereupon, she would set about him and qualify for another session in the ducking-stool poised over the Roch near the Wellington Hotel. It was dismantled about 1820.

This town of surprises has the widest bridge in Europe and half the motorists trundling through the centre are unaware of a river flowing beneath their wheels. The turgid Roch was covered in four stages between 1903–25, providing useful work for the unemployed in slum clearance and an inspired public scheme. The Victorian Gothic town hall, commenced in 1866, is ranked as one of the most magnificent in the country, with a soaring grandfather clock-tower, an elaborately carved facade graced by gilded lions and an array of craftsmanship within that is utterly superb! The corner-stone was laid by Rochdale's own golden-tongued son, John Bright, M.P., who was distraught upon losing his bride, Elizabeth, after two years, from tuberculosis, until a Manchester Alderman, Richard Cobden, reminded him that many were dying of starvation because of the Corn Laws. That shocked him into action. Cobden and Bright formed that famous Victorian Liberal duo which successfully espoused so many good causes. Bright, the orator, was returned three times to Parliament, lastly serving as a minister under Gladstone, but his links bound him to

Rochdale where he worshipped in the Friends' Meeting House in George Street in a seat bearing his name, and where he was buried in 1889 with his fellow Quakers.

Up Toad Lane in a quaint little building preserved as a museum twenty-eight red-faced Chartists doggedly opened their premises, "The Pioneer Stores", for business after a hard-working day at the mill, in December 1844. In the aftermath of a bitter strike and a bosses' lock-out, flannel-weavers had been forced to crawl back and resume working for the same, or less, pay than before. During a Sunday afternoon Chartists' meeting, Charles Howarth suggested a co-operative store where customers could share out the profits. Unfortunately, no-one had £1 to put down and the launching was delayed until each faithful Pioneer had contributed that amount by 2d. and later 3d. instalments. Ridicule of neighbours was hardest to bear, but that quickly changed when the first "divi" was paid out and within six years the Pioneers opened their first flour mill in Rochdale. That first little Co-op Shop attracts visitors from all over the world.

The site of St. Chad's Church, 122 steps above the town, was determined, according to legend, by "Goblin Builders" who repeatedly shifted materials overnight from the banks of the Roch below. The church, consecrated in 1170, was as black as jet twenty-odd years ago, when I first knew it, but it gleams, golden as a biscuit, after a clean-up, and clearance of the weathered gravestones begun in 1970. They left "Tim Bobbin's" railed off grave undisturbed, where he lies at peace with his Mary after their matrimonial ups and downs. Their son, Tom Collier, lived at 51 Packer Street below. Despite many alterations, you can feel the age of St. Chad's which has remnants of Early English and Decorated work and some fine memorials including a rare one, signed by Wm. Coleburne, c. 1715 and reckoned to be one of Lancashire's best.

The old parish covered many townships, all involved in the old rush-bearings of late August when the church floor was sweetened by the strewing of freshly gathered rushes. Carts piled many feet high and topped by floral decorations, processed with their attendant crowds towards Mother Church, a dozen or more dwindling to one or two by the 1830's.

Among its many clever offspring, Rochdale produced Gracie Fields, Cyril Smith, M.P., Sir James Kay-Shuttleworth, founder of our popular system of education, Professor John Milne, an authority on earthquakes, Dr. Henry Brierley, Registrar to the Wigan County Court and an exponent of the Lancashire dialect and Sir Samuel Turner who presented Falinge Park to the town and who was the first to recognise and develop the industrial potential of asbestos. The famous poet, Lord Byron, was Lord of the Manor of Rochdale until he sold out in 1823, his ancestors having held it from Commonwealth times.

Along with pride in achievements, Rochdale clung to traditional legends . . . of a Fairy Chapel at "The Thrutch" where the Spodden brawls and foams through a cleft, north of the town; of an apparitional bunny, "The Baum Rabbit", once regularly cavorting about the churchyard of St. Mary's which was built on the old "baum" (balm) fields where apothecaries used to gather herbs for their nostrums, and apparently impervious to pellets and gunshot!

Oldham Metropolitan Borough

I met her on the Fylde coast, a cheerful little blonde body who sang as she bustled about her work, spreading happiness among the residents of an old folks' home. But she didn't belong there. "I come from Oldham . . . Owd'am", she added with a grin, "Worked in the mill from leaving school till I got made redundant . . . five times! Then I moved!"

I had instant horrific visions of those "dark Satanic mills" in what was the greatest cotton spinning centre of the world, with over two hundred chimneys belching pollution into the ether and unendurable din and vibration, floor upon floor; and naturally supposed she wouldn't be sorry, escaping from all that? The answer was prompt. "I would go back tomorrow, I would THAT! It was grand. Hard work, but the comradeship! We had many a laugh!"

The rot set in with a vengeance about 1950, but there were rumours long before that and the workers could see it coming. Regular exports of machinery and expertise to the Far East could only add up to one thing, the decline of Lancashire textiles. Delegations went up to London. Operatives stated their case. Employers were advised to modernise and, at great expense, they did; but, by that time, cheap Commonwealth imports had doubled and trebled.

In 1957 the United Textile Factory Workers published their "Plan for Cotton" promoted by the then

Harold Wilson, M.P. It proposed too little, too late. The damage was already done. Traditional export markets had been lost and the industry's productive capacity was in surplus. The Centenary History of the Oldham Master Cotton Spinners' Association Ltd. (1866–1966) by the Secretary, J. E. Longworth, J.P., relates the sorry downfall of King Cotton. Mr. Longworth, a kind and knowledgeable gentleman, spared the time to discuss the sad situation of Oldham, a Metropolitan Borough including Crompton, Shaw, Royton, Chadderton, Middleton, and Failsworth, since 1974. In this area, in the 1920's, there were 250 mills going at full blast, compared with about 25 in 1981. The operatives are inured to it by now. Formal announcements of closure, in canteens, before all the staff, are quite as often ignored. "We know what you have come to tell us", they will remark wryly, having experienced it twice or thrice before. But five times? No, really, that WAS unusual.

In war-time when men were called up, the industry had to re-organise. In 1939 over 40 mills closed and machinery was mothballed in 11 others. With peace restored, began recruitment campaigns, removal of controls and revival of the old traditional skills. The future looked good. "England's bread hangs by Lancashire's thread", was the confident slogan . . . until pressures built up to the watershed years of 1953/54. Then, closures began, though the Korean war provided a fillip. There were signs of obvious slump; optimism wilted, employment figures sank steadily from 32,140 in 1954 to 19,820 in 1959 and by that time the Unions had agreed to voluntary redundancy financed by employers, based on years of service and spindleage. Curiously, in that year began another of those upward four-year cycles followed in 1963 by another down-turn with more closures and relentless decline. It was heart-breaking to watch perhaps half those fine mills falling to the demolition men, though a few were put to other uses — galleries, supermarkets, craft centres, Mail Order warehouses, etc., while those remaining were beautifully streamlined to survive.

Bolton was always traditionally a fine count spinning area. Oldham from the 1900's was a coarse count spinning centre with some weaving of fustians, velvets and corduroys on the side. They were Mule mills from the 1920's until 1959, changing to ring-spinning when modernisation became imperative, with open-end spinning being gradually introduced in the late 1960's, as at Maple and Lilac Mills. These new machines, once made in Czechoslovakia, are now manufactured in Accrington.

The decline of Oldham's textile industry has affected the whole infra-structure. The dust extraction system was introduced here and, in general, a very happy relationship existed between employers and workers before the combines, as evidenced by a record of no major strikes or lock-outs between 1933–1966.

So, what is it like to-day, this Oldham through which Romans were marching nearly 2,000 years ago along their main road from Manchester to York? This centre of many thriving crafts in the Middle Ages which became important with the turnpiking of roads in the 18th century and is now skirted by the trans-Pennine motorway, the M62? It is an up and down place, I can tell you! A distinct shock to the calf muscles of softies from the Fylde Coast where the only hills are railway bridges! From whichever viewpoint, wherever the eye travels, you are gazing upon hills, the Pennines, green or hazy grey or blue in the distance. Puffing and panting, you struggle up by the old Town Hall, a dignified pile in the style of a Greek temple, completed in 1879 (the new Civic Centre is a tower block) . . . and head for the Parish Church of St. Mary, a bold Gothic piece of stone architecture on an elevated site, only to find it locked against the vandals of whom Oldham has no more, and no less, than other comparable places. The disappointment is mitigated only by the recollection that St. Mary's was entirely rebuilt in the 1820's and was restored about a century ago. Anciently, Oldham was a chapelry attached to Prestwich, its first church being so dilapidated by 1476 that the Rector of Prestwich commissioned the building of a new one. A gallery was added in 1703 to accommodate the increasing population.

Oldham linen weavers are listed as early as 1592 and there are 17th century entries in the church registers referring to "linen websters". These were the cottage craftsmen and farmers forced to augment small incomes by toiling at the loom. Daniel Defoe, inveterate traveller and observer, popular and prolific novelist and pamphleteer in the early 18th century, noted the lusty fellows, the "little maisters" in the countryside around Oldham, some at the loom, some at the dye vat, others dressing the cloths of both wool and cotton. Women did the spinning, hence the word "spinsters", and from the moment baby hands could be trained, children were set to carding, for it was a case of pulling together for sheer survival.

The first mill was established by Ralph Taylor at Thorpe Clough, Royton, in 1764; another at Lees Hall

OLDHAM, the Blue Coat School (Henshaw's Charity) from an engraving in the 1830's.

about 1778 by William Clegg of Westwood. Whether they were mills or converted houses is difficult to say. Mills were driven by water power in the first instance, steam power later, though a few started off with horses. As the 19th century dawned, expansion was more rapid in weaving than in spinning, particularly in velveteens and "substantial fustians". By 1839 there were 200 cotton mills employing 15¼ thousand workers. Population increased eightfold from 10,000 in 1794 to 80,000 in 1866 when Oldham boasted 3,000,000 spindles busily and profitably at work.

The rest is a story of decline, but you cannot write off a place as clever and hardworking as Oldham simply because one industry bites the dust. Oldham is close to all the main conurbations in the north of England. It is linked by motorway to the principal industrial centres and the port of Liverpool. It has been prepared to diversify, channelling 43% of local labour into engineering and utilising skills creatively in preference to the service industries. Large stores have moved into the Town Square Shopping Centre opened in 1981 and the Council is operating an Industrial Loan Scheme attractive to small firms.

Educationally, Oldham has a fine record, beginning in 1611 with the foundation of a Free Grammar School by the Asshestons of Chadderton so that children could be "instructed in the English, Greek and Latin tongues, and withal in good manners". The 18th century produced many bequests for specific charities — for the poor, for apprenticeships, for doles of woollen cloth, for schoolmasters' salaries or for the purchase of bibles and catechisms. John Walker gave £600 in 1755 for teaching Oldham's poor children. In 1807/08 Thomas Henshaw, a wealthy Oldham hat manufacturer, envisaged the establishment of a Blue Coat Charity School in either Oldham or Manchester and set aside £20,000 for that purpose. The foundation stone was laid in 1829 on the lower part of Oldham Edge of one of the most romantic and graceful buildings in the district which is still called the "Blue Coat School" despite efforts to turn it into "Henshaw's Comprehensive". The Oldhamers would have none of it, persisting with the old honoured title until they won the day! The elegant pile with battlements, turrets and gables, gazes down over the township from its lofty situation and the steep breezy pull, which taxes those beyond the first green flush of youth, must also knock some of the cockiness out of the pupils before their toes connect with the front doorstep. I was informed with pride that the old traditions are still kept up, along with strict standards and celebration of Founder's Day. There is also an accomplished School Band — making music is as natural as breathing, in these parts, and it was ever so in hard-working Lancashire.

The native Oldham character, to my mind, is admirable. It may modify but does not lightly change. It speaks its mind with courage and is full of common sense. Fiercely loyal and equally passionate in its loves and its hatreds, it mourns the decline of its early Radicalism, the emergence of "middle-class refeenment", the pandering to materialism, the degeneration into booze-ups of old cotton town traditions like the Wakes, the insidious campaign against the memorable Whit Walks in the "Godless years", the 1950's and

1960's, on grounds that they disrupted traffic, till they ceased, only to be replaced by the Parochial Walks on Whit Sundays when the crowds turn up as of old.

It takes pride in its church life, strong as ever, very few lost. Old churches surrounded by new estates become the centre of community life, with a good mix of Anglicans, Roman Catholics, Non-conformists, a couple of Moravian churches and a Mormon temple thrown in for good measure. There are mosques and temples too, serving the coloured inflow. The Oldham folk are tolerant and kindly, and while they love their moorlands and the beautiful villages on the outskirts in the foothills of the Pennines — Greenfield, Diggle, Delph, Dob Cross and Saddleworth, where old customs like Morris Dancing and Rush-bearings persist, they are touchily conscious that it is "all middle-cass, now!" As for Saddleworth, birthplace of that gifted dialect minstrel, Ammon Wrigley (to whom there is a stone memorial up at Standedge), the War of the Roses is still in full swing. "The fashionables make their money in Oldham, then stick their noses up and go and live in Saddleworth", I was told. "They like to think they are Yorkshire — it has swung to and fro — but we won't let them go!" If there is an edge between the two counties separated by the Pennines, it is blunted by the Lancastrians' good humour and sense of comedy.

Motoring "over the tops" from the west and avoiding the motorway, the approach to Oldham is magnificent — another poke in the eye for those who ignorantly dismiss Lancashire as a county of unending ugliness and a perpetual sunless "Coronation Street" slum with railway arches, front doors on the street, cramped rear yards and littered back alleys smelling of tom-cats! All that is Man's doing . . . he who also devised the magical hypnotic box. But these hills, gaunt and bare and beautiful, these jutting rocks and dipping vales, these perpetually shifting hues and shadows, are Nature's works and of an artistry sublime.

The mental image of Oldham as a dismal work-stained industrial town also falls wide of the mark. Sure, it has its dingy areas, particularly as it merges into Failsworth; and even Failsworth, which produced its own gifted band of Lancashire bards, is rescued from total dreariness by its "little miracle" that defied all laws of chance! Inexplicably, when industry exploded in Oldham and Ashton-under-Lyne and land was gobbled up by mill building and housing and canal cutting, a few acres escaped where Nature reigned serene in Medlock Vale. Thither after a toilsome week hurried the old-time cotton operative who found solace on the Sabbath away from the whirring wheels and jarring clatter of Mammon. In the 1850's, poet Ben Brierley returned from such an outing with mind still uplifted by the sight of a brave and abundant crop of daisies. His first book, "A Day's Out" (1856) referred to this magic place and suggested it should be called "Daisy Nook", and so it has been ever since. It is near Failsworth's eastern border with Ashton-under-Lyne, is now officially a Country Park owned by the National Trust, which first acquired 15 acres in 1938 and added more later. Here you will find a sylvan dell, beautifully landscaped, with a nature walk and a footbridge over tranquil waters and you could fancy yourself deep in the countryside instead of tide-trapped by a sea of commerce.

Oldham, in any case, launched a "Town in the Countryside" project in 1974, began planting trees and flowering shrubs, improving parks, adding a dramatic blaze of colour in tulip time to Alexandra Park. It has already captured the coveted North West "Britain in Bloom" award, no mean achievement and showing that Oldham means business. There is a fine modern Swimming Stadium on a hillside overlooking the church and, quite apart from the splendid shopping area, everyone must have heard of the famous Tommyfield Market, operating thrice weekly, all 3½ acres of it teeming with life on Fridays, when some 450 stallholders try to coax cash from customers, with a wonderful variety of merchandise and produce.

Head for the villages around Oldham at Whitsuntide and renew contact with old Lancashire traditions like bowls and hoops, whips and tops, pea-shooters and sherbert dabs, Sunday School processions, brass band concerts — more than a dozen to choose from — with boys' bands, youth bands, big-name bands, music-on-the-march bands and smartly uniformed bands assembled on village greens or downing pints after a performance. Famous names crop up — Fairey Aviation, Manchester C.W.S., Leyland Vehicles, Besses o'th'Barn and a host of lesser known but not less dedicated music makers converge on the foothills of the Pennines and blow themselves breathless until daylight fades, and to the accompanying fragrance from a mobile fish and chip stall.

Oldham is close to the Peak District National Park, the Pennine Way and those breezy uplands which separate it from the old West Riding. Perhaps it was from their old-time enemies and near neighbours that the South-East Lancastrians learned to speak out with fearless honesty, and yet with the comic good humour for which the Red Rose man is famous. Les Dawson, Eric Sykes, and Cannon and Ball come from the Oldham area, and Dora Bryan was educated at Hathershaw Council School, according to her entry in "Who's Who". Oldham was the birthplace of Sir William Walton and opera star, Dame Eva Turner, and produced firebrands like J. R. Clynes, Labour M.P. for Manchester North-East, 1906–1945. He was a minder in a mill, worked his way to power from the Trades Council and textile unions into the newly formed Labour party. Oldham inspired off-comers like Mrs. Mary Higgs (1854–1937), a Girton scholar and woman of high ideals, who married the Congregational minister at Greenacres. Dressed as a tramp, she enquired into vagrancy, walked to all the doss-houses and workhouses, sampled the roving life at first hand and gave evidence before a Parliamentary Commission; and as a result, wrote "Glimpses into the Abyss" (1906). She organised Play Centres, founded Poetry and Historical Societies and the movement for "Beautiful Oldham". There was never any shortage of culture in this breezy, hearty town which, for years, supported its own Repertory Theatre and which still has its Coliseum. Football support is divided between Oldham Athletic and the Watersheddings ground which is the spiritual home of the Rugby League fans. Choosing where to live cannot be easy if you are torn between those durable workers' stone cottages as at Upper Mill, Diggle, Delph and Dob Cross, and the executive type properties in the Saddleworth villages.

Coal was important to Oldham, once upon a time, more than sixty collieries operating, many rat-ridden, and all but eight worked out by 1900. From the 1830's engineering developed — textile machinery and tools, to begin with, motors, electrical gear and accompaniments of the internal combustion engine later, the famous "Bradbury" motor bikes and sewing machines, washing machines and kitchen ranges from 1900 onwards. "Smoky Owdham" was a great place for clogs and clog making, in the old days, when children lay in bed of an early morning listening to the heavy tramping of the men going to work at Platt Works and womenfolk hearkened for the return of the clogged brigade in the early evenings. There was only 3% unemployment in those days but the realities were stark. A man worked 48–60 hours for about 26/- (£1·30), less than half of to-day's average in real terms and the work was incomparably harder, and industrial diseases and accidents infinitely higher. Cotton mills particularly were dangerous, accounting for 40% of the 500 fatal and 60,000 non-fatal accidents between 1900–20, in Oldham alone. Silicosis and nystagmus, leading to blindness, stalked miners in poorly lit collieries; "Weavers' cough", chronic bronchitis caused by inhalation of cotton dust, led to premature death; oil thrown by spinning machines caused "Mule Spinners' cancer"; the compressed air tool often resulted in "Boilerman's Deafness"; and curious deformities developed from unnatural and repetitive movements in both mill and mine.

Early in the 1980's we have higher unemployment. But there is a definite feeling that the recession will pass, industry will recover and Oldham will always keep its end up. Incidentally at Hollinwood, along Manchester Road, a former landlord of the "Help the Poor Struggler" inn was Albert Pierrepoint, the last of the public hangmen. He was a spinner at Failsworth in the 1920's when Marlborough Mills went on short-time which prompted him to write an application, successfully as it turned out, for the job of public executioner . . . an occupation not to everyone's taste but it ran in the family — his father and uncle were notable hangmen — and it could be run as a sideline. Afterwards, this dedicated and discreet professional who never discussed his gruesome "other work", regularly slipped away to despatch infamous murderers like John Haigh, Neville Heath and John Christie, and War Criminals after the Nuremburg trials. He retired at length to Southport and his autobiography was published in 1975.

On a happier note, the late Helen Bradley M.B.E., the apple-cheeked, bespectacled primitive painter of bustling Lancashire scenes, haunted by the pink-clad "Miss Carter", was born at Lees, Oldham, in 1900. She was an instinctive artist, dabbling merely until L. S. Lowry encouraged her to specialise on recollective scenes of her childhood in the Edwardian era, and by then she was in her sixties. Her quaint style took off in a big way in the 1970's with reproductions in book form, including "Miss Carter Wore Pink" and "The Queen who Came to Tea". The area which had inspired most of her works also premiered her exhibitions at Oldham's Art Gallery and there was a national sense of shock when the bubbling conversationalist, with an almost childlike zest for life, died suddenly at the age of 79, having endeared herself to the telly-viewing millions.

Long before that, in the mid 15th century, Bishop Hugh Oldham of Exeter, founder of the Manchester Free Grammar School, was born in Goulburn Street, Oldham and grew up in the household of Thomas, first Earl of Derby, having himself descended from an ancient family. This friendly, wise and pious chap, somewhat "rough in speeche" and jealous of his rights, also helped to endow Corpus Christi College and furnished the library at Brazennose College, Oxford. He died in 1519 and was buried in his chapel in Exeter Cathedral.

Less illustrious but more familiar, was Blind Joe Howarth the Bellman, who cried Oldham's news through the streets for upwards of forty years, and was so revered that they erected a statue of him in Alexandra Park and gave him two M.P.'s for company, Robert Ashcroft and John Platt. That park, incidentally, provided work for operatives laid off during the tragic Cotton Famine of the 1860's.

Oldham also has its happy royal connections with the island of Tonga, for which a local engineering firm has completed important projects. After travelling to Britain to attend the wedding of the Prince and Princess of Wales on 29th July, 1981, in St. Paul's Cathedral, the 25-stone monarch, son of the late and very popular Queen Salote, came to Oldham to visit the engineering works five days later and received a right royal, flag-waving warm-hearted welcome. He made it clear that if he ever had to settle in Britain, he would choose Oldham with its trees and hills, in preference to London; and in return, the Oldham folk who had worked alongside the Tongans, thought them "fearless, brave, god-fearing men and smashing fellows!"

Just beyond the boundaries of Oldham, but visible for miles, is Hartshead Pike, a tall pepperpot tower built in 1863 to commemorate the marriage of an earlier Prince of Wales and Princess Alexandra. As July 1981 approached and the whole nation was smitten with Royal Wedding fever, a Salford firm, Commercial Blast Clean Ltd., set about removing the accumulated grim and graffiti of decades as a labour of love. Let us hope that no-one will be tempted ever again to deface this long-and-well-loved landmark.

Ashton-under-Lyne

In a busy industrial town on the north-east outskirts of Manchester, you would scarcely expect to discover one of Old Lancashire's most persistent legends, a canal with a distinctly Venetian flavour — you half expect to see gondolas proceeding through Portland Street Basin (which is the junction of Ashton and Peak Forest Canals); a church begun about 1400 and the finest medieval glass in the north-west.

At Ashton-under-Lyne lived James Bibby, International Champion Porridge-Eater — 6 pints in 20 minutes — who defeated a Scottish contender in 1880 for a prize of £2. Here John Wroe, a Bradford woolcomber, established his Christian Israelite Church in 1822. The sect still functions, in Australia whither Wroe fled after alleged immoral practices with young maidens of the congregation. Ashton still holds its open air market — the Charter dates back to 1284 — has a multi-million pound Civic Centre under construction, a famous landmark, Hartshead Pike, and unexpected bonny corners.

For many centuries the good folk turned out every Easter Monday to enact "Riding the Black Lad" in bitter memory of a local tyrant, Ralph de Assheton, who married a Middleton heiress. He returned regularly, inspected his manor and imposed severe penalties on tenants who had failed to clear his lands of corn marigold. They loathed the black-armoured, black-hearted knight and celebrated the anniversary of his death by parading a straw effigy of "The Black Lad" on horseback, and afterwards using it as a target for those possessing fire-arms, a tradition that persisted into last century. The old hall of the Asshetons, an ancient turreted and gabled stone manor house, which stood near Park Parade Railway Station, was demolished in 1890. An ancestor, Sir John de Assheton, M.P., an Agincourt veteran, began to build the church of St. Michael and it was completed c. 1500 by his grandson, Sir Thomas de Assheton, who is depicted along with his three wives in one of the magnificently painted glass windows. They are the outstanding wonders of this edifice which was almost entirely restructured in the 1840's in "florid Perpendicular" style, and the tower with a great peal of a dozen bells was replaced in the 1880's.

Ashton-under-Lyne was once a great cotton town with all the old worthy Lancashire traditions. At weekends, operatives headed for the hills or sampled the sweet delights of Failworth's Daisy Nook — that is, if they still had sufficient breath and energy left after a gruelling week in the mill and a Friday night spent cleaning, polishing, washing windows, scrubbing and donkey-stoning front doorsteps and even, in some cases, the front pavement. The donkey stones of brown, or white or cream, came from the Ashton company of Eli Whalley that only went out of business in 1979 . . . (sic transit gloria mundi). A bronze statue of Hugh Mason commemorates a kindly millowner who cared deeply for his work-people, forbade them to drink, join a trade union or skive off work. The brave fellow risked his life by reading the Riot Act when religious mobsters ran amok in 1868.

16. BETWEEN RIBBLE AND MERSEY

Leyland

Village-cum-town-cum-industrial-sprawl just about sums up Leyland, part of the Central Lancashire New Town project of 1972 to foster economic growth and population increase in the north-west. Statistics don't interest me. History does! I am attracted to Old Leyland, mentioned in Domesday, held by Edward the Confessor, woodland then, two square miles of it, with an "aerie of hawks", and a priest who officiated heaven knows where, possibly in some humble Christian edifice, though there were several crosses dotted about. By the 13th century, the Church "de Layland" belonged to the Abbots of Evesham who collected tithes and fees and supplied monks from their daughter house, Penwortham Priory. This liberated the parishioners from oppressive domination by the Faringtons who had held half the manor of Leyland from John o' Gaunt's time. The Abbots presented the Vicars from 1332 until the Dissolution.

We can only speculate about life here in medieval times. Not all Abbots were good and Evesham's were no exception. Off-shoot houses, such as Penwortham, were often dumping grounds for recalcitrant brethren, many of whom had less taste for religion than talent for surviving in safety behind monastery walls. Life was a pretty coarse and cruel business when St. Andrew's Church came into existence, c. 1220. The villagers would scarcely be enthusiastic about a rush-strewn, unheated, unlit barn of a building with a thatched and, possibly, leaking roof, no pews to sit in, and services gabbled in Latin, which might as well have been Greek for all they knew and perhaps cared! The gritstone chancel, re-roofed in 1956, has triple sedilia, piscina, aumbry and a "leper squint" which may have been a spy-hole for the priest whose cell was close by.

The 15th century tower had "Faure Greete Bells" in 1552, six in 1863 and a couple added for the Diamond Jubilee, all re-cast in 1929. The tower was repaired with ffarington money by Seth Woodcock, chaplain to the great Cardinal Wolsey, during his Vicariate, 1488–1516. His emblem, a woodcock, appears in stone in the west wall. The Rev. Seth is supposed to have furnished the rose-shaped Tudor font which went missing, turned up in Worden park and was returned to the church in 1910. By then, the Misses Farington had provided the present 19th century font and the relic of Henry VIII's time was transferred to St. John the Divine's Church, Earnshaw Bridge (1969) where, doubtless, it will be treasured for ever.

What a pity that the Faringtons of Worden Hall, whose home and park of 147 acres were acquired by the local authority for the townsfolk, thought fit to raze and rebuild the nave in "gothicised Georgian" in 1817. This well-meaning meddling virtually destroyed a venerable structure which might, with care, have stood for all time. The old stubborn walls had to be blasted with gunpowder, and the present huge nave with the ffarington chapel in place of the old chantry of St. Nicholas, is a poor substitute for the original which left its roof marks on the tower wall.

Yet, there are treasures galore to be enjoyed. Four chained tomes encased beneath a window containing precious fragments of medieval stained glass; good brasses, memorials to past Squires and worthies, coats of arms of Leyland district gentry. Once overrun with swine and grazing cattle and "negligently kept", the churchyard is a happy hunting ground for the antiquarian. There are ancient carved stones beneath the east window. One, engraved with a Saxon cross, served as a footbridge over a stream until it was rescued and returned by a former Vicar. South of the chancel, look for a table tomb and the crude outline of William Walker, "Batchelor of Musick", a jovial fellow, one feels, Parish "clarke" for 25 years and an able teacher, by whose Will —

> *"everie one that is a scolar at Leyland scole at the*
> *tyme of my death shall have one halfpenny in silver"*

What a thrill for those young Elizabethans in the year of the Armada (1588).

A small flat stone nearby, commemorating Elizabeth Redhead, sets me wondering how this venerable spinster — she died in her 92nd year in 1866 — came to be ending her days in Leyland? She was Preston personnified, had kept a tuckshop in Mount Street for 45 years, knew all the "Nobs", was an uncompromising Tory and at election times came in handy, rooting out impersonators at the polling booths. Betty could trace everyone back for three generations! She could hob-nob as easily with chimney sweeps or society ladies, was respected by the great Derby family and the county folk whose opponents she denounced in forthright terms, for she had been born in 1774, knew what was what, upheld the old settled order. Mr. R. Townley-Parker once linked the old lady up Fishergate to the Bull Hotel, introduced her to the candidate, and sent her home in triumph in a cab, to the admiration of the neighbours.

I have a photograph of Old Betty Redhead seated in long grey skirts, with shoulder shawl, frilled white cap and starched cotton pinny, a working dame of considerable self possession who was "at home" with her betters, scornful of the plebeian and handy with the besom when youngsters misbehaved. Did she take ill, suddenly, during a visit to Leyland? Did she end her single days in one of the Almshouses with which the village was generously provided by the Faringtons and others? Such speculations, and sly reminders like — "Thou art as I was, I am as thou shalt be!" — are half the joy of poking around old churchyards.

I think of Robert Charnock, 17th century R.C. priest whose forfeited estates were granted to Leyland parish. According to the inscription, he was esteemed for qualities above "birth or idle pedigree", a devout Christian who "shone forth beyond his fellows" and was buried near his parents in 1670. And was he really "a man almost divine", as the legend above the old priests' door proclaims, or in the 1680's did his brief Vicariate lend enchantment to the memory of the Rev. George Walmsley? Where also, among the saints, and sinners, lies "Robin o'Jack's" (Robert Robinson), the local burglar who was tried, sentenced and hanged at Lancaster in 1825, and whose funeral service attracted great crowds and packed every pew in the great new nave for the very first time?

A dozen years ago, a dilapidated building stood rotting in a churchyard corner. To-day, thanks to the South Ribble Authority and the Job Creation Scheme, it is a local museum of immense charm and interest, an L-shaped 17th century building with a small walled yard and Master's quarters added in 1790. Chantry priests once taught a handful of scholars; then in 1546 Incumbents were enjoined to "kepe one fre Gramar Skoyle in the Church", with emphasis on plain song, grammar and Latin. Early schoolmasters received less than £4 p.a., and in the 17th century the school was destitute of books "save a Dixionary", having "not any libraries about us worth the writinge of". Yet from here went Richard Cuerden, later Vice-Principal of St. Mary Hall, Oxford, who practised medicine in Preston and wrote five columes of Lancashire history before his death in the 1690's.

I think kindly of Thomas Moon, Master here for sixty years before his death in 1776 and whose philosophy I wholeheartedly share:

> *He seldome grieved at worldly loss,*
> *Gold, he esteemed as gilded dross.*
> *No change of fortune did destroy*
> *His peace of mind and heartfelt joy.*

A happy man and a witty one who could rise above worldly considerations and be remembered for "sound learning . . . and probity". Edward Marsden succeeded, a Classicist and Mathematician, almost equally long-serving, who meted out corporal punishment to his 30 pupils, when needful.

The difficulties of teaching in a single large classroom were manifest in the 1860's when a dozen girls, curtained off from 35 boys, were taught sewing by the Master's wife. Roman Catholics had to be otherwise employed while the rest were at church, and though most pupils were above common social standing, the Commissioner's Report credited them with "very little intelligence". Additionally, the building was deteriorating and ceased to function in 1874. Afterwards it was used for parish functions until restoration work began in 1976, revealing its mullion windows, clam-staff-and-daub partition walls, and blackened ancient timbers leaning at crazy angles.

Wander along Fox Lane where the cellars of the cotton workers were once a-clatter with their contraptions. The old village atmosphere survived into the era of the internal combustion engine. There

LEYLAND:
St. Andrew's Parish Church (above).
The Old Grammar School (now a museum) in course of restoration (below).

were even a couple of farms redolent of chickens and pigs between the Cricket Club and the "Seven Stars" as late as the 1920's. Periodically, some expert mechanic rattled by, testing a chassis, leaning this way or that and listening intently to the tuning of the engine. There were half a dozen fish and chip shops, many small family businesses long before the supermarkets, where you could buy everything from fresh fish to a new Sunday hat, or commission every craftsman from a cobbler to the bespoke tailor. There were two cinemas, now taken over by multiples or Bingo, and gone are the days when everybody knew everybody else by name, because folk move about in isolating metal boxes with wheels at the corners, instead of swarming on to the buses for a sixpenny-return shopping spree to Preston!

What does not change, however, is the warmth, helpfulness and hospitality of the Leyland people, a "gradely" lot, as you would expect of a Lancashire community that once made its living from "cottons".

The Father of Leyland Motors

From the beginning of Time, Man dreamt of conquering the air. His urge to create a horseless carriage came later. Ramsey and Wildegoose applied for a patent in 1619! Cugnot, Trevithick and a host of original thinkers who followed were held back by Parliaments determined to ban these bizarre contraptions which could only cause accidents and damage highways and bridges. Victorians venerated the Horse, blacksmiths and wheelwrights were as busy as modern breakdown garages, and Elias Sumner, clanging happily away at

This fascinating photograph from the archives of Leyland Vehicles shows the first run of James Sumner's steam tri-car, a three-wheeler fitted with a lawn mower engine, for the famous biscuit manufacturer, Mr. Theodore Carr of Carlisle in 1895. It was a great success and despite the "red-flag" law, Mr. Carr ordered an improved model the following year.

the anvil in his Leyland smithy, never suspected that by the time the business fell into the hands of James Sumner, in 1892, the horseless carriage would have passed from the dream stage into reality!

By the 1890's, the smithy had given way to the Sumner Works complete with steam hammer and lathes, supplying brass and iron castings and employing a score of engineers at 28s.0d., for a 61-hour week, with brief breaks for meals. Those splendid craftsmen laid the foundations for an enormous manufacturing enterprise beyond the wildest fancies even of young James Sumner, a visionary, if ever there was one. In 1884 he had designed a 5-ton steam wagon to convey coal to Stanning's Bleachworks. Unfortunately, it broke down on a 15-mile test trip to Ormskirk. Brother William acted as red flag man and the intrepid pair landed up in Court charged with leaving the wagon unattended. That was its last trip, but it heightened Sumner's determination to succeed with steam, even after his eyes were permanently damaged by a boiler explosion during experiments. Soon, he was working hard on a small two-cylinder engine with an oil-fired boiler attached to a second-hand two-seater "twopenny-farthing" tricycle. It zipped around at a spanking pace, flummoxing the Police and landing the brothers, once again, in the dock. Half in exasperation, half in fun, the magistrates fined them only a shilling!

The next effort was a steam unit fitted to a lawn mower used on a local estate, a ridiculous Emmett-like contraption which bagged first prize at the Royal Lancashire Agricultural Show. Orders poured in, from Rugby School, from Cricket Clubs all over the country. A similar unit drove a three-wheeled car in 1895 for Carlisle's famous biscuit manufacturer, Theodore Carr, who promptly ordered another. At this point, the Sumner Works linked up with Coulthard's, the Preston engineers. Then, in 1896, Henry Spurrier returned from Florida, whose brother George had taken over Coulthard's interests.

That year, an Act of Parliament favouring road vehicles was passed and Henry Spurrier and James Sumner formed the Lancashire Steam Motor Company, precursor of Leyland Motors, and financed by Henry Spurrier, Senior, whose sons, and Sumner, joined the board. Their new 30-cwt. steam van earned the highest award in Manchester trials in 1897. Even the Prince of Wales was impressed and the young designers, cock-a-hoop, walked off with more awards in 1898. Orders for their 3-tonner and later, a 4-tonner, poured in from far and wide. The work-force swelled to 160 and in 1902 the Company bought three acres of land and began building the North Works. They were exporting Royal Mail vans to Ceylon in 1901 and proving beyond argument that steam transport was infinitely cheaper and more efficient than horse-drawn! The Motor Car Act of 1903 gave added impetus and the petrol engine, introduced experimentally in 1904, gradually gained ground, particularly when orders for London buses arrived as early as 1905. They built well at Leyland, too! Many of those original vehicles were still in splendid condition, and still working, in 1921. Steam lawn mowers had lapsed into fond memory. Trucks, vans, buses, fire engines, even tram cars, rolled off the assembly line; and the quaint jaunty old "chara" jounced around the countryside at 12 m.p.h. taking trippers to the seaside.

By 1914 "Leyland Motors Limited" had a work-force of 1500 and thousands of petrol driven and steam wagons to their credit, besides specialist vehicles for the War Office. At the end of hostilities, they were geared up for the civilian market, with exciting prospects until the slump of the early 'twenties brought losses and short-time working. With the upswing, a year or two later, appeared the Trojan, a 10 h.p. solid rubber-tyred comical looking vehicle, butt of music hall comics, but reliable. It sold more than 80 a week until 1928, by which time Leyland trucks were bouncing over the Western prairies and the Australian outback, and Leyland buses were going to Russia and other parts of the world. Workers' houses had swallowed up surrounding green acres. Branches had been opened in Australia, New Zealand and the East.

Blindness darkened "Owd Jimmy Sumner's" latter years but his acute engineering perceptions never forsook him. He retired in 1919, having exceeded the most exuberant ambitions of his young days, his life a triumph, his contributions to industry incomparable. He was Lancashire to the last fibre and he deserves to be remembered!

Chorley

The story of St. Lawrence's Parish Church, which originally belonged to Croston, reaches back to 1362 when the first priest was allocated. Since then it has been rebuilt several times, notably in 1859, though the tower, the oldest part, has survived since 1400. Chorley was holding markets 600 years ago, and there is still that very special excitement on Tuesdays and Fridays when stallholders unpack and lay out their merchandise for inspection. Cattle markets came later when pigs and cows were sold in the streets. All this marketing probably explains why the townsfolk are warm and welcoming and friendly to newcomers whose trade they have always valued.

Close to the town, along the Preston road, stand the gates to the attractively wooded Astley Park which was donated to Chorley in 1922. The grounds are lovely, a green oasis; and Astley Hall, the ancient home of the Charnocks, the Brookes of Mere and the Towneley-Parkers, is a jewel. In Tudor times it was half-timbered with a central courtyard. The superb Jacobean frontage, like Hardwick Hall "more glass than wall!" was built in the 1660's and is handsomely reflected in a small lake, but the visitor has no conception of the merits of Astley until he has gazed upon those magnificent and most elaborate plaster ceilings which must be the best in the county and among the finest in the land. The Great Hall rises two storeys high and the Long Gallery which extends across the frontage accommodates a 23½ft. shovel-board table, the finest in existence, its solid timbers supported on ten pairs of legs! There are old family portraits, coats of arms, Cromwell's great carved oak bed and a portrait of the Protector, some fine furnishings, special interests rooms and an Art Gallery with a good permanent collection, including pottery and glass, where regional artists are invited to exhibit.

The Stanleys, Earls of Derby

The rise of this illustrious family, who were Lords Paramount of the soil of West Lancashire, owes as much to downright cleverness as to good fortune. They skilfully trimmed their sails, steered clear of the political rocks on which many of their contemporaries foundered; they married well, their heirs survived, their conduct was courtierly and they entertained on a sumptuous scale. Their principal home was as commodious as a king's palace and neighbours accorded them the respect due to the Sovereign. They were a power to be reckoned with and no monarch dared leave them out of his councils.

The dynasty was founded by Adam de Audithley and his sons, Lydulph and Adam, who came over with the Conqueror. As a reward, Adam senior received Red Castle, Salop, and his family later built Healey Castle in Staffordshire. Lydulph's son married Mabella, daughter of Henry de Stoneley whose seat was situated near the head of the Trent and when Henry died, Adam, the son-in-law, became Lord of Stoneley, while his grandson, James, became the first Lord Audley of Healey Castle. A complicated exchange of estates between Audithley cousins following the marriage of Joanna Stanley of Stafford and William de Audithley, whereupon "in honour of his Lady" he took the name of Stanley and made Stoneley his seat, resulted in the Lancashire Stanleys who have occupied a unique position in the county for almost 600 years. Judicious marriages to Derbyshire, Cheshire and Cumbrian heiresses further advanced their fortunes and by the 14th century the head of the family was Chief Forester of Wirral with a coat of arms, three stags' heads on a bend, adapted from the ancient bailiwick of Wirral Forest.

It was that "brave and Valiant Gentleman", Sir John Stanley, veteran of Poictiers under the Black Prince, who set the clan firmly on the map. Edward III gave him a knighthood after a successful duel at Winchester with a haughty Frenchman. The tale goes that Isabel, the fabulously wealthy heiress of Lathom and Knowsley, was among the spectators, and that she fell in love with the bonny fighter upon whom Destiny and four monarchs were to shower honours like manna from heaven. They were married in 1385 and twenty years later Sir John received from Henry IV (Bolinbroke, Duke of Lancaster), for loyalty during the Percy Rebellion, the Lordship of Man "with the Castle and Peel of Man, and all Royalties, Regalities and Franchises &c" . . . in exchange for a cast of falcons at each coronation. He was Constable of Roxburgh Castle, Lord Justice of Ireland, Knight of the Garter and Knight of the Shire before his death in 1414.

The Legend of the Eagle and Child

The Lords of Lathom and Knowsley were established before the Conquest. Sir Robert de Lathom founded Burscough Priory. His great-grandson, Sir Thomas Lathom married a Dunham Massey heiress who produced only Isabel, whereas he had fathered several bastards. His favourite was Oskatel, son of Mary Oskatel, a young gentlewoman with whom Sir Thomas had enjoyed a love intrigue. Longing to recognise the child, the crafty fellow "had recourse to a pious cheat", arranging for the swaddled babe to be left in or near an eagle's nest within Lathom Hall Park. Then, taking his lawful lady a-walking and hearing cries, he sent a servant to investigate who discovered a human babe, and a male child, at that! Good Dame Lathom, probably not one wit fooled by the ploy, feigned gratitude for this gift from heaven, whom she tenderly reared as her own.

Oskatel grew up in his father's household and the doting knight would have made him his heir but for Isabel who was betrothed to Sir John Stanley.

The Stanleys, however, were powerful enough to insist that the endowments came with the bride or the deal was off! . . . and that is how they came into those vast estates centred upon Lathom and Knowsley. Oskatel did well enough, growing up a "compleat Gentleman", receiving a knighthood, inheriting Irlam, Urmston and other desmesnes from his natural father, and founding the Alderley branch of the family.

There are two versions of the Eagle and Child crest of the Stanleys. One states that the wily Sir Thomas Lathom adopted "an Eagle upon the wing turning her head back and looking in a sprightly manner as for something she had lost" . . . to give credence to the supposed miracle. The other suggests that Isabel's family, "in contempt and derision of their spurious brother", adopted an eagle with a cradled babe in its talons. Throughout Lancashire you will discover inns named in memory of these 14th century goings on, and it may occur to you that if Family Planning had operated 600 years ago, history would have turned out a good deal duller and tamer!

★   ★   ★   ★

Having secured the Lathom fortunes, the Stanleys enjoyed the confidence of successive monarchs. Prudent marriages increased their estates, one bringing Hornby Castle into the family; and Sir Thomas Stanley was made a baron in 1456. Stanleys led the Lancastrians in the Wars of the Roses. The second baron, Sir Thomas, "a wily fox", daintily negotiated that minefield that brought many to the block, despite his first wife being related to Warwick the Kingmaker! His second marriage to Margaret Beaufort made him step-father to the future Henry VII who was already over in France seeking assistance against Richard III. Richard had enemies galore. He was suspected of murdering the two little princes. His dilemma was painful, for here was a Stanley eloquently protesting his loyalty, too powerful to be shoved around, yet wed to that potentially dangerous lady, great-grand-daughter of John o' Gaunt, whose Plantaganet blood had passed to her sly and scheming son, Henry!

Craftily, Sir Thomas pleaded sickness and the need of good country air and went off to recuperate at Lathom, leaving his son and heir, Lord Strange, behind as a hostage. The Lady Margaret, meantime, was rusticated, deprived of attendants and cut off from her son who was planning an invasion. Henry Tudor landed at Milford Haven on 7th August, 1485, conferred a fortnight later, 6 miles short of Bosworth Field in Leicestershire, with his stepfather who had miraculously recovered! On the historic 22nd August, Sir Thomas openly sided with Henry against Richard, who threatened to slay the hostage. But, "having greater work in hand", failed to do so. The action was resolved by Sir William Stanley (brother to Sir Thomas) who rushed in with 3,000 fresh men and turned the tide in favour of Margaret Beaufort's pup. Richard III could have cut and run. Instead, he charged the enemy's standard-bearer and was dragged down and hacked to death. His crown, a golden ornament worn on particular occasions, rolled under a gorse bush where it was spotted by Sir Thomas Stanley. He placed it upon his step-son's head crying: "King Henry! King Henry!" and afterwards for this favour, or treachery, depending on how you regard it, Sir Thomas was created Earl of Derby and appointed Lord High Steward of England at the coronation of Henry VII in October 1485. Two years later, he was godfather to Prince Arthur, the King's first-born son.

The new Earl discovered it was no disadvantage to be the king's stepfather. Lucrative offices, benefits from forfeited estates and guardianship of the young Harrington heiresses enhanced the wealth of the Stanleys. They set about renewing Warrington bridge over the Mersey in 1495, and rebuilding an old hunting lodge in Knowsley deer park. Knowsley Hall, a jumble of architectural styles added by practically every generation for 500 years, incorporates a portion of the first Earl's re-build, though little is obvious from pre-17th century and the present title-holder has moved to a more modest property within the park.

In the dangerous post-Bosworth period, Sir William Stanley, who tipped the scales for Henry, was suspected of siding with Perkin Warbreck, who claimed to be one of the young murdered Princes. He lost his head for that in 1495, and his estates were snatched by the king. The first Earl died peacefully in 1504 with his head still secured to his shoulders, and was buried at Burscough Priory, as were his descendants until the Dissolution. His tomb and effigy were later shifted to Ormskirk Church to join later Stanleys.

Edward, the 3rd Earl, succeeded as a minor in the retinue of Cardinal Wolsey. By request of Henry VIII, his step-kinsman, he suppressed the Pilgrimage of Grace, seized Whalley Abbey, supervised the Dissolution of Lancashire monastic houses. He was trusted by Protestant Edward VI, went over to Rome for Mary Tudor who made him her Lord High Steward, and returned to the Anglican church to become Elizabeth's Privy Councillor and right-hand man in the county. This "great and honourable Earl" married thrice, fathered many children, lived in splendour maintaining 200 servants and feeding 60 aged and decrepit characters twice daily. On Good Fridays, some 2,700 received meat, drink and money and, indeed, all were welcome, for his gates were ever open and his hall swarmed with gentry and honest yeomen. Entertaining cost this tall benevolent man £4,000 per annum above the income from his two large parks, but he paid his bills on the dot and died, sincerely mourned, in 1572. For magnificence and pageantry, his funeral was unparalleled in the north, hundreds of notables, singing men, gentlemen, servants, yeomen and poor men processing from Lathom to Ormskirk "with weeping and tears".

LATHOM HOUSE in all its magnificence and as it must have looked in that halcyon period before the outbreak of the Civil War.

His son Henry, the 4th Earl, married Margaret Clifford, a descendant of Henry VII, but fortunately the lady had no dynastic ambitions, being content with life at Lathom — house-guests, family gatherings, preachers, politicians and match-making parents and their offspring forever arriving and departing. In addition to 4 sons and a daughter begot by his lady-wife, his lusty Lordship fathered 3 natural children by Jane Halsall, a young woman from Knowsley. They were well provided for and married suitably, and the Earl passed his happy and busy life between Lathom, The Tower at Liverpool, the Isle of Man and London. He was Lord High Steward of England, Lord Chamberlain of Chester, and died in 1594.

His second son succeeded, Ferdinand, the tragic 5th Earl "who went off the Stage of this World in the Flower of his Age, to the great loss of his Prince, Family and Country . . . an exalted genius . . . one of the most hopeful peers of the Age". And THAT, rumour would have it, by witchcraft! A waxen image with hair of his colouring and belly pricked with a pin was found in the sick chamber. Four months earlier, Richard Hackett, one of Elizabeth's exiled enemies, had pleaded with Ferdinand to snatch the crown of England. There was Tudor blood in his veins and the Queen was a confirmed virgin! Ferdinand scornfully declined and soon after fell foully sick, with such vomiting of "a dark rusty colour" that friends suspected poison or witchcraft. His Gentleman of Horse fled with one of his best mounts, never to be heard of again, and Ferdinand passed away leaving a wife, Alice Spenser of Althorpe and 3 young daughters.

His younger brother William, the 6th Earl, was the odd-ball of the family whose wanderings were talked about by folk who would "make themselves merry therewith". Twenty years or more, he was absent and assumed dead, his property settled on Ferdinand's daughters under the Guardianship of 4 Bishops and 4 Lords. When he returned eventually and claimed his birthright, only a few aged tenants recognised their true Lord. It took several years to sort things out, the Queen intervening on William's behalf, the girls being provided for, the Earl retaining Lathom, Knowsley, sundry castles, manors and property in

Lancashire, Cumbria, Yorkshire, Cheshire, Wales and London. In the early years of James I he also had his title to the Isle of Man confirmed and in 1637, infirm and full of years, he withdrew from "the hurry and fatigue of life" and died peacefully on Deeside in 1642.

A tragic destiny awaited his son and heir, James, Lord Strange, the 7th Earl (see Bolton). Yet, his youth was charmed, his marriage to a spirited French woman of high quality and noble birth most felicitous. Health, intelligence, the high regard of their peers, mutual affecton and pride in their brood of promising youngsters, blessed them with hopefulness for the future. Between brilliant court festivities and home life at Lathom they enjoyed the friendship of Prince Charles and Henrietta Maria, and when Charles inherited in 1625, they never anticipated the rift between monarchy and Parliament widening at last into bitter Civil War. When that happened, none stood more firmly for Charles Stuart than James Stanley, the 7th Earl. Where his illustrious ancestors might have neatly side-stepped, he fought the king's cause and forfeited his life. Letters to his son and heir reveal the commonsense of a deeply affectionate father, and his counsel is valid to-day as it was over 300 year ago.

> *Use great Caution in the choice of a Wife . . . a Man can probably err but once . . .*
> *Enquire well into her disposition . . . nor Chuse an uncomely Creature for Wealth, for it*
> *will cause Contempt in others and loathing with you . . .*
> *Chuse not a dwarf or a fool . . . As to your Housekeeping, let it be moderate rather*
> *plentiful than niggardly . . . Banish Drunkenness as a bane to health . . . and remember,*
> *the needy Man can never live happily . . .*
> *Bring your children up with Learning and Obedience yet without Austerity: Praise them*
> *openly. Reprehend them secretly . . . Be not scurrilous . . . nor satirical . . .*
> *Remember . . . That War is soon kindled, but Peace very hardly procured . . .*
> *Of all things, seek ye to know the Word of God . . . for he who is false to GOD, can never*
> *be true to Man.*

Charles, the 8th Earl, inherited an estate in confusion and disorder. Lathom House, that princely stronghold, had been destroyed, its park despoiled, the estate sequestrated. Similarly with Knowsley. Poor recompense for the loss of a father who had spent a fortune in support of the monarch and his son (Charles II) who was living in exile. Even at the Restoration in 1660, when Royalists anticipated the return of their estates, "nothing could prevail upon that ungrateful King (Charles II) to give his Royal Assent". A sad Earldom, one feels. He was succeeded by his sons, William and James, 9th and 10th Earls of Derby.

James succeeded in 1702. He embarked on major improvements at Knowsley, the royal slight to his late father still rankling and being immortalised in stone on the new elevation. This cultured gentleman of great artistic sense and organising ability, died without male heir in 1736, and the title passed to Edward Stanley of the Bickerstaffe branch, descended from the 1st Earl, born at Preston in 1689. After a long life of public service he was succeeded by son Edward, the 12th Earl, a sporting fellow who bred fighting cocks, founded the Derby in 1780 and raised a few eyebrows by taking a delightful Drury Lane actress for his second wife. It turned out well. The Earl was Lord Lieutenant of Lancashire for 58 years and twice Chancellor of the Duchy.

His son, Edward Stanley K.G., the 13th Earl, established a menagerie at Knowsley, famous for rare birds and mammals, delighting house-guests including Edward Lear who wrote many of his nonsense rhymes here, and justifying the outlay of £10,000 per annum. His son, Edward Geoffrey Stanley, 14th Earl from 1851–1869, brilliant scholar, great statesman and leader of the Conservatives after the fall of Sir Robert Peel following the repeal of the Corn Laws, was a superb all-rounder. He followed the Turf; his translation of Homer's Iliad was a runaway best-seller, he was Premier three times, resigning in favour of Disraeli, and was plagued by that old enemy of high-livers, namely gout! But he enjoyed his biblical span and was succeeded by his equally brilliant son, Edward Henry Stanley, the 15th Earl, who entered Parliament at 22, held high office, leaned towards social reform and pleaded fair-play for Jews and dissenters.

His brother, known affectionately as "The Honourable Fred" became 16th Earl in 1893, a man of warm heart and devotion to duty, immensely popular with those who met him at local functions, particularly along the Fylde coast for which he had a special affection. His son, Edward George Villiers Stanley, 17th Earl (1865–1948) is the one I clearly remember, a large benevolent gentleman who opened Queen Mary School, Lytham, when I was a brown-gym-slipped schoolgirl, one of those privileged and eager-eyed ones who were admitted in that September of 1930. His size, the black or dark grey which he habitually wore; the hats — somewhere between a topper and a bowler — and the atmosphere he brought with him, simultaneously kindly and regal, rendered him memorable. "The King of Lancashire", Randolph Churchill called him, and so he was, in terms of respect and affection. The previous week he had opened a new phase of Lytham Hospital. He was told that our two school courtyards had been named, at the wish of the scholars, after the Princesses Elizabeth and Margaret Rose. It was a pretty compliment which he proposed to convey to the proud grandparents, King George V and Queen Mary. He went further, took possession of a splendid framed photograph of the Queen, took it to London and had it signed, "MARY, R". It is one of the School's proudest possessions. The gallant old gentleman also added to Knowsley, placed the Eagle and Child crest in stone on the main block, and bowed out of public life after 50 years' service. Never was great noblemen more genial, more beloved, and the spirit of Lancashire paled a little with his passing.

His grandson, Edward John Stanley, M.C., who fought gallantly on Anzio's beaches, is the 18th and present Earl. He was Lord Lieutenant of the county, 1951–1968, but freed himself to work unrestrictedly for Lancashire in a swiftly changing world where hearts and hard-headedness often come into conflict. Knowsley was too large. Reality had to be faced, and despite the family motto "sans Changer", the palatial hall passed to the Lancashire County Constabulary, the Earl and Countess occupying a smaller property within the park which is positively HUGE! Visit the Safari Park and you will see what I mean; note that estate wall, miles of it, those acres of thick woodland; those vast areas occupied by exotic beasts, from lions and tigers (the notices advise you to KEEP GOING because they CAN damage your tyres!) to rhinos and giraffes; from eland and zebra, to cheetahs, elephants, ostrich, buffaloes and baboons! The White Hunter always handy in emergencies!

Nice to see these fascinating creatures living, fighting, playing, breeding, without interference from menacing homo sapiens. Lovely to see the landscape rising and dipping, and glorious clumps of woodland, green as emeralds, and dappled deer, and sun glinting on a quiet lake dotted with waterfowl; and rabbits, in their MILLIONS! Even the smallest babies don't budge an inch when vehicles drive by. Day in, day out, they've seen it all before! But of Knowsley Hall itself, not a glimpse, not even at a distance. A disappointment; the rest, pure joy! And the marvel of the vastness of Knowsley Park, 14,000 acres where Earls and their courtly connections rode, hunted, dallied in a green domain, a whole world apart from the hum-drum!

Side wings, Lathom House.

The great Lathom House mystery

Pilkingtons', the world's greatest name in the manufacture of flat glass, began at St. Helens when John Mackay & Company established a casting hall at Ravenhead in 1773. Nearly two centuries later they built Research and Development Laboratories on an elevated site once occupied by Lathom House, Royalist fortress, home of the 7th Earl of Derby whose gallant Countess, a woman of spirit and sparkle, defied Parliament and achieved immortality as one of the romantic heroines of history.

Afterwards, this vast establishment, with its ample food, coal and water supplies, totally disappeared so that arguments even raged about its actual location. A later Lathom house, dismantled in the 1920's, was built for Sir Thomas Bootle in the 1720's with a central block and two side wings of which one, used as stabling, remained when I last visited. But the original site remained a mystery until Dr. Geoffrey Copley, Materials Science department manager, who joined Pilkingtons' in 1961, became curious enough to examine the evidence. Drawing inspiration from Broxap's work and various learned papers, and cheerfully admitting: "I am not a historian — I just approach a problem scientifically to find an answer!", a typical boffin's reaction, he began investigating, not with the spade "which could cause serious damage", but by resort to aerial photography which seemed to indicate foundations, a moat and entrenchments, probably Parliamentarian, and making calculations based on 17th century firing power.

In November 1980, I met Dr. Copley and an equally enthusiastic colleague, John Alderson, with whom I spent a convivial hour or two going through the evidence, including grids, maps, aerial and ground photographs, notes of excavations by Holly Lodge 6th Form pupils, records of musket and round-shot picked up in neighbouring fields, male skeletons unearthed in the 1850's and 1860's, a carved fragment of the Derby crest, chunks of masonry and numerous foundations, all discovered within a neglected area known as "Spa Roughs". The surrounding land is cultivated which suggests that "Spa Roughs" was the original site of Lathom House, the rubble after demolition making ploughing too difficult for local farmers. Dr. Copley's revealing article on the subject, published in the company's house-organ, "Pilkington News" (10/1/79), makes fascinating reading and suggests that "an important historical prize could be waiting on the company's doorstep".

★   ★   ★   ★

A short distance from R. & D. Laboratories is the ancient Chapel of St. John, founded by the 2nd Earl of Derby, consecrated in 1500 A.D., and a cluster of picturesque 18th century almshouses adjoining. During the Civil War, Roundheads stabled their horses in the chapel and the screen is scarred with their bullets. Visiting this little community, set back from the highway, is like travelling back through the ages, proof again that dear Old Lancashire is far too modest for her own good; does not lay all her goods in the shop window, bragging, boasting, and button-holing the passer-by to come and view her ancient treasures. But they are there, all the same, lying not far from every beaten track; and the chap who is tired of finding them out is not only tired of Life! . . . but I would respectfully suggest that he is already DEAD!

The flatlands and Martin Mere

Motoring across the Lancashire plain south of the Ribble reminds me of the flat-lands of Over-Wyre; or the "low spongie" acres of Marton Moss, behind Blackpool, where reclamation began in 1731 and gathered momentum in the late 18th century. As a result, Marton Mere, once 6 miles by 1½, diminished steadily and valuable acres were put under "Whete" which, in Leland's day, was "not veri communely sowid in thes partes".

Across the Ribble, its counterpart, Martin Mere covered 12 square miles with "islands" poking up here and there and a circumference of 18 miles in a rainy spell. To the east, flood waters tumbled into the River Douglas, Rufford being the old ford over the outfall. Traveller Celia Fiennes avoided the infamous "Martin's Mer" which was "hazardous for Strangers to pass by it".

Thomas Fleetwood of Bank Hall, Bretherton, was the first to tackle Martin Mere which wasted so much fertile land. In 1692 he proposed to cut an outlet through to the Ribble Estuary with flood-gates to hold back the sea at high tide. Problems developed, however, and those gates were adjusted several times before Thomas Eccleston of Scarisbrick Hall entered the lists, c. 1778. He was a passionate agriculturist. He knew John Gilbert, the Duke of Bridgewater's ingenious Agent. By fitting three pairs of flood-gates, slicing a channel through the bed of the Mere and cutting 8 miles of ditches per day with a guttering plough drawn by teams of horses, the farming Squire lived to see reclaimed acres yielding cereal crops and good grazing, long before his death in 1809. Meantime, Thomas Hesketh of Rufford was using a steam engine to pump flood-water into the sluice and thence into the river at Crossens.

Full credit, however, to Thomas Fleetwood, that well-loved pioneer who, 300 years before one brick had been set upon another at Southport, "converted the immense Martonian Mere into firm dry land, a deed which older generations dare nor attempt and future will scarcely believe". He was buried in 1717 in St. Cuthbert's Church, North Meols (Churchtown), the "Mele" of Domesday, the Mother of Southport and,

BANK HALL, BRETHERTON (top), part of Lord Lilford's estates, is an imposing brick house dating back to 1608 with early 19th century additions. From *c.* 1200, it passed from the Banastres to the Fleetwoods and in 1717 to the Leghs of Lyme. The lower portion (right) became offices for the Agent.

SOUTHPORT'S mother village of Churchtown (North Meols) (bottom) has a number of picturesque thatched and whitewashed cottages which have survived from the days of the old fishing community from which the sea gradually retreated.

to my mind, the most attractive community in Old Lancashire. Strangely, the majority of visitors are oblivious of its existence. Ride up Roe Lane to the Botanic Gardens (where, incidentally, the Local History Museum has a collection of early water colours that will charm the very eyes out of your head!) . . . and there you are! At the old fishing village — meols means sand-dunes — from which the sea receded, with charming olde-worlde thatched cottages from which old dames once trundled, bucket in hand, to the pump; and youngsters played on doorsteps, and cats snoozed on window sills, and barefoot men walked to their boats or mended their nets and dried them in the sun.

The de Coudrays owned the manor until A.D. 1200, then the Aughtons, the Bolds, and the Heskeths of Rufford whose descendant married the Fleetwood heiress from Rossall. Here, between 875–883, rested the precious remains of St. Cuthbert to whom the church, completely rebuilt in the 1730's, is dedicated. It has many interesting features and memorials, including an attractive monument to Roger Hesketh, by Nollekins. John Linaker, the Hesketh Agent, erected the stocks, now railed off near the church, in 1741. They were last occupied in 1861 by a local drunk! Two handsome old white inns complete the village picture, the Hesketh Arms and the Bold Arms; and across the way, behind entrance gates brought from Bold Hall, stands the ancient manorial house, Meols Hall, smaller now than formerly, where the famous Jesuit, Edmund Campion, took shelter in 1581.

Southport

The story of Southport's founder, William Sutton, the Churchtown innkeeper, has been told ad nauseam and yet deserves to be briefly sketched. The jovial fellow was probably as startled as anyone when strangers came to bathe in the sea! Like all other coastal communities, the isolated village was entirely fixed in its ways. It had been a hot-bed of recusancy; and in the 18th century it clung to the old suspicions of bathing in any form! However, Blackpool had been attracting sea-bathers for fifty years and when it dawned on Sutton that the craze had come to stay he erected a wooden hut in the South Hawes sand-hills for the use of his patrons. "The Old Duke", as he was nicknamed, little dreamt in 1792 that he was founding the most elegant resort in Lancashire and, possibly, in the north of England. The fastidious had not yet appeared. The "lower orders" dossed down among the fisherfolk. Within six years Sutton leased half a dozen acres round his bathing hut, built a new inn (they called it "The Duke's Folly"), and summoned his cronies to a house-warming. Wine flowed free! Dr. Barton, lately retired from Ormskirk, presided, smashed a ceremonial bottle of port and proposed health to this new "South Port". The convivial party promptly renamed a watercourse which ran outside the "Folly" and spilled on to Birkdale sands after the famous Egyptian river, having recently heard of Nelson's Victory at the Nile. A tablet commemorating Sutton's activities can be found embedded in a wall at the southern Lord Street–Duke Street corner. Lord Street, one of the most dignified shopping thoroughfares in the kingdom, was originally Lords' Street, in deference to joint landowners. It developed in the 1820's in a wide low-lying "slack" between two lines of sandhills and set the tone for gracious streets, fine properties, splendid parks that emerged in the ensuing years.

Formby

Formby, seven miles south of Southport, has survived drastic visitations, human and non-human. About 2600 B.C., a storm destroyed the great forest near the River Alt. Norse settlers arrived early in the 10th century . . . the name comes from Forni's byr, meaning homestead or settlement . . . the sea encroached in the Middle Ages; the Alt and Downholland Brook frequently spilled over, there were marshes around Martin Mere and the Douglas once emptied into the sea here. In more recent centuries, blowing sand was a menace, blocking drains, destroying farmlands, even overwhelming the graveyard and the early 12th century chapel of Ravenmeols, bringing its life to a close in 1739. Three years later, they built the attractive Georgian Church of St. Peter, well away from the tides, using some ancient original stones, a bell of 1661 and the sundial that stands near the porch.

Formby Hall, the attractive manor house of the ancient family of Formby who settled in the 12th century, was rebuilt in 1523, embellished with battlements in the 18th century and modernised in Victoria's reign. It is used now by the Brontë Society as a holiday home for Liverpool children, and stands in secluded woodlands to the north of Formby. Female descendants of the Formbys built St. Luke's Church beside the old sand-invaded graveyard when the area was expected to become as popular as Southport. I am fond of this "Little Chapel in the Dunes" (1855) where so many Formbys are buried. A "rose" window in the west wall depicts floral species common to the area. A Norman font with a 23-sided base and carvings worn away by farmers sharpening implements was unearthed from a boundary cop after the sand-blow. The porch houses the tombstone of Richard Formby, a giant of a man, Armour Bearer to the King, who died in 1407. It was smashed during a fire at York Minster in 1840 and returned to Formby.

There was a homespun charm about the place a hundred years ago — plenty of thatch, a couple of windmills, stocks and a village cross on Cross Green. There is a hint of it still, though the stocks and a wooden replica of the cross, encased in zinc, were brought to St. Luke's churchyard for safekeeping. The Formby tombs are there from the old church and William Percy French, composer of the Irish songs, "Phil the Fluter's Ball" and "Mountains of Mourne", was buried here in 1920, having died during a visit. The outstanding curiosity is the Godstone, a pagan relic which Christian missionaries made respectable by having it carved with a Calvary cross topped by a circle. It was the custom in old times to carry a corpse around it three times in the direction of the sun to prevent the departed from haunting loved ones. Among one of my W.E.A. groups was a gentleman who had noticed a coffin being carried thrice round the churchyard, prior to interment, in Holland, suggesting that old superstitions have not quite died out! Formby to-day is famous for asparagus growing, its pine-woods and wildlife.

Ince Blundell, Sefton, Lydiate

South of Formby, an area flat as a fenland and as treeless except where landowners had bothered to plant was dominated by Blundells whose ancestors arrived with the Conqueror. The Crosby Hall family, who still occupy their ancient seat, were ardent Catholics, hounded, punitively fined, imprisoned and even banished for their Faith. Yet they gave sons to the church, maintained the first R.C. Chaplain in Lancashire, harboured priests from 1568–1708 — a Jesuit arrested here in 1590 died in Lancaster Castle of gaol fever — and had the Mass said secretly for the devout of the district. They were dedicated scribblers, adding to the Great Hodge Podge covering nearly 3 centuries and begun in the 1590's. William the Cavalier and Nicholas the Diarist, between them, noted family doings for almost 100 years up to 1728. In 1708 Ned Howerd's cottage in the village (identified by a cross on the gable) served as a Mass centre until 1720 when the Diarist built a chapel discreetly referred to as West Lane House. It became a school and convent when St. Mary's R.C. Church, rich in Blundell memorials and paintings of English Martyrs, was built in 1847 by Nicholas's great-grandson William. The present Crosby Hall, mostly Georgian, has a splendid library and stands embowered in conspicuous woodlands.

The Blundells of Ince Blundell (meaning Blundell's island), like their namesakes, were Catholics, Royalists and Jacobites who suffered much even, for a time, being forced into Irish exile. They planted fine trees for privacy, for shelter from the sea-winds. Their handsome hall, rebuilt in early Georgian style, was a Jesuits' centre, and a palace of treasures in Henry's time, he being as obsessive a collector of antiquities as his chum and fellow-Jacobite, Charles Towneley of Towneley. When a specially built garden temple overflowed, Henry Blundell added an entrance hall in the form of a Pantheon, with niches to house carvings from ancient cultures. Alas, they have departed, some to Liverpool Art Gallery. The Weld Blundells also left after the last war and the property is now a convalescent home used by Augustinian nuns.

Pre-Reformation, the Crosby Blundells heard Mass in the fine old embattled Parish Church of Sefton, built in the 1530's though the soaring spire is 14th century. Here in 1698, a great gathering of Blundells brought the old "Cavalier" to be buried in the family vault beneath the north-east aisle. Here are the most magnificent medieval and Tudor monuments of Old Lancashire, effigies, brasses, tombs and monuments of the great Molyneux family whose ancestor "de Molines", came over with William. Richard was knighted at Agincourt; Sir William fought nobly at Flodden. They rest in goodly company. Carvings abound here, in the canopied rood screen (early 1500's), the elaborate Sefton pew, the chancel stalls, the canopied pulpit (1635). Only the moated site remains now of the illustrious family's great hall.

Lydiate, near the Leeds–Liverpool canal, has the "Scottish Piper", claimed to be Lancashire's oldest inn, and two interesting ruins. "Lydiate Abbey", so called, was the small church of St. Katharine, built by Lawrence Ireland with a buttressed tower in the 1460's and dismantled at the Reformation. A figure of the Saint and reredos carvings are in St. Mary's R.C. Church built in the 1850's by the Weld–Blundells facing the ancient remains of Lydiate Hall. The oldest portion burned down two centuries ago. Plaster gradually

SCOTCH PIPER INN, LYDIATE (above) on the A567 between Southport and Liverpool, claimed to be the oldest pub in historic Lancashire, dating back to 1320 and built round a massive tree which still supports part of the roof. One family, the Moorcrofts, held the licence for 500 years until 1945. The name was changed from the Royal Oak following the 1715 Jacobite Rebellion, when a wounded Highlander fell in love with and married the Innkeeper's daughter. Beer is drawn from the wood. There is no cellar here.

SCARISBRICK HALL (right) designed by Augustus Pugin in 1840 and completed in 1868 by his son Edward Pugin must be one of the most exciting buildings in the north-west. The Scarisbricks were in possession until 1948 when the hall was converted into St. Katherine's Training College which closed in 1963 in which year Headmaster C. A. Oxley, M.A., and Mrs. Oxley, bought the Hall and 50 acres for a non-profit-making independent day and boarding school. It operates on sound Christian principles and now has 700 pupils of both sexes from 4 to 18.

decayed from the wooden skeleton of a 15th century house where archaeologists have been occupied during the last year or two.

The new West Lancashire District

Behind Southport and Formby, the new West Lancashire District spreads from the Ribble Estuary marshes to Aughton and Bickerstaffe in the south, and eastwards beyond the modest hills of Parbold and Harrock to Wrightington where lived the Dicconsons, Catholics caught up in Jacobite plottings and ardent enough to join the royal exiles at St. Germain. No peace of mind for this family for generations, but Wrightington Hall is more famous now for miracles of modern orthopaedic surgery and renewed hopes of mobility for many.

At the heart of the District, on an old Roman route, Ormskirk has been holding street markets (Thursdays and Saturdays) since 1286. Was a settlement really founded here by Orm, the Viking, as they locally believe? Domesday did not include it, though it was the administrative centre of West Derby Hundred. In Abbey Lane off the A59 road to Burscough, beside parked caravans, rises a residual fragment of Burscough Priory, an Augustinian house founded in the 12th century and stripped to the ground after the Dissolution. From 1190, Burscough brethren served Ormskirk Church until a Vicar was appointed in 1286. Fashionable Tudor families had town houses at Ormskirk, the Stanleys occupying the Mansion House in St. Helen's Road. Young Will Shakespeare performed for the Lathoms of Lathom House and for Ormskirk folk in a theatre behind the old Ship Inn in Moor Street, now a shop, in 1577–8. A grammar school stood north of the churchyard in 1610, the old town cross being replaced in 1876 by a clock tower. When the Town Hall (now shops) bearing the Eagle and Child crest was built in 1799, Ormskirk was an important coaching centre with numerous inns and 30 vehicles per day clattering off in all directions until the railway opened in 1849. An influx of poor Irish labouring families created slum conditions leading to fevers and the deadly cholera.

The town's pride is the Parish Church, a combination of Saxon, Norman and Perpendicular. It is unusual in having a spire, a separate tower and a legend about two sisters who could not agree which to choose, so they built both! Not so! The steeple is 15th century. The massive buttressed tower, c.1540, was built to accommodate Burscough Priory bells from masonry lugged from the same source. The great Stanleys, screened off in the Derby chapel, had their vault here after the Dissolution. Henry VII worshipped here after Bosworth. The hexagonal font was donated by the courageous Countess of Derby who defied Parliament for so long during the Civil War, one of the highlights of that grim and bitter business. Afterwards, Lathom House was so totally destroyed that even the site became a subject for debate.

Over to the west, the A567 leads to Halsall, a farming parish with a beautiful Church of St. Cuthbert dating back to 1250 and containing some of Old Lancashire's best work from many periods. A Decorated doorway, 15th century stalls with misericords, 14th century alcove tomb and early Perpendicular tower and spire are among the features that deserve to be seen. The choir vestry was an Elizabethan Free Grammar School founded by the Halsalls and Sir Henry Halsall, who married a Stanley lady, appears in effigy on a table tomb of 1523. Tucked away in an unspoilt corner of the Liverpool diocese, it comes as a pleasant shock to discover craftsmanship of such high quality.

Two or three miles north, on the A570 Ormskirk–Southport road, pleasure boats cruise along the canal at Scarisbrick, and a monstrous tower, vaguely reminiscent of Big Ben's, soars 100 feet above a skyline that is pure flight of fancy. A jungle of wrought iron, a gaggle of gargoyles, crockets, finials, gables, pinnacles and weathervanes, vie for attention with a clutch of winged angels perched on a turret by virtue of a rich eccentric's passion for Gothic ornamentation. Plumptious! . . . Fantabulous! . . . words have to be specially coined for Scarisbrick Hall, a veritable Palace of Treasures, home of the Scarisbricks from the 12th century until 1945 and now an Evangelical Day and Boarding School for boys.

Linger a while. From the gates or from the lake formed early last century, gaze upon this phenomenon, this patchwork of European treasures welded together by House of Commons Designer, Augustus Welby Pugin (the Elder). Consider that, after the family departed, the property was transformed at colossal expense into a teachers' training college, then abandoned as uneconomic! Afterwards, the whole conglomeration of ancient and modern was sold, metaphorically "for a song" to a Liverpool headmaster with the proviso that everything remains in situ. The unique character of the place, for the forseeable future, should therefore be safe.

Like their neighbours, the Scarisbricks were devout Catholics, maintaining priests, treading warily through political and religious minefields, swelling their acres by draining portions of Martin Mere. Their hall was crumbling by 1814 and Foster, the Architect, began rebuilding and was still at it when his patron died in 1833. A bachelor inherited, Charles Scarisbrick, High Sheriff of Lancashire, a strange fellow, somewhat of a recluse. Yet, with Pugin the Elder he scoured chateaux, cathedrals, monasteries and churches from the Netherlands to Italy, ransacking, crating up and shipping home for the next stage of the project. The result is a glorious Gothic mish-mash, an architectural absurdity and an extravaganza befitting one of the richest commoners of his day.

When Charles Scarisbrick died suddenly while seated before the dining room fire in May 1860, his last playful prank was revealed in the reading of the will which instructed the undertakers to bear his corpse in a perfectly straight line from the hall to Bescar Chapel where he had left a puzzling gap in the Presbytery garden wall. Accordingly, the mourners proceeded on foot across planks over ditches, through gaps slashed through hedges, across a meadow, a wheatfield, a potato patch and finally through the gap, which was afterwards closed.

Charles's equally wayward sister Anne (Lady Hunloke) succeeded, "the fairest woman in Europe", declared George IV during a visit to Preston Guild in 1822. She took over where he left off, employed the architect's son, "Pugin the Younger", and dreamed up even more elaborate notions. The original clock tower plan, designed as a run-up to "Big Ben", was jettisoned in favour of that assertive, cloud-nudging, disproportionate pile that looks heavy enough to pull the whole building over on its side!

If the exterior is magnificent, an incomparable feast awaits the eye within! Massive doors, 6″ thick and deeply carved on both sides, gilded ceilings, hand-printed wallpapers bearing the initials A.S. (for Anne Scarisbrick), a magnificent Drawing Room, the King's Room where monarchs are painted on panels beneath an elaborate ceiling, and other priceless mementoes, recall the Scarisbrick adventures. When Gladstone visited before Christmas in 1867, Lady Anne ordered the whole neighbourhood to be illuminated with Bengal Lights, while the hall's ornamental features were bathed in red, green, blue and white lights when estate workers and their wives clambered over roofs waving torches and touching off flares. Sheer exhibitionism, wanton extravagance, a glorious exercise in eccentricity but what a performance!

Winging eastwards to Rufford, ancient seat of the Catholic Heskeths, we can visit their hall, National Trust property now, an amalgam of 15th century "magpie" and Carolean, with a splendid timber-framed great hall unchanged for five centuries, where the young Shakespeare performed, and priests were hidden, and a resident "grey lady" is still on duty long after perilous illicit visits and persecutions. The area is watered by Rivers Yarrow and Douglas that rise in neighbouring nurseries in the haunted heights above Rivington, near Winter Hill. Yarrow ("rough water") skirts Chorley, bumbles towards Eccleston and Croston, both having churches reaching back to the Angles. Croston actually has a cross at the entrance to a little unspoilt village street leading to St. Michael's church with its massive 15th century tower and a superb early 18th century Rectory, impressive and elegant, as befitted the incumbent of a once wide-spreading parish.

The River Douglas, one of the earliest rivers to be improved by "navigations" in the pre-canal era (1720–1742), wanders down to Blackrod and Wigan. It was useful for transporting coal from the heart of Lancashire to the Ribble Estuary and thence to Ireland and the north. The Douglas (alias Astland) collects Yarrow near Bretherton and soon after receiving the little Lostock heads for marriage with the Ribble opposite Freckleton Naze. It is a historic river. According to Nennius, a 9th century monk, the legendary Arthur fought the invaders on the banks of "Dubglas", and there are rumours of the Celtic chieftain and his valiant Round Tablers haunting the Holmeswood area of Rufford, at the edge of dark.

There is much to interest folks like me along the busy Liverpool–Preston highroad. At Tarleton, the manorial courts were once held at The Ram's Head (1640). Halfway down the hill which is a notorious accident black-spot stands the attractive little Georgian Church of St. Mary (1719) which replaced an earlier crumbling Tudor structure. It is usually closed, used only for occasional funerals and for the obligatory annual service to keep the licence on the fourth Sunday in August. The Lord of the Manor built it there for his own convenience. The Tarleton villagers were less enthusiastic about a long slog up a muddy country lane and in the end they rebelled, built another church, smack in the village, in the 1880's, and kept the old place only for burials. They were a dogged lot, "some of the hardest workers and best ale drinkers in England" was how Hewitson, travelling last century, described them. I included both in my "Country Churches" broadcasts, delighted at last to gain entry into the "old" church, equally pleased to visit the "new" which has eight of the sweetest toned bells in Old Lancashire, and a splendid team to ring them!

Where the highroad crosses both canal and river, then turns sharply left, Bank Hall, rebuilt in 1608, hides among trees, a fine building gone to seed with woodworm and dry rot working their mischief. It belongs to Lord Lilford's estate and a portion is still used as offices by the Agent. Apart from that, it is silent, with grounds somewhat overgrown when last I visited, and a grandeur still in a great brick building with curved gables, Victorian additions, and a tower bearing chess-pieces carved in stone, silhouetted against the sky. The Banastres were here, then the Fleetwoods, including Thomas, the drainage pioneer, and afterwards the Leghs of Lyme. A little nearer Preston, a picturesque tower windmill has been converted into a home, and the older cottages, of brick made from local clay, have an attractive warm russet hue.

At the junction of Carr House Lane, a bonny bow-frontred toll-house is a left-over from the old Turnpike days. Carr House, one of our historic houses was built by the Stones brothers, Thomas and Andrew, in 1613 for their brother John, a sheep farmer, for they were all somehow connected with wool. This lovely early Jacobean house was derelict, with woodwork ripped out, floorboards and stair-treads knocked up and dead sheep lying about, twenty years ago when I and my W.E.A. enthusiasts discovered it and took it to our hearts. There was a ghastly rent down the facade and such a prevalent air of decay that we rejoiced mightily to hear that it was to be restored and used to house Barry Elder's Doll Museum (now at Lancaster). In fact, we were the first members of the public to be allowed in before the official opening, and many exhibits were contributed by my eager friends to whom the house was significant on account of its association with Jeremiah Horrocks.

This young genius, a self-taught astronomer from Toxeth, came as curate to St. Michael's Church, Much Hoole, built in 1628 as a Chapel of Ease to Croston; and probably augmented his income by tutoring the Stones' youngsters at Carr House where he lodged in the room above the porch. By October 1639 he suspected that the planet Venus would pass between Earth and Sun, a phenomenon never before noticed. Of all ill luck, it was due to happen on a Sunday, 24th November, 1639, and one can imagine the fevered youth wrapping up the services, locking up and galloping back along muddy field paths to his lodgings, hoping to witness this Transit of Venus by means of the most primitive equipment and only if the weather conditions allowed! He and his friend, William Crabtree keeping vigil at Broughton, Manchester, were privileged to witness this rare occurrence which led indirectly to Captain Cook's adventures and discoveries in the 18th century. Jeremiah Horrocks, "The Pride and Boast of British Astronomy . . . one of England's most illustrious sons", died shortly after at the age of 22 and is commemorated in a stained glass window and a mural tablet at St. Michael's, Much Hoole, which, to me, is the cosiest, best cared for and most attractive of all the county's little country churches. The tower (1720) has a sun-dial as a memorial to that inspired Toxeth youth who rose above agonising doubts, lack of tutors and isolation from kindred spirits, to complete his life's work for which he will ever be remembered and honoured. Carr House, part of the Lilford estates, is now privately occupied.

Wigan

This was Roman "Coccium" where roads met and marching legions rested, where brave Arthur fought the invaders and Anglo-Saxons settled — yet, it was omitted from Domesday! After the Conquest, Wigan belonged to the Barony of Newton, became one of Lancashire's earliest free boroughs with its own Guild Merchant in 1246, Monday markets from 1258 and Friday markets from the 14th century. The magnificent Parish Church of All Saints, likened to "a small cathedral", was rebuilt last century with many left-overs. Portions of the tower are 700 years old, thicker than a man's height, and contain a fragment from a Roman altar. Towering above the Market Place, the church constantly reminded stallholders of their Christian obligations.

In the grounds of a Girls' School up Standishgate, a curious relic known as Mab's Cross commemorates a 14th century marital hiatus. Sir William Bradshaigh, husband of heiress Mabel Norris of Haigh, fled into exile after engaging in the Banastre Rebellion of 1315. Years later, he stole back disguised as a palmer, discovered his lady, supposing him dead, had been coerced into an unhappy union with a wicked Welshman. Whereupon, he pursued the usurper, slew him at Newton-le-Willows and was very quickly pardoned and re-instated. Lady Mabel's confessor, however, with perhaps typical medieval male chauvinism, subjected her to the public humiliation of trudging barefoot and bearing a lighted candle to the Standishgate, two miles away, "onst a week" in penance for her supposed bigamy. Fortunately the couple were reunited and appear in effigy upon their tomb in the parish church.

During the Civil War, Royalist Wigan suffered much, an outbreak of plague in 1648 crowning the town's miseries. After the monarch's execution, when his son (Charles II) returned, the Royalists recklessly rallied again to the Earl of Derby, lately come over from his safe Island, and at the approach to the town along Wigan Lane on 25th August, 1651, were ambushed by Roundheads. The Earl survived, two horses shot from under him, and escaped, with a few companions; but his deputy and colleague in many a campaign, Sir Thomas Tyldesley of Myerscough Lodge, was mown down along with many others. An obelisk was raised at the very spot, years later, by a young Cornet, Alexander Rigby, when he became High Sheriff of Lancashire. It proclaims Tyldesley's greatness in admiring terms, exhorts his descendants "to follow the noble example of their Loyal Ancestor".

Afterwards, Sir Thomas's son, Edward Tyldesley, built Fox Hall, now a pub, as a summer home on the Blackpool sea-front. The Cavalier's grandson, another Thomas, a jolly Jacobite, diarist and socialite, left records which are full of interest and amusement. His death at the end of 1714 preserved him from the trauma of the approaching Rebellion. Wigan Jacobites were deeply involved in the Lancashire Plot of 1690–4 to restore James II, in the fiasco of 1715 and the tragedy of 1745. In advance and retreat, Charles Edward Stuart is reputed to have lodged twice in the Hallgate.

In 1678, Wigan was the first English town to market field-crop potatoes and was fast becoming famous for pewter, porcelain, clock and cabinet-making, brass and bell-founding, a small degree of ironworking and coal. In Henry VIII's time, Leland had noted "summe Marchauntes, sum Artificers, sum Fermers" and the discovery of "moche Canal like Se Coole", ("cannel" which provided heat and light for the poor and was also used for roofing, flooring and ornamental carvings.) Coal-getting became a cottage-industry, householders burrowing in their backyards, to the annoyance of neighbours, and many pits being sunk around Wigan.

Georgian Wigan became famous also for textiles, for every kind of bedding, canvas, coverlets and rugs. A Cloth Hall was opened in 1784. Local chalybeate springs turned the place briefly into a Spa until coal-workings caused contamination. The improvement of the Douglas (1720), the construction of a canal in 1727 and its extension to Liverpool in 1772 (purchased later by the Leeds–Liverpool company), bolstered local trade. Eight cotton mills operated here in 1818 and the town was an important coaching centre. In 1780 the Earl of Crawford and Balcarres married the Bradshaigh heiress and settled at the earlier Haigh Hall which their son rebuilt in the 1830's after mining subsidence. The gracious mansion was crammed with treasures and priceless writings, (many now in Manchester's Rylands Library), and its fine park, acquired by the Corporation in 1947, contained 244 acres of woodland, gardens and banks of brilliantly coloured azaleas and rhododendrons. As if it were yesterday, I recall a bitterly cold winter's Sunday when I and my cheery band clambered aboard the tractor-train and toured the grounds as snow-flakes swirled down, promising to come back and enjoy the shrubs in full bloom.

Wigan has seen much action. Luddite risings, Chartist riots in the 1840's, Cotton Famine sufferings of the 1860's, and the founding of the first two miners' unions here in 1862. Yet, they scoff, who don't know better, and snigger at out-worn allusions to "Wigan Pier", a short stretch of canal wharf, incorporated into the Music Hall act of one born at Ashton-under-Lyne, the illegitimate son of a drunken mother. James Booth became "George", adopted the name Formby from a coal-wagon in Wigan sidings, married Eliza Hoy from Wigan where their son, George Formby Junior was born in 1904. "The Lad from Wigan" or "The Wigan Nightingale" was how the chronically bronchitic, George Senior, was billed. He died after a fatal coughing spasm in February 1921. George Formby Junior was pure box office magic, as popular to-day as in life, with many impersonators, some little more than toddlers and several coming tantalisingly close to that special magic. We adored the naive grinning gormless appealing fellow with teeth like marble tombstones hanging out to dry, an artless innocence with saucy lyrics and an infectious twanging technique on the ukulele. Nobody could wear a magnificently-cut suit like George, whose apparent "daftness", (over which he must have been chuckling all the way to the bank), often obscured the plain truth that he was simply loaded with Sex Appeal!

During their latter years, George and Beryl Formby were near neighbours, living "round the corner" on the Promenade, Fairhaven, near Queen Mary School, supposedly the most devoted couple in Show Business. The bitter truth emerged after Beryl's death on Christmas Day 1960. She had spotted his potential in 1923, and, Svengali-like, had developed his genius, master-minded his success, married him and kept him in total subjection, summoning him for meals with a police-whistle, doling out 25p a day pocket money and jealously driving away any female competition. Within weeks came the shock announcement of his imminent re-marriage. When I commented involuntarily: "Don't worry! Beryl hasn't finished with him yet!" my Mother, suspicious of anything "spooky", demanded an explanation and I couldn't give one. But the answer came on 6th March 1961 when George Formby died of a heart condition, having striven vainly to marry his sweetheart on his hospital death-bed.

In the bitter family wranglings that followed, it could only have been the lawyers for whom it "Turned Out Nice Again!", to quote the famous catchphrase. Tragically, George's fiancee, the principal beneficiary, died in her early 40's in 1971.

★　　★　　★　　★

Those two industrial monarchs, King Coal and King Cotton, finally expired in 1967 but their demise was predictable and Wigan had switched to new industries in engineering, the rag trade and food production. The town is as addicted as ever to Rugby and all the ball games, athletics and pigeon fancying. Culturally, Wigan is very much alive, warm-hearted and welcoming as ever and it will take a lot more than a mere recession to knock the stuffing out of this historic Borough which locally they call "Wiggin".

Haigh Hall, Wigan.

17. TWO GREAT CITIES

Manchester

Like a snail retreating into its shell, I shrink from the bustle of great cities, but when I travel in by rail, I marvel anew at Manchester's vitality and its great contributions to this Modern Age of Change. Down the centuries everything happened here. Ancient Britons camped beside the Irwell. Romans established Mamucium (corrupted to "Mancunium"), built linking roads and departed c. 400 A.D. Angles and Danes clashed or coexisted and Norsemen filtered in from the west. Christian missionaries saved souls and a church was recorded in Domesday within Salford Hundred. In the hey-day of Monasticism after the Conquest, an off-shoot of Lenton Priory (Notts) functioned at Kersal Cell. The Grelleys were Lords of the Manor, followed by the La Warrs, then the Wests who once entertained Henry VII after Bosworth; and finally the Mosleys who held feudal sway until the Corporation purchased the manorial rights and privileges for £200,000 in 1846 and embarked upon long overdue improvements.

Leland described Manchester as "the fairest, best builded . . . town of all Lancashire". It was linked with Salford across the Irwell by a three-arched bridge upon which "is a pretty little chapel" and the townsfolk lived by "finishing" woollens produced in outlying towns, or weaving coarse linens from locally grown flax. A free grammar school was founded here in 1515 by Hugh Oldham, the Lancastrian Bishop of Exeter, but there was no hint then that Manchester would become one of the world's leading centres of Science, Scholarship, Medicine, Reform, Commerce and Music.

In the 17th century this "most industrious" town, noted for "civility and religion" turned from woollens to fustians. Its Radicalism stems from Civil War days when the majority supported Parliament, but the King's execution and Cromwell's dour influence won them back to Jacobitism, and there was a degree of support in 1745 for Bonnie Prince Charlie who is supposed to have lodged here.

In the 18th century, Mancunians concerned themselves with the practical application of Science. The inventions of Kay, Hargreaves, Arkwright and Crompton plunged the town into the Industrial Revolution. Industrial architecture swallowed up whole areas. The focus on the manufacture of machinery attracted Welsh, Irish and Scottish migrants seeking exciting new careers. A Newcomen engine pumped water for Arkwright's mill here in 1780 and by 1800 there were numerous cotton mills, many kinds of steam engines, workshops and specialist engineers concentrating on producing new tools and machines. This heady challenging period transformed Manchester into the Industrial Workshop of the World! . . . and much more beside!

As the population shot up, concern increased for community health. Puerperal fever was a bane. Sub-standard conditions, overcrowding and pollution belched out by a thickening forest of chimneys, caused Typhus epidemics in the 1780's and 90's. Manchester, which now ranks with Edinburgh in the field of medicine, began with a 12-bed Infirmary in Withy Grove in 1752; replaced it four years later with an 80-bed hospital amid flower beds on the site of Piccadilly Gardens, but those "radiant little garden city" days were short-lived. The boom town of the 1780's bred boorishness, jealousy and suspicion. Blackspots developed, narrow streets of smoke-blackened brick where families lived among their accumulated filth within the deafening din of machines, where wage slaves alternated between depravity and despair.

"A great nasty manufacturing town", Lord Torrington called it in 1790. Yet, there was culture also. Manchester acquired New College in Mosley Street in 1786 and the Portico Library (1806) where the great Dr. Dalton had free access in exchange for winding up the clock! But a new century brought new troubles; Luddites, loom smashers, riots and hungry mobs, soup kitchens and strikes, weavers drilling with sticks and staves, and Reformers inflaming the passions. Henry "Orator" Hunt addressed crowds in St. Peter's Field in January 1819, and again in the August with the disastrous result of the Peterloo massacre. On that spot, in 1839, the first Free Trade Hall was built in wood and replaced in brick three years later. The Repeal of the Corn Laws was announced there, for which great men had fought and pleaded for years on end.

In the slump of the 1820's, workers came to a state of near-rebellion and only the influence of the good

MANCHESTER'S magnificent Town Hall covers nearly two acres and cost £1m. by the time it was completed in 1877. It was formally opened on 13th September and three days of celebrations concluded with a procession of 40,000 members of trade societies. The architect was Alfred Waterhouse, A.R.A., one of the competitors who submitted designs to the City Council in 1866. The mid-Victorian Gothic extravaganza is as impressive within as it is imposing without and probably ranks as Waterhouse's masterpiece.

Methodists preserved Lancashire from disaster. But confidence returned with Victoria's reign. Leading architects designed splendid buildings befitting the new merchant princes. The name of Alfred Waterhouse was bandied about, a "Gothic" man, greatly in demand, whose plan for Manchester's Town Hall was chosen from 130 competition entries in 1866. It took ten years to build, a feast for the senses within, a joy to the eye without, particularly since the great clean up when the city went "smokeless".

Besides manufacturing, retailing entered into fiercer competition. Partners, Thomas Kendal and James Milne, catered for the carriage folk and gentry; David Lewis's new store opened in 1880, and attracted such hordes of working folk that police reinforcements had to be summoned. The Queen opened the Manchester Ship Canal (1894) linking the Docks (at Salford) with the sea, and it became fashionable for magnates from Cottonopolis to park their families in fine residences on the sea coast, at Lytham or St. Annes, and travel in daily by Club Train. In the slump of the 1920's many lost all, and pampered daughters who had decorated cafe society, the tennis club or the dansant, became shop assistants, glad of a few shillings a week. Like the rest of Lancashire, the post-war demise of Cotton dealt Manchester a grievous blow and though it is still an important commercial centre, it has slipped below Birmingham in the Big City Stakes.

The Arndale Centre, creation of the 1970's, ("A lavatorial monstrosity", some call it!) obliterated many time-honoured specialist shops, covers 14 acres, claims to be the most stupendous shopping centre in Europe, and is almost a town in itself, fabulous, mesmerising, but not for the likes of me! Give me reminders of Manchester's proud and ancient past, the Cathedral, Chetham's which I first visited in school days, the old Wellington. Let me pause by its great statues, winkle out its "hidden gems", and experience the joys of discovery, which I did, only a year or two ago, at Droylsden, of all places, surely one of the most dismal areas in the north-west. And there it was, heartrendingly lovely. Fairfield's Moravian Settlement, founded in 1785, the oldest in England, an 18th century oasis of gentleness, orderliness and charm. The treat in store is well worth the journey and there is not a discordant note in this sedate Christian community whose originators planned and built the houses, planted trees in the cobbled streets, and provided such necessary services as the shop, the church, the doctor, the night watchman. Unmarried Brethren ran the bakehouse. Single Sisters worked in the laundry or farm. There were no dogs running loose and children had to be indoors by 8 p.m., and the same sober living prevails to-day. Even in death, the sexes are sedately segregated, a pathway dividing the Sisters on the one side from the Brethren on the other. Old Lancashire can show you no place more charming and felicitous to the eye than this Conservation Area, lovingly tended by those who are privileged to live there, where the very bricks and stones are steeped in two centuries of goodly living.

Liverpool on the Mersey

Liverpool owes everything to the Cheshire-born river, once the southern boundary of Old Lancashire, formed when two small streams meet near Stockport. Bollin and Weaver flow in from the Cheshire side and into its northern banks pours the Tame, bringing in the waters of the Irwell which has collected the Roch near Radcliffe and the Medlock at Salford.

This great city at the Mersey mouth was always different from the rest of Lancashire; had its eyes on distant prospects, an easy acceptance of incomers and time-honoured trading links with Wales. Its mayor, from Tudor times, might be a Welshman; even its name "Llerpwll" (place by the pool) derives from the Welsh. Here is the oldest Chinese community in the kingdom. Jews and immigrants from Russia and every country in Europe rubbed shoulders with starving Irish who poured off vessels during the great potato blight and, in the absence of a passage to America, settled in the worst slums, the lowest paid work, drowning their miseries in countless sleazy pubs and beershops.

Liverpool was an escape hatch for thousands of worthy Lancashire folk in the desperate 1840's, and again during the Cotton Famine miseries generated by the American Civil War. Last century it seemed a golden gateway to a new life in that land "flowing with milk and honey" promised by Mormon evangelists who proselytised in Lancashire in the late 1830's during the lifetime of their "prophet", Joseph Smith, and lured multitudes of Saints to their "earthly paradise" at Nauvoo up the Mississippi. James Greenlagh fell for their blandishments, a cotton spinner of Egerton, near Bolton, married with four young children aged between one and seven. He sold up, arrived with portable belongings in 1842 and boarded ship with 270 others bound for New Orleans and thence by paddle steamer up river to St. Louis and Nauvoo.

Ten harrowing weeks later, the exhausted family arrived, bumped up against harsh reality and, "being satisfied that something was wrong here", the understatement of the century, determined somehow to get back home. Many Preston folks, particularly from Longton where the persuasive and polygamous Brigham Young had all but emptied the village churches, were gloomily resigned to their fate but, twenty-three weeks after setting out, the Greenlagh family arrived back in Liverpool, penniless, in debt to a fellow passenger, but safely reaching Egerton "the same night, to the joy of our friends". Joseph Livesey published a detailed narrative of the misadventure, yet converts continually headed for Liverpool.

The city's history cannot be compared with that of Manchester. Liverpool did not appear in Domesday, for the simple reason that there was nothing worth recording. The castle was completed in 1237. A few streets gradually developed, but 300 years later a plague nearly wiped out the population. From the 17th century, prosperity came from "black gold", the capture and shipping of African slaves, each survivor, only

LIVERPOOL. Two of the city's principal treasures — the Town Hall (above) (mid 18th century) by John Wood of Bath, with replenishments after a fire in 1795, by James Wyatt and John Foster whose interiors were magnificent, as befitted a thrusting successful city: and St. George's Hall described as "among the finest Renaissance buildings in the world". It was designed and begun in 1838 by the young Harvey Lonsdale Elmes who died before its completion in 1854. Photographs kindly supplied by Liverpool Corporation Public Relations Office.

one in three, returning £1 clear profit. The same ships returned laden with sugar, rum and tobacco. Conditions aboard the slavers were appalling, the stench unendurable. Dead and dying were thrown over the side; compassion went out of the porthole. Slaves toiled on the southern plantations whose harvests fed Liverpool's cotton auctions, the greatest in the world, and kept the Lancashire operatives in employment.

Professed Christians waxed fat on traffic in human misery but a faint uneasiness was stirring. William Wilberforce, the Hull merchant's son, championed the enslaved ones, but the Society for Abolition was founded in Liverpool in 1787, by men of the calibre of William Roscoe and William Rathbone. The slave trade was illegalised in 1807, totally abolished in 1833, in which year even young Gladstone, whose father employed slaves, was slightly ambivalent, pleading in his maiden speech to the House, at the age of 23, for financial compensation to the owners.

The Industrial Revolution and the rising importance of cotton encouraged the Duke of Bridgewater and James Brindley to cut a canal linking Liverpool and its American and West Indies trade, with Manchester, the centre of manufactures. The opening, at the end of 1772, slashed transport costs, syphoned traffic from the turnpikes, created one of the busiest ports in the country and turned the Mersey into its busiest river, apart from the Thames.

Under Jesse Hartley, inspired Dock Engineer, an elaborate system of docks and warehouses developed, including Albert Dock, opened by the Prince Consort in 1845. In that decade, hordes of half-starved Irish refugees added to the city's vast Catholic population, 300,000 in 1847 alone! A reputation was quickly established for "drunkenness and crime . . . over every other seaport in the country". Emigrants still poured in and from 1899 steamers of the White Star Line left for Australia, every month. The port had progressed beyond belief, second only to London, handling imports and exports amounting to £252m. annually, as the century closed. In the first decade of this century, grandiloquent building operations coincided with rising optimism about passenger shipping. It was an exciting era of maiden voyages and magnificent new waterfront buildings, the Docks offices, the Liver Building and Cunard headquarters.

Long before the first 2½ miles Mersey Tunnel ("Queensway") was opened by H.M. King George V and Queen Mary in 1934, or the second 1½ miles "Kingsway" Tunnel was opened by their grand-daughter, H.M. The Queen in 1971, Liverpool inaugurated its overhead electric railway, since replaced by a road, the very first of its kind in the world, in 1893.

The May 1982 visit of Pope John Paul II was a graphic reminder of the religious fervour which persists in a city which, otherwise, appears — temporarily, we hope — to have run out of steam. Two closely positioned, totally different, equally impressive Cathedrals rise up, linked by Hope Street, the Anglican Cathedral, commenced in 1904, startling in its sheer solidity and size; the R.C. Metropolitan Cathedral of Christ the King, post-war ecclesiastical rotundo, with its tapering tower of coloured glass thrusting through a conical roof, giving the impression of a giant tepee, hence the nickname "Paddy's Wig-wam" or "The Mersey Funnel".

It becomes immediately obvious that "Scousers", a kaleidoscopic mixture of cultures, creeds and colours, think, talk and sound like no-one else on earth, clamping the teeth together and forcing the words up through the tonsils. But the droll, dead pan, zany babblings of the Liverpudlians, breed natural comics and the city's list of funny-men grows by the year.

Like Manchester, which has slid back in the Big City Stakes, Liverpool, which has suffered from the recession of the 1970's, and from horrifying street violence of the early 1980's, particularly in Toxteth, still has plenty going for it, superb architecture — St. George's Hall is recognised as the "finest Greco–Roman building in Europe" — splendid theatre, fabulous shops, the largest collection of paintings outside London, a University (1878) which has attracted some of the world's most eminent thinkers, markets operating somewhere every weekday; Speke Airport on the doorstep, 3,000 acres of public parkland, and innumerable temples dedicated to the god Bacchus. No city can touch Liverpool for opulent pubs! Its dockland is changing, part will become a vast Maritime Museum and Park, with models and exhibits, walks, guided tours and memorabilia from the romantic days of the great ocean liners.

Liverpool must prove again to the world that it has the stamina to stand up and the vitality to fight back and succeed; and, of course, it WILL . . . for there is an inherited sub-stratum of Lancashire grit and sinew . . . and qualities of cleverness and compassion which place the old Red Rose County second to none!

ACKNOWLEDGEMENTS

HAVING devoted half a lifetime to the study of Lancashire, it would be impossible, for considerations of space alone, to list all the published works which I have consulted at some time or another. It would, however, be safe to assume that the items in any comprehensive Lancashire library have become as old and treasured friends to me and many of them jostle for space on my bookshelves.

Down the decades, also, an army of helpful and hospitable individuals have borne with my enquiries and put information my way, earning my deep gratitude and affection. Times without number, their old photographs, documents and personal recollections have set me off wandering, reading, and researching as, I hope, this book, in its turn, will do for others, some perhaps too young yet to appreciate the treat lying in store.

Yet there are those who simply must be singled out and mentioned for their generous and cheerful assistance in the preparation of this work, and to whom I freely acknowledge my indebtedness. Kath Jones prepared the charming pen sketches. Stanley Brown gave useful criticisms and suggestions, acted as navigator and provided valuable introductions to sources of material. Frank Dean, as always, supplied many splendid photographs and Ted Gray prepared photographic prints. I am grateful, also to Peter G. Crowther and Ian Ward of Lancaster City Architect's Department and to my late and most dear friend, Jean Hanson, some of whose photographs have been chosen to commemorate our long-shared enthusiasm for Lancashire. I pay tribute also to the following, in alphabetical order, who generously and freely supplied the illustrations as under:

(Numbers are page numbers. B = bottom; C = centre; L = left; R = right; T = top)

Miss Ada Blackhurst: 29(TL).
Blackpool Borough Publicity Department: 34(B).
E. H. Booth & Co Ltd, Fishergate, Preston: 29(TR).
Dr Geoffrey Copley, R. & D. Pilkington Group, Lathom: 124.
Frank Dean: 10(T;B) 25, 38(T), 58(TL;TR;C;B), 60, 66(T;B), 69, 75, 87(T;B), 107, 128(T).
Roger Frost: 95.
The late Mrs Jean Hanson: 38(B), 63(T;B), 70, 90(T;B), 119(T;B), 131(T).
Harris Library, Art Gallery & Museum, Preston: 6, 27 (and S. Sartin for additional information).
Charles Wilson, Lancaster City Architect and Planning Officer; his Technical Librarian, Peter G. Crowther; and Ian Ward: 42(TL;TR;BL;BR), 45.
Lever Brothers (Unilever), Port Sunlight: 108.
Leyland Vehicles Ltd: 120.
Liverpool Corporation Public Relations Office: 140(T;B).
Bob Owen: 39(T).
C. A. Oxley: 131(B).
Dr G. Sumner: 77(T;B).

★　　★　　★

Pen sketches specially drawn by Kath Jones: 5, 22, 33, 40, 50, 53, 57, 67, 68, 71, 74, 76, 86, 126, 136, 143.

★　　★　　★

Photograph on page 128(B) from Southport Local History collection appears by courtesy of the Metropolitan Borough of Sefton.

Wycoller Hall fireplace.

INDEX

Abbeystead   76
Abbey Village   88
Accrington   91
Achievements   11–15
Agecroft Hall   109
Ainsdale   56
Allen, Cardinal William   37, 40
Altham   72
Arkholme   57
Arkwright, Sir Richard   27
Arthur, King   133
Ashton, Lord   44, 45
Ashton under Lyne   116
Assheton of Downham   65
Aughton   59
Aviation   11

Bacup   98–100
Bamford, Samuel   81
Bashall   65, 67
Beecham family   13, 14
Belmont   88
Bispham   35
Blackburn   89, 91
Blackpool   33–36
Blundells of Ince   130
"Bobbin, Tim" (John Collier)   79, 81
Bolton   105–108
Bolton-le-Sands   53, 54
Booth, Edwin Henry   31
Bradley, Helen   115
Bradshaw   84
Bradshaw, George   12
Bradshaw, Mabel   134, 135
Bramwell, William   62
Brazil, Angela   61, 88
Bretherton   134
Bridgewater, Duke of   8, 141
Brierley, Ben   81, 82, 114
Bright, John   62, 110
Brindley, James   141
Bromley Cross   85
Brontë, Charlotte   50, 57, 71, 97
Brookhouse   59

Burnley   71, 92–94
Burscough Priory   122, 132
Bury   109, 110

C.H.A. & Holiday Fellowship   97
Calder, River   61, 67, 71
Carnforth   55
Carr House, Bretherton   134
Caton   56, 59
Catterall   78
Cheeryble Brothers   100, 101
Chetham, Humphrey   11, 84
Chetham's Music College   11, 14, 84
Chipping   62
Chorley   56, 121
Churchtown (Fylde)   40, 78
Churchtown (Southport)   127, 129
Clarke, Allen   33, 35
Claughton (Hornby)   59
Clifton of Lytham   36
Clitheroe   64, 65
Cliviger   92
Cobden, Richard   110
Cockerham   40, 61
Cockersand Abbey   40, 61
Collier, John ("Tim Bobbin")   79, 81
Colne   95–97
Cook, Captain   65
Cooke, Alistair   12
Co-operative Society   111
Cowan Bridge School   57
Crompton, Samuel   106–108
Cromwell, Oliver   25, 62, 64
Cronshaw, Joseph   83
Croston   56
Cuerdale Hoard   23
Cuthbert, Saint   36
Cutler, Ann   62

Daisy Nook   114, 116
Dalton of Thurnham   8, 26
Darwen   85
Darwen, River   61, 76
de Hoghton   24

Derby, Earls of   105, 122 et seq.
Dickens, Charles   14, 32, 101
Dolphinholme   78
Douglas, River   76, 133
Downham   65
Dunkenhalgh   70

Eagle & Child   122
Elswick   37, 62

Fairfield (Moravians)   139
Fleetwood   24, 37
Formby   56, 129–130
Formby, George   135, 136
Fylde   33 et seq.

Garstang   78
Gaskell, Mrs Elizabeth   14, 32, 49
Gawthorpe   71
Gladstone, W. E.   12, 141
Glasson   46, 60
Grant Brothers   85, 100, 101
Great Harwood   72, 73
Greenhalgh Castle   78
Gressingham   57
Gunpowder Plot   8

Hackensall   78
Hacking Hall   70
Hale   9
Hall-i-th'Wood, Bolton   106
Halsall   132
Halton   59
Hargreaves, James   86, 91, 106
Hartley, Wallace   97
Hartley, William   96
Hartshead Pike   116
Helmshore   86
Henry VI   67
Hest-with-Slyne   54
Heysham   51, 52
Hodder, River   61–64
Holcombe Harriers   85
Holcombe Tower   85
Holme   71, 94, 95

Hornby   59, 123
Horrocks, Jeremiah   134
Horrocks, John   26, 32
Hurst Green   64
Hurstwood   94

Ince Blundell   56, 130
Irwell, River   98, 110

John o'Gaunt   20, 21, 43
Jollie, Rev. Thomas   72

Kay, John   110
Kay-Shuttleworth, Sir James   12
King, Lieut. James   65
Kirkham   37, 40
Knowsley Safari Park   126

Lancashire artists   14
Lancashire Authors' Association   79,81
Lancashire dialect   16 et seq., 81
Lancashire witches   41, 43
Lancashire writers   12, 13, 33, 79, 81, 99
Lancaster   41–47
Langho   68
Lathom   122, 123, 126
Lathom House   126
Laycock, Samuel   82, 83
Leck, River   57
Leonard, T. Arthur   97
Lever W. H. (Lord Leverhulme)   86, 108–109
Leyland   117–119
Leyland Motors   119–121
Lingard, Dr. John   13, 59
Liverpool   11, 139–141
Livesey, Joseph   12, 28–30, 139
Longridge   12, 62
Loud, River   62
Lune, River   57–60
Lydiate   130
Lytham St. Annes   15, 36, 56

Macara, Sir Charles   15
Manchester   11, 137–139
Manchester Ship Canal   138
Marsh, George (Martyr)   106
Martholme   73
Martin Mere   56, 127
Marton Mere (Blackpool)   56, 127
Melling   57
Mercer, John   73
Mersey, River   61, 139
Methodism   62, 89, 138
Mitton   64
Moravians (Fairfield)   139
Morecambe   50–51

Morecambe Bay   50 et seq.
Mormons   32, 139
Much Hoole   134
Myres, T. Harrison   7

Nelson   95

Oldham   111–116
Oldham, Hugh   115
Ordsall Hall   8
Ormskirk   8, 132
Over Kellet   55
Overton   60

Padiham   71
Pankhurst family   11, 12
Parrox Hall   78
Paslew, Abbot John   41, 68, 71
Peel, "Parsley"   91
Peel, Sir Robert   12, 85, 109
Pendle   8, 45, 65
Pilkington's (Glass)   8, 126, 127
Pilling   40
Poictou, Roger de   41, 64
Portus Setantiorum   78
Poulton   40
Preesall   78
Prescot   8
Preston   7, 22 et seq.

Quakers   45, 46, 54, 62

Ramsbottom   100, 101
Rawtenstall   104
Red Rose of Lancaster   20, 21
Ribble, River   61, et seq.
Ribchester   73–76
Rivington   86 et seq.
Rochdale   81, 110, 111
Rossall School   37
Rossendale Valley   98
Royce, Henry   14
Rufford   8, 133
Rylands, John (Library)   11

St. Annes   15, 36, 44, 45
St. Michael's-on-Wyre   40, 78
St. Patrick   52
Salford   138
Samlesbury   8, 76
Sawley Abbey   65
Scarisbrick Hall   132
Scotsmans Stump   85
Sefton   130
Shard Bridge   78

Shireburne family   62–64
Shuttleworth of Gawthorpe   71
Slyne   54
Smithills Hall   106
Southport   129
Spenser, Edmund   94
Stanley family   105, 122 et seq.
Stonyhurst   62, 64
Stout, William   41, 53, 54
Stydd   75
Suffragettes   11, 12
Sumner, James   120
Sunderland Point   56, 60, 61
Sutton, William   129

Tarleton   133, 134
Tate, Henry   12
Thompson, Francis   32
Thornley   62
Thornton Marsh Mill   40
Thurnham Hall   8, 26
Tockholes   89
Towneley family   12, 93, 94, 130
Towneley Hall   93
Tunstall   57
Turton Tower   84, 85
Tyldesley, Sir Thomas   135

Walmesley family   70
Walton-le-Dale   23, 25, 41, 61
Warton (Silverdale)   55
Washington family   55
Waugh, Edwin   81
Weavers' Triangle, Burnley   92
Webb, Beatrice   100
Wenning, River   59
Whalley   67 et seq.
Whitaker, Dr. T. D.   94, 95
Whitewell   61
Whitworth Doctors   102–104
Wigan   134, 135
Wildlife   56
Winter Hill   88
Wiswell   68
Worsley   8
Wray   59
Wrea Green   37
Wrigley, Ammon   83
Wrightington   132
Wycoller   96–97
Wyre, River   76 et seq.
Wythenshawe   8

Yarrow, River   76, 133
Yealand   8